CURRENT ISSUES IN CLINICAL PSYCHOLOGY 1987

Current Issues in Clinical Psychology 1987

The Annual Merseyside Conference in Clinical Psychology

Edited by
DAVID GLASGOW
and
NADINE EISENBERG
Regional Forensic Psychiatry Service
Liverpool

Avebury
Aldershot · Brookfield USA · Hong Kong · Singapore · Sydney

Published by

Avebury

Gower Publishing Company Limited
Gower House
Croft Road
Aldershot
Hants GU11 3HR
England

Gower Publishing Company
Old Post Road
Brookfield
Vermont 05036
USA

ISBN 0 566 05742 5

Contents

Preface

This volume represents the proceedings of the seventh 'Current Issues in Clinical Psychology' conference, an event which is held annually within the Mersey Regional Health Authority. Each year, the organising committee selects topics for inclusion which will offer practicing clinicians the opportunity to keep abreast of new developments and research in clinical psychology.

In 1987 the symposia included: psychotherapy in institutions, cognitive therapy, training in clinical psychology, family therapy with schizophrenic clients and 'empowering the client'. The chapters within this volume correspond to these symposia.

The first chapter addresses the issue of whether psychotherapy is possible within the confines of an institution, given the many constraints presented by what may be an inward looking, restrictive and even repressive regime. Contributors discuss issues related to confidentiality, trust and the ability of the institution to adapt to individuals needs and demands rather than clients being required to conform to expectancies of the system.

The chapter on training considers current thinking and directions in clinical training - particularly the conflict between current areas of interest as opposed to the long term development of clinical psychology. Another problem discussed is that of maintaining psychologists interest in research, a vital yet easily forgotten task amongst the many competing demands of a clinician's time once they are in post.

Chapter three considers the current status of cognitive therapy and recent developments in the field. Established models are critically evaluated and future directions and applications are discussed.

The chapter on family therapy brings together four very different perspectives on working with families with a member regarded as schizophrenic. A significant aspect of this chapter is that it includes consideration of not only families where the identified client is the child, but also the less widely discussed problems raised by the schizophrenic member being a parent in the family system.

The final chapter was convened in somewhat different circumstances than the other symposia, in that it was organised in memory of Albert Chambwe by the psychologists who trained with him. The papers are very disparate and yet all address the issue of how to empower our clients in the face of debilitating and dehumanising processes - ranging from the fatal consequences of AIDS to institutional resistance.

Acknowledgements

Many thanks to the following members of the Conference Steering Committee for their various contributions towards making this publication possible: Richard Bentall, Gus Baker, Sarah Gregory, Sue Hingley, Pauline Johnson, Danny Reid and Austin Sinnott.

We would also like to give special thanks to Denise Conroy who prepared the manuscript.

Contributors

CARR, Sally. Research Psychologist, Department of Psychiatry, University of Oxford.

DABBS, Alan. Senior Lecturer in Clinical Psychology, Department of Psychiatry, University of Leeds.

DOUGLAS, Angela. Principal Clinical Psychologist, Lynefield Mount Hospital, Bradford.

EL-JAZAIRI, Laraine. Principal Clinical Psychologist, Moss Side Hospital, Merseyside.

GOMERSALL, James. Senior Lecturer in Psychotherapy, Whiteley Woods Clinic, Sheffield.

JONES, Elsa. Family Therapist, Family Institute, Cardiff.

KENNEDY, Fiona. Senior Clinical Psychologist, ATC, Wythenshawe, Manchester.

LETHAM, Jane. Clinical Psychologist, Child Development Centre, Charing Cross Hospital, Fulham, London.

MILLER, Ann. Principal Clinical Psychologist, Marlborough Family Service, London.

MILLS, Irene. Senior Clinical Psychologist, Department of Psychology, Rainhill Hospital, Merseyside.

MORLEY, Stephen. Lecturer in Clinical Psychology, Department of Psychiatry, University of Leeds.

NG, Kee-on. Senior Clinical Psychologist, Wilson House, Sale and Brooklands Hospital, Sale, Cheshire.

PARRY, Glenys. Regional Tutor, Wessex Regional Health Authority.

SALKOVSKIS, Paul. Senior Clinical Psychologist (Research), Department of Psychiatry, University of Oxford.

VAUGHN, Christine. Research Clinical Psychologist, MRC, Social Psychiatry Unit, Institute of Psychiatry, University of London.

WARBURG, Richard. Senior Clinical Psychologist, North Manchester General Hospital.

WEBSTER, Jeni. Lecturer in Psychiatric Social Work, Manchester University.

WILKS, Jenny. Clinical Psychologist, Maudsley Drugs Training Unit, Denmark Hill, London.

WOODWARD, Roland. Senior Psychologist, H.M. Prison and Youth Custody Centre, Grendon Underwood.

YOUNG, Jackie. Clinical Psychologist, Whole Woman Clinic, London.

PART I
PSYCHOTHERAPY IN INSTITUTIONS

Emergent themes in psychotherapy with special hospital patients

L. EL-JAZAIRI

The inherent contradictions and dilemmas, both acknowledged and denied, that exist within the total institution that is the Special Hospital have a profound and crucial impact on any therapeutic endeavour within this setting. Berman and Segal (1982), in discussing the practice of individual psychotherapy within a psychiatric hospital identify these dilemmas as follows:

1) the patient cannot be truly voluntary.

2) the therapist is bound to experience conflicts of loyalty.

3) confidentiality and exclusivity between patient and therapist cannot be preserved.

4) therapist 'non-directiveness' and 'neutrality' are not maintained due to the pressures upon therapist and patient to set and meet certain 'goals'.

5) the unfolding transference and countertransference are confounded by 'real' relating during daily institutional life.

They conclude that whilst no hospital setting can ever do away with the dilemmas affecting psychotherapeutic practice within institutions, the adoption of principles of the therapeutic community could provide a facilitating environment for psychotherapy within such settings.

Pilgrim (1988) looks at the question of psychotherapy within secure settings from a sociological/political perspective and concludes that conditions within secure institutions are largely antagonistic to the deployment of individual therapy. Against the background of the social development of both psychotherapy and secure provision in Britain, he emphasises the social control function of both. Pilgrim is of the view that the double-think rhetoric surrounding the process of decision making within and without the Special Hospital results in a highly mystifying regime. He concludes that such an analysis:

> will probably lead to the conclusion that so much of our present secure provision requires dismantling, rather than that such provision should deploy more psychotherapy.

He concedes, however that this prospect is highly unlikely in the forseeable future. The choice seems to be therefore, between abandoning the practice of psychotherapy in this setting altogether, or continuing to explore psychotherapeutic possibilities within this context.

Whilst there is a plethora of psychodynamic/psychoanalytic 'explanations' of deviance, offender behaviour and criminality, sadly there is little published work about the actual process of dynamic psychotherapy in secure settings apart from that of Murray Cox, Consultant Psychotherapist at Broadmoor Hospital. Cox views offender-therapy as a specialised field of psychotherapy, which overlaps, but is not coterminous with psychotherapy undertaken in a secure setting (Cox, 1976). His work is largely concerned with the exploration of the dynmic process within group psychotherapy with offender-patients, and in his writing there is a central recurrent theme as to the significance for the patient of the experience of being confined for an unknown duration:

> The cardinal distinction between psychotherapy of a known duration and psychotherapy 'without limit of time' is, in itself, bound to influence the content of therapy, irrespective of who sets the time limits.
> (Cox, 1976)

More recent work has included a description of working within the 'Associative Mode' with the schizophrenic offender patient (Cox, 1982) and the contribution of the psychotherapist to the assessment of dangerousness (Cox 1982). Whilst not ignoring the question of psychotherapeutic outcome, he views the question of research in this area as being fraught with difficulties (Personal Communication 1986).

It is to the question of the process of dynamic psychotherapy within the setting of the Special Hospital that this paper is addressed. By 'process' in this setting I refer principally to exploration within the perameters of the therapeutic relationship in terms of what could be seen as 'therapeutically indicated deviations of technique' (Langs,

1973). More importantly I am concerned with the space within the therapeutic relationship, one central theme being the need for this 'space within' to survive in a non-conducive environment. After briefly describing the setting of Moss Side Hospital and outlining some major patient characteristics, I shall discuss aspects of the process of psychotherapy within this setting under the following headings:

1) The institutional context.

2) Factors present and emerging within the patient.

3) Processes in the therapist.

4) Emergent themes within the therapeutic relationship.

SETTINGS AND PATIENTS

Moss Side Hospital is one of four Special Hospitals in England in which patients are detained because they are deemed to 'require treatment under conditions of special security on account of their dangerous, violent or criminal propensities' (Mental Health Act, 1959).

As of August 31st, 1987 there was a total of 302 patients in the hospital, 212 male and 90 female. A survey of the characteristics of the patients carried out by Jackson, Bentall and Reid (January 1986) yielded some valuable descriptive data. At that time there were a total of 272 patients, 71 of whom were women. Patients were relatively evenly distributed across the major categories defined by the Mental Health Act (1983), thirty one per cent being mentally impaired, twenty seven per cent mentally ill, twenty seven per cent psychopathic personality disordered, and thirteen per cent having combined diagnoses. (for a discussion of the terms used by the Mental Health Act, see Jones, 1985). This data updated as of 31st August, 1987 (El Jazairi, September, 1987) shows a five per cent decrease in the number of mentally impaired patients and a seven per cent increase in those identified as psychopathic disorder. A comparison between male and female patients (August 1987) reveals major differences in these two categories: only thirteen per cent of the women are diagnosed as mentally impaired as opposed to thirty one per cent of the men and more women are in the psychopathic disorder category (forty eight per cent as compared to thirty two per cent of the men).

The majority of patients are admitted on account of management difficulties (twenty seven per cent) with arson and assault together accounting for a further forty six per cent of identified index offences (arson twenty five per cent; assault twenty one percent). Only thirteen percent of patients are sex offenders and nine percent have committed homicide. Approximately half of the patients are under thirty years of age, almost a quarter of the total number being aged between twenty and twenty five years. The majority of patients are admitted from local hospitals (thirty three percent) with prisons and remand centres accounting for nineteen per cent and thirteen per cent of admissions respectively (total of thirty two per cent). A further sixteen per cent of patients are transferred from other Special Hospitals. The average length of stay in hospital is about six years.

A statistic of particular importance with respect to psychotherapy with these patients is that twenty seven per cent of them were under three years of age when first taken into care and this increases to thirty seven per cent up to the age of six years. This gives some idea of the severity of emotional deprivation experienced by the patients.

Initially, patients are taken into an assessment ward which also functions as a high dependency (disturbed) facility. Progress through the hospital is from secure to less secure areas, with a system of increasing privileges. It should be noted that security is contained within each ward, and that there is no unescorted movement within a secure perimeter (parole system). Patient services are organised into multidisciplinary teams, the 'care team meeting' or 'case conference' being the focus. A care plan for each patient is formulated by the team and psychotherapy is offered as one option among a number of treatment strategies within the context of the overall management of the patient. However, for a variety of complex reasons the 'treatment' the patient receives often falls short of their actual needs.

THE INSTITUTIONAL CONTEXT

Clearly the major contradiction within the context of the Special Hospitals is that inherent in the question of their function. Put simply, the contradiction is threefold and is expressed in the dilemma of the conflict of role which affect <u>all</u> staff in contact with patients.

1) the treatment function.
2) the custodial function.
3) the protection of society function.

Arguably, psychologists are more marginal than nursing staff and therefore less subject to this dilemma of role conflict, the psychotherapist even less so having no actual team responsibility. Nevertheless issues of role conflict, particularly in terms of the patient's expectations/fantasy inevitably arise and need to be addressed within the therapeutic relationship. I shall return to this later in discussing the question of confidentiality.

In discussing contextual factors affecting the process of psychotherapy, it must be realised that no psychotherapy actually takes place within a vacuum. To appreciate this one only has to consider the increasing constraints and pressures affecting the practice of outpatient psychotherapy in the present monetarist climate which prevails within the National

Health Service and which by and large has been 'swallowed whole' by the new breed of managers within our own profession. I believe that a secure environment such as the Special Hospital in fact forces confrontation with these contextual issues which affect the therapeutic relationship in a far more explicit and direct way.

What are these contextual factors within the Special Hospital? Clearly the fact that the patient may be detained 'without limit of time' is crucial, primarily in terms of the existential dilemma this presents to the patient. This seems to be reflected within the psychotherapy in terms of the blurring of therapeutic time boundaries, the themes of aimlessness and sameness which recur, often punctuated by periods of preoccupation with 'demarcational' events within institutional life. The fact that the patient may view the therapist as being able to influence or make decisions about discharge or aspects of the patient's life within the hospital (which may in fact be the case) leads inevitably to (early) confrontation with the patient's motives for psychotherapy. It is vital that the therapist is aware of this, since feelings of helplessness and powerlessness together with the wish to 'prove' oneself to the patient can lead to being seduced into 'doing for' rather than 'being with' the patient. Such powerful contextual influences can lead to what must be viewed essentially as acting out on the part of the therapist.

The perception of the therapeutic relationship held by the ward staff can, and does, directly affect the process of psychotherapy and leads me to the firm conclusion that in order to protect the therapeutic space, it is essential to maintain a good working relationship with them. Problems of survival seem ever present and are reflected in the stream of the therapeutic discourse. Quite literally, it can be a struggle to preserve the actual space in which the session takes place and I have held sessions in the dining rooms, day rooms and even 'on court' in fine weather. I am constantly amazed that despite these problems the work seems to continue. Linked to this is the necessity of viewing the one or two hours of psychotherapy per week against the other 166 hours in which the patient experiences hospital life. The intensification of this experience within the total institution means that 'hospital life' can become a major theme in psychotherapy, a theme which can lead patient and therapist away from psychotherapy to exhortation, or simply therapeutic inertia. This seems to happen because the institutional setting exerts such a powerful influence on patient and therapist that the therapist can easily listen to the material in the session only in terms of its 'reality' content and lose touch with the underlying unconscious themes.

FACTORS PRESENT AND EMERGING WITHIN THE PATIENT

Just as general diagnostic categories shed little light on underlying psychodynamics, no unitary psychopathology or object relational constellation underlies type of offence or behavioural disorder. Patients frequently have a history of profound early deprivation/abandonment including emotional, physical and sexual abuse. The latter is particularly, though certainly not exclusively, prevalent in the women's histories. This inevitably results in a lack of basic trust in the sense described by Erikson, such that the theme of lack of trust becomes a pervasive one in therapy. Thus the patient continually reminds the therapist that she can trust no-one with inevitable consequences for the psychotherapeutic relationship. I have found that it is helpful to move beyond the issue for the patient that nurses, doctors, other staff cannot be trusted to consideration of the patient's profound inability to trust because of early life experiences. This has been alluded to by Cox (1974). Viewed in this light the issue is made accessible to exploration in the therapy rather than becoming enmeshed in the question of who or who is not to be trusted, with the therapist needing to 'prove' their own trustworthiness.

A major factor which has been identified as necessary to the formation of a therapeutic alliance and for a positive therapeutic outcome is motivation for insight. It has been argued that this, by definition, is lacking in confined patients and indeed it is in some, just as it is lacking in patients who present for psychotherapy in other contexts. And yet, my experience suggests that patients in the Special Hospital setting can be and are motivated to achieve insight and a genuine understanding of their difficulties. This is not to deny that many patients, especially initially, have other motives for engaging in psychotherapy and inevitably there is a period in the beginning of therapy in which the therapist seeks actively to establish a therapeutic alliance with the patient. This work takes different forms depending on the sort of patient one is working with but I commonly employ techniques outside the usual 'verbal communication' to facilitate this bridge building between patient and therapist. A patient I am currently working with is silent, anxious and potentially very dangerous and yet I have been able to establish a tentative link with her by using her gift for art and encouraging written communication after each session. In each session her schematic drawing of herself and myself in the session is placed between us and is added to by her in the light of themes discussed in the session. The act of maintaining a link with her outside the session is crucial because initially it seemed that when I left the session I ceased to exist for her.

A final factor of significance with patients at Moss Side is their difficulty in tolerating certain inner feelings. This can be seen in the 'overcontrolled psychopath' as a total denial of feeling, or at the other end of the spectrum, the acting out of the self mutilator or violent patient. The focus of therapy must still remain 'to put the patient in touch with as much of his true feleings as he can bear' (Malan, 1979) and yet for these patients their feelings can be truly unbearable. Thus the timing of confrontation can have disastrous consequences both in terms of aggressive acting out possibly towards the therapist and in 'losing' the patient. I learned this to my cost in my very first sesion with a young woman in my first few months at Moss Side who left the session and never returned. What for a more 'intact' patient may be merely a clumsy indiscretion can have potentially disastrous consequences for such 'damaged' patients.

A low level of self esteem is common to many patients, but I have found in working within the confines of the Special Hospital this can amount to a total disregard for the self, self loathing and self hatred. Often the patient has an image of the self as worthless, guilty, without hope, needing to be punished. This lack of self esteem has a profound affect on the course of therapy not least because of the therapeutic pessimism which can result from the patient's sense of worthlessness. The fact that the therapist can care for the patient in itself leads to a reconsideration of the patient's sense of worth. I make a particular point of saying to one of my patients who has a profound sense of worthlessness 'take care of yourself' as I leave a session. Murray Cox (1975) is of the view that the task of increasing/maintaining the patient's self esteem at an optimal level is of central importance. He also points out that signs of increasing self esteem within the patient are of prognostic value.

PROCESSES IN THE THERAPIST

A central question for the psychotherapist is how much of the patient's true feelings can the therapist bear? This question has two aspects. The patient may lead the therapist to confront aspects of themself which are anxiety provoking and unacceptable. Thus, for example, the sexual or violent fantasies of the patient may force confrontation with one's own potential for sexual perversity or violence. There is also the related issue of the problem of maintaining an empathic link with the patient who begins to confront the facts of their offence. The example of a female therapist working with a violent rapist illustrates this difficulty.

Another very pertinent issue for the therapist is the actual threat of violence, the point at which the therapist becomes afraid of the patient. As Murray Cox (1974) has pointed out, with the homicidal or aggressive patient, fantasy has become fact at least once with dire consequences and theoretically there is no reason theoretically why this could not be repeated. Fear of the patient is manifest also in the way the therapist can (be made to) feel responsible for an aggressive incident caused by the patient or responsible for self mutilatory behaviour on the part of the patient. Therapeutic pessimism, a sense of hopelessness and despair can result and be added to by the patient's own sense of inertia. Thus we return to the issue of survival within the psychotherapeutic space.

Finally, the level of deprivation/lack of basic trust in these patients can lead to the fantasy on the part of the therapist that one can actually be the good parent the patient lacked and lead to acting out on the part of the therapist alluded to earlier.

EMERGENT THEMES IN PSYCHOTHERAPY

Lack of basic trust

As mentioned previously, an initial period of work aimed towards establishing a therapeutic alliance seems invevitable in working with patients who lack a sense of basic trust. Aspects of psychotherapy with the borderline patient as discussed in a previous paper (El-Jazairi, 1986) provides some useful insights. I am thinking particularly of the need for consistency of boundaries, the issue of the survival of the therapist and the containment and holding function of the therapist as opposed to the interpretive function. In a setting in which boundaries are constantly invaded, this fact needs to be actively worked with throughout the therapy.

Patients within Special Hospitals often have little or no experience other than life in instituions or relationships based on exploitation, resulting in them becoming victim or perpetrator. Thus the patient can be said to have no conception or experience of the potential within a therapeutic relationship. Hopefully a learning process takes place as the therapist offers consistency and achieves the appropriate balance between support and confrontation leading towards awareness and self disclosure on the part of the patient.

Confidentiality/therapeutic boundaries

The limits of confidentiality in my view need to be discussed with the patient at some point and will inevitably be a recurring theme in psychotherapy. These limits can be 'tested' by the patient in a number of ways, and it is vital that the therapist both confronts the patient with this testing out and reminds him/her of the boundaries of confidentiality. This can become extremely difficult when the question of disclosure of information, for example in the context of a forthcoming Tribunal, becomes an issue. It is my practice to discuss everything which might be said with the patient if this is a source of anxiety. However, it should be borne in mind that the only required evidence is that contained in the report of the Responsible Medical Officer (RMO). I have been fortunate in that the RMO's of patients I am working with in psychotherapy are thankfully sensitive to this issue so that as yet it has not presented any real problem.

The theme of guilt

My experience to date suggests that the issue of guilt is a central dynamic in psychotherapy within this context which takes a number of forms. The victim of sexual abuse for example, experiences guilt and self blame and must be helped to re-assess their role in the abusing relationship. Often guilt is experienced in relation to the index offence for example one of my patients, a twenty one year old man, murdered his best friend in a frenzied attack with a knife when he was sixteen years old. His confinement to Moss Side for years is experienced as deserved punishment. The difficulty in therapy is that confronting and discussing the index offence leads to a flood of guilt and remorse which he experiences as intolerable.

Guilt may be imagined rather than real leading to an almost delusional state of self blame. An example of this is one of my patients, a young woman who has spent all her life in institutions who is convinced she 'killed' her grandfather. He was the one positive figure in her life and he died whilst she was in Holloway through her offences. One task in therapy is that of enabling her to 'hold on' to this good experience rather than have it destroyed by guilt. Thus in the 'here and now' of the therapeutic relationship I am working actively to help her 'hold on' to the hour as a potentially good experience within the context of institutional life.

The question of whether the patient is actually innocent or guilty (and therefore deserving of punishment) in terms of the reasons for admission is often a theme which seems to be linked to the patient's wish that the therapist 'do something' for them. This is a difficult area within psychotherapy, in which the therapist is positioned between the need to prove oneself on the one hand and the necessity of interfacing with other workers concerned with the total care of the patient and the therapist contributing to this total care.

Finally, there is the difficulty of a total lack of a sense of guilt present in some patients who are closest to the description of the psychopathic personality. The one assessment I have carried out with such a patient led me to conclude that it would not be possible to work with him in psychotherapy for a number of reasons, the most salient being he refused to see me!

The experience of confinement

From what has already been discussed it is perhaps obvious that the experience of confinement is a pervasive theme in psychotherapy in the Special Hospital context. This emerges within the process in various ways, sometimes in the form of a total preoccupation in the sessions with daily ward events. This is similar to the outpatient setting in which the patient seems unable to go beyond daily events often viewed as 'superficial ' by the therapist.

The problem in the secure environment is not the technical handling of such material but rather seems to be that the therapist is also subject to the constraints and influences of the institution in a way which is experienced as far more direct and pervasive than in many other settings. Further, there is the profound sense that the therapist <u>should</u> set to rights what is wrong within the institution which does or may have a deleterious effect on the patient. This conflict often prevents the therapist from 'hearing' the unconscious theme so that she/he too becomes preoccupied with day to day 'reality' events.

I should perhaps make it clear that I am not arguing for total analytic neutrality but merely pointing out the way in which insitutional pressures not only impinge on the therapeutic space but have a profound influence on the process of psychotherapy. Such pressures can all too easily lead the therapist away from therapy. The question of what is or is not actually in the best interests of the patient is central here.

CONCLUSION

Whilst acknowledging the constraints and dilemmas which affect the process of psychotherapy within the setting of the Special Hospital, it seems that somehow it is possible to foster and preserve the psychotherapeutic relationship within this often hostile environment.

Psychotherapeutic events undoubtedly occur within one-to-one therapy and it seems possible to establish a working alliance with patients in this context.

The need for the therapist to be fully aware of and to resist institutional pressures to abandon psychotherapy and offer 'practical help' is of paramount importance, and the establishment of a good working relationship with all staff is essential in preserving the therapeutic space.

ACKNOWLEDGEMENT

My remarks concerning the process of psychotherapy with Special Hospital patients should be viewed under the broad heading of 'preliminary observations' which are based on twelve months work with individual patients at Moss Side Hospital. I am indebted to my colleagues in the Psychology Department who have contributed to these observations both directly and indirectly.

In particular Claire Maguire, Senior Clinical Psychologist, has made a direct contribution in offering her insights within ongoing discussion of both her own and my own clinical work. I should also like to thank John Birkett and Julie Ross, trainee clinical psychologists, who have enabled me to learn more about the psychodynamic process through supervising their work with patients at Moss Side. Finally I am indebted to my patients who have continued to work with me despite my lack of any real understanding and in the face of extreme difficulty both within and without the therapeutic space.

The views expressed in this paper are personal and do not necessarily reflect those of the Department of Health and Social Security.

REFERENCES

Berman, E. and Segal, R., (1982), The captive client: Dilemmas of psychotherapy in the psychiatric hospital. _Psychotherpay: Theory, Research and Practice_, 19, 1, 31-41.

Cox, M., (1976), Group psychotherapy in a secure setting, _Proceedings of Royal Society of Medicine_, 69, 215-220.

Cox, M., (1982), I took a life because I needed one: Psychotherapeutic possibilities with the schizophrenic offender patient, _Psychother. Psychosom_, 37, 96-105.

Cox, M., (1982), The psychotherapist as assessor of dangerousness in Hamilton, J.R. and Freeman, H. (eds.), _Dangerousness, Psychiatric Assessment and Management_, Gaskell.

Cox, M., (1984), The psychotherapist's anxiety: Liability or asset? With special reference to the offender patient, _British Journal of Criminology_, 14, 1-17.

El-Jazairi, L., (1986), The borderline personality: An introduction and overview in Eisenberg, N. and Glasgow, D. (eds.), _Current Issues in Clinical Psychology_, Gower, Aldershot.

Jackson, H., Bentall, R and Reid, D., (1986), Moss Side patients' survey. In preparation.

Jones, R.M., (ed.), (1985), Mental Health Act Mannual, Sweet and Maxwell, London.

Langs, R., (1973), _The Technique of Psychoanalytic Psychotherapy_ Vol. 1.

Malan, D., (1979), _Individual Psychotherapy and the Science of Psychodynamics_, Butterworth.

Mental Health Act (1983), HMSO, London.

Pilgrim, D., (1988), Psychotherapy in British Special Hospitals: A case of failure to thrive, _Free Associations_, 10.

Creative asylum: psychotherapy, the individual and the institutions?

A. DOUGLAS

INTRODUCTION

Institutions providing Mental Health care are going to be with us for some time and psychotherapy has a wealth of theoretical models and clinical expertise which can be applied to a variety of institutional settings. The process of 'de-institutionalising' mental health has been on the agenda of the National Health Service since the 1959 Mental Health Act and is now on the top of the list for District Health Authority operational policies. There have been gains over the past twenty years in terms of humanising hospital conditions, unlocking wards, shorter hospital stays, less compulsory treatment, extended community care, group hostels and preventative mental health care. In the 1980's the move is towards community mental health centres, in the hope that these will gradually replace the larger institution. These centres, whilst free from the restrictions and limitations of large hospitals remote from the community being served, will nevertheless be institutions, evolving structures and routines that enable groups of staff to function as a team and provide a service to large numbers of people. The psychotherapists employed by the NHS are going to be called upon to apply their clinical knowledge to patients who were previously seen as medical cases only and who depend on the institution.

I hope that in moving away from the horrors of the old 'asylum' we will develop methods of healing and caring for the acutely disturbed person as well as for the person who can more easily engage in counselling, psychotherapy or cognitive therapy. Moving house will not remove the distress or underlying causes of severe psychological disturbance, though it will undoubtedly ease the burden on those who suffer, both patients and relatives.

The institution within which I work is a small psychiatric hospital, opened in the 1960's as the way forward from the old asylum. In my own practice I use psychodynamic, object relations, cognitive, spiritual and holistic models in formulating the problems and processes experienced by individuals, and what follows is an account of two cases where I attempted to use the institution as a potentially healing environment.

Case 1: Phyllis

I owe a great deal to Phyllis. She aroused my interest in acutely disturbed psychological states and did me the honour of responding to my psychotherapeutic endeavours. This encouraged myself and other staff in the hospital to continue in our efforts to apply psychotherapeutic methods in treating seriously disturbed patients. She also happened to have a consultant psychiatrist who was well aware of the caring involved in his patients' recovery, irrespective of any medical intervention. Phyllis was thirty eight years old and had received a variety of medical and therapeutic treatments over nine months, including talking over her problems in day centre groups and assessment by the family therapy unit. She had deteriorated consistently, and finally quite dramatically, so that she had to be hospitalised. She had originally asked for help in dealing with a two and a half year old daughter and was now in a state of total retreat from reality, apparently unable to communicate verbally. She was locked in seclusion on an acute admission ward, in a desparate attempt by staff to protect her from herself. She was unpredictable, uncooperative and incontinent of urine and faeces. When allowed out of seclusion she attacked other patients, stole cigarettes pulled their clothes and jumped on their backs.

In referring Phyllis to me, the consultant psychiatrist had pointed out that all treatment had failed over several weeks and that he was being pressed by nursing and medical staff to use electroconvulsive therapy and make further medical investigations such as brain scans. He was particularly struck by the way all the staff involved in her care found themselves fluctuating between despair, anger and helplessness, resenting this patient's 'manipulation' (i.e. she 'would not' respond to treatment plans).

I studied my three meetings with Phyllis. On the first occasion she had spoken two sentences to me: 'Both my parents are dead', and 'I cook and clean at home, that's all I do'. This was the only verbal communication I had about herself. In the first two meetings she had wanted to kiss and touch me and her few words had been spoken in a childlike voice. She had run away from me or wanted cigarettes, a comb or anything in my pockets. Saying 'No' to her demands triggered violent outbursts. In our third meeting she wept, was confused and seemed to have no memory of how long she had been in hospital or how she had behaved. She didn't run away and wanted to know how her boyfriend and daughter were.

I realised that I had a young child in front of me for most of that short time we met. It was a toddler who searched through pockets and developed a tantrum when people said no. On the other hand, she was also a realistically distressed adult, concerned about her boyfriend and child.

I guessed she was telling me something about her condition and that she needed to be treated both as a toddler and an adult. She had also told me the reason she was like this: her mother had died very recently and her father died when she was two years old; in addition, she had never faced that painful business of how to satisfy her intellectual and social needs whilst caring for a small child at home.

I felt there was hope for this woman, even though her adult self was so overshadowed by the toddler. At the end of our final meetng she said 'It's too late, I'm too ill!' I replied that she had indeed been very ill but that she would get better.

I wanted to communicate with Phyllis in a way that showed I understood her language. We couldn't have a conversation. However, I could attempt to arrange her environment in such a way that she would feel taken care of as a toddler and also appreciated as an adult: the institution could become therapeutic for her. The staff needed a means of integrating and holding the feelings generated in working with such disturbed behaviour. I shared my interpretation of her condition with them. I briefly explained about regression and its curative function. I admitted my inexperience in dealing with such severe regression, but offered support in terms of team discussions and supervision of individuals' relationships with Phyllis. Negative feelings were to be expected and worked with. The team hadn't quite expected this kind of interpretation, and the sceptics stared open mouthed. The optimists, however, enjoyed the fun of deciding how they should care for a toddler. Enthusiasm and caring nurses carried the day. They were prepared to try anything.

Interpretation and guidance were needed in developing an overall treatment plan that used a close relationship between staff and patient. Guilt and blame were high on the list of personal reactions to the use of a seclusion room. I proposed that this action could be seen in a positive light. Several nurses had noticed that Phyllis asked to return to seclusion when out on the ward for short periods. Here was the toddlers need for security, protection and a 'safe place'. Why not make it a homely place to be? She was moved to an ordinary room that could be locked but which she was encouraged to use as her own room. Personal belongings, photos and furnishings were provided to create a homely atmosphere. She was given a clock so that she could be aware of the general structuring of her day and so that the adult could be encouraged, as well as the toddler.

Nurses devised toiletting, dressing and eating programmes, providing constant care and attention between two nurses on opposite shifts. They followed their natural inclinations to be warm and affectionate, giving hugs and kisses when wanted and reassurance and encouragement when needed. They were also firmly rebuking when appropriate e.g. there were several tantrums as this woman began to recover when she threw bedclothes out of her window, smashed the clock and refused to wear only one set of clothes instead of four or five at once. Occupational therapists maintained their contact with her, sharing conversations, and simple activities. The doctor set aside regular time to talk to her and see if her adult side could be encouraged to share and explore her feelings.

Within a week this woman was continent, dressing herself and eating and mixing with other patients. She started to structure her care plan according to her own wishes with the reassurance and encouragement of her nurses.

I continued to work with staff feelings and also to interpret developments for the key nurses and the team as a whole. This included the emergence of this woman's grief in sudden fearful outbursts, and the reactions she showed to staff absences and changes. Photos were used to stimulate memories of her parents and encourage grieving. I continuously stressed the positive aspect of her difficult behaviour for those staff who were given the angry or depressed response when the 'special' nurses were absent. The important aspect was that we, the institution, could contain, hold and integrate all her feelings without disintegrating into conflict or despair.

Within a few weeks, occupational therapists and nurses together helped her to face her first meetings with her three year old daughter, advising on how to handle the toddler's awkwardness and tantrums. They accompanied her through her first steps of going home. Medication had been progressively decreased and electro-convulsive therapy had never been used. She was discharged from hospital six weeks after first being confined in the seclusion room. She left the ward a sophisticated, if somewhat nervous woman.

It is now two and a half years since I was first asked to see Phyllis and over a year since the account of this case was published (Douglas, 1986). On returning from maternity leave a few weeks ago, I was told that she had recently suffered what was described as a 'manic' episode, following her decision to leave her boyfriend. Unfortunately, she had no out patient care at that particular time and had gone abroad. Her behaviour led to her being returned to this country by the Consul. She lost a custody case for her child. She had had a sufficiently good relationship with the ward staff in the hospital, however, to enable her to come and ask to talk about these events. She visited the old seclusion room. Her second crisis had not been nearly as bad and she was asking for help in dealing with her feelings. A psychotherapeutic framework had clearly enabled the institution to provide an environment that could enable this woman to grow.

This first case raised many issues about the use of psychotherapy during acute illness. We had been successful in providing an alternative, psychotherapeutically based treatment whilst Phyllis was an in-patient. I was left rather uncertain however about the role of psychotherapy in her long term care. I was unable to offer the intensity of psychotherapeutic treatment which is recommended when treating people with 'borderline' conditions by authors such as Kernberg (1984). Long waiting lists and other responsibilities of a job based in an NHS clinical psychology department cannot accommodate many individuals who need several psychotherapy sessions in a week.

Case II: Sandra

In this second case, I decided to investigate the kind of psychotherapeutic involvement I could offer for someone who was at risk of breakdown and hospital admission and whether this might be of value. Sandra had specifically asked to see a female therapist because she had recently felt overwhelmed by memories of childhood sexual abuse which she didn't think she could discuss with a man. She waited six months to see me, after first mentioning the problem to her Consultant Psychiatrist. In her initial session with me she talked of needing to let out all that had happened but fearing that things were getting out of hand. She was beginning to see messages about rape and incest in everything that surrounded her: advertisements and bill boards, the way people responded to her at work, on the bus, in the street. She had recently been accused of being 'overly physical' in her contact with adolescent boys in her job. She felt this accusation to be totally unfounded, saying that she was merely comforting and befriending children who were greatly deprived of physical contact and warmth in their home lives.

This contrast between the way she described her behaviour and the way others described her, later proved to be one of the signs I associated with the process that was attempting to work its way through inside her. Her childhood experiences were being re-enacted and she could not hold on to her existence in the present.

We had only five weeks of regular individual sessions before this process took charge. She talked of issues from the past which were refusing to be overlooked. Focussing on the here and now did not help her to contain these experiences and feelings and she felt she had never faced her past adequately. There was unresolved grief over abortions she had undergone eighteen years earlier, fear and hatred of men stemming from family incest, current grief over a separation from her husband, which she felt had been brought about through her psychological state.

In the fifth week of sessions her mother died, ending an eighteen month illness. The sheer number of significant losses finally tipped the balance and Sandra could no longer face the increasing visions, voices, hallucinations and persecutory experiences that crowded into her life. I suggested admission to hospital and she took up the offer with tears of relief.

Hanging on to the idea that a psychotic breakdown can be beneficial was not easy! I already felt a failure. I was also bewildered by the distance that the process was creating between us. Sandra could relate to me in a rational, appropriately emotional way letting me into her past but she found it much harder to open up about her present chaos. Letting me into her disturbing thoughts, voices and visions required more trust than we had yet built up.

I began to work on my feelings. The sense of personal failure about the hospital admission was undoubtedly linked to my institutional setting, where the aim is to prevent a breakdown or crisis occurring, in line with good preventative mental health ideas. I had also sensed this attitude in Sandra herself, her determination to hang on to the appearance of normality, the shame and guilt she felt about her inability to function in a 'socially worthy' way. She, too, classed herself as a failure.

As a therapist I needed to rethink, to discover the positive role I had played in enabling Sandra to bring out her symptoms. It was quite simple, I had merely asked Sandra what she would like to aim for in therapy, then attempted to give her the space to do this. She had talked about her family background, concentrating on the repeated experience of incest and sexual exploitation on the one hand and the overbearing pressure to achieve, on the other. The general message seemed to be one of intrusion from both men and women, allowing no opportunity for her to discover herself, her own abilities and interests, likes and dislikes. When she talked she became enraged, shouting and crying. She was angry about her hospital treatment, also. She felt she had been pressurised during previous hospital stays, expected to return to normal life and full time employment too soon. As soon as she seemed to be functioning 'normally' on the outside she was assumed to be well. Inside she felt suicidal, unable to see the point of returning to a meaningless marriage and a restricted, isolated existence which contained no joy. For twenty years she had struggled to keep herself in one piece on the outside. She 'performed' in her job then returned home to let out the despair and anguish. Her first admission to a psychiatric hospital had been within a year of her second abortion, about sixteen years previously. There had been many admissions to hospital since then. She had increasingly lost confidence in herself and placed her husband in the position of adviser, parent and sage. Her breakdowns and admissions to psychiatric hospitals proved to her and all around her that she was not able to function as a 'normal' human being in society. Her recent separation from her husband proved that she couldn't keep a man and wasn't good enough to be loved.

From these accounts, and an examination of the role institutions had previously played in Sandra's treatment, I gradually formed ideas as to the positive role our institution could play in her treatment. I did not yet understand her symptoms but hoped to as the process inside her unfolded. Her anger was about intrusion and restriction. Presumably, any close relationship would trigger the fears and feelings related to this.

I interpreted Sandra's plea as one for space, as well as

support, interest and availability of staff within the institution when needed. Any progress in developing relationships within the institution would undoubtedly trigger her fears related to intrusion and possibly worsen her symptoms. I felt we needed to allow her to manage this process, withdrawing or approaching as she could. Unfortunately, asking for staff to 'follow the process' does not fit in with the usual acute admission ward policy. Psychiatric admission is generally about controlling illness, symptoms or behaviour and bringing it back to normal. Hence the sympathetic and enthusiastic response by the ward team to the psychotherapeutic interventions in the first case described. The multidisciplinary team repeatedly returned to this issue of following rather than controlling Sandra's condition during her hospital stay. This request for 'unconditional love' proved to be an extremely wearing task much of the time, sometimes an alarming one, too. For Sandra there was the pressure of employment and her home circumstances. Allowing herself to be out of action meant loss of earnings and could have led to her losing her job. She decided to sell her house during her stay and became temporarily homeless. For the team working with Sandra there was the continual feeling of helplessness as they watched her make decisions which they feared could ruin her future happiness. Even more frustrating for them were the long periods where it seemed she was doing nothing positive about her circumstances, merely using the hospital for 'bed and board'. Much of the time she did not discuss issues with staff or seek their help. When she did she was usually in a state of acute grief or upset over incidents which she couldn't talk about.

During her six months stay she continued to see me for individual psychotherapy sessions. She began to examine her visual and auditory experiences. She knew these were separate from her actual experience at the time but could not escape their persecutory nature. Her reason for wanting to be admitted to hospital was protection from the visions and voices that haunted her at night. Her house had become a chamber of horrors: dead bodies were under the floor boards, murders were enacted in the garden. Mutilated bodies surrounded her. She was terrified of sleeping alone in her house.

Scene by scene we pieced together the significance of these experiences. They were alarming because they were intrusive, uncontrollable. Sometimes she felt they had a psychic nature in that they depicted events she would later read about in the newspaper. Sometimes she felt they faced her with episodes from her past or people she was trying to block out of her memory. This was particularly the case with her mother. She always perceived these 'visitations' as menacing. I encouraged her to concentrate on the positive function these visitors might have. Were they encouraging her to examine issues that she had left unresolved, such as her feelings towards her mother, toward violence from the past or towards her own potential violence? I felt my own fear in exploring these psychotic states and began to understand the terrifying nature of these experiences. I turned to literature on psychic experiences to look for possible ways of helping Sandra to deal with this creative process. There were many parallels between her experiences and those of mediums and spiritual healers. They have the advantage, however of a system of protection from unwanted 'callers'. They see themselves as receivers of thoughts and 'vibrations' transmitted by both the living and the dead. They believe they can tune in to these 'vibrations' in a particular state of consciousness. They also talk of the dangers of being 'blown open' to such vibrations, through drugs or severe stress. Various methods of 'closing oneself' have been described, which include visualisation, contact with nature through walks in the country or gardening and mundane practical tasks that help focus concentration on external reality.

As we examined the uses of this kind of thinking, Sandra began to talk about her mother's craziness. Her mother had, she believed been psychic. She had also been frightened of strangers and burglars. She went through periods of avoiding all contact with people, locking herself and family inside the house. Gradually Sandra faced her grief over her mother.

During her hospital stay Sandra experienced various crises, many involving her dealing with other patients. These were examined by the staff team in relation to her early childhood experiences of incest and abuse.

Towards the end of six months Sandra decided that the institution was bad for her health. She wanted to choose her own food, eat more healthily, and get away from other patients. She asked for help in finding a flat. After some weeks she decided she would have to find a place herself since the social worker wasn't having any luck in doing this. We continued our psychotherapy sessions on a regular weekly basis. She returned to a fulltime job and faced the despair and depression she associated with her work. During her hospital stay she had begun to write poetry and short stories. She now lived alone for the first time in twenty years. She started to look for social outlets and ways of developing new relationships.

It is two years since my first contact with Sandra. She is currently examining extremely painful material related to her illegal abortions. She is now able to do this without being taken over by psychotic symptoms. She recently identified the situations that can lead to her overinclusive thinking and grandiose theories of the universe. One involved sexual attraction to a man, the other being rejected by a woman. Throughout therapy she has had the back up of the institution in one form or another. Day centre staff involved her in various creative activities and groups, at her request her consultant psychiatrist arranged to see her periodically to demonstrate his continued interest in her progress. She is also examining the role the institution has had in her healing process. She has described at length the benefits of being able to socialise with other people experiencing psychotic states. She emphasised the value of these distant but empathic relationships and their contrast with the terrifying experience of ordinary relationships in the outside world. She could approach and withdraw at will as a visitor to the hospital after she was discharged.

From these two cases it is clear that assessment of the individual psychotherapeutic material is necessary in order to decide upon the appropriate kind of therapeutic intervention and environment within the institution. In the first case, a structured environment was essential for regression to be contained. In the second case unstructured space was essential to enable a woman to discover her 'self' unhindered.

On the basis of these and similar cases I have worked with over the past three years, I am beginning to develop a personal 'working' model of psychotic or schizoid processes for use in clinical practice.

PSYCHOTIC PROCESSES AND INSTITUTIONS: A MODEL FOR CLINICAL PRACTICE

Initially, I attempt to identify and understand the individual's experience and the response of those around them i.e. the family, friends and society as a whole, so that the experience and the response can be acknowledged and worked on by the individual and the institution during a hospital stay. Often, the individual will have spent the period prior to admission in a state of ignorance, denial, avoidance or fear, gripped by symptoms that cannot be explained logically to others. There is seemingly no awareness of the symptoms being part of the self and they become increasingly separate from the person. It is as if the individual has been 'taken over' or occupied by an invading army. The constant barrage of voices, visual hallucinations and chaotic thought distances the person from those around.

The reactions of others is generally a mixture of confusion, despair and anger with someone who apparently behaves in a way which has no regard for them and their feelings. They may see sadness, anger, violence, preoccupation and lack of concern shown in varying degrees, often without any explanation from the individual and an apparent disregard for effects, even on those who are emotionally close. Further, the relationship they thought they had with this person might no longer exist and they no longer know the rules by which he or she is operating.

The 'symptoms' may take over completely, breaking down communication between the individual and those around. The 'sane' can no longer understand what is happening and the so called 'insane' either seek or are persuaded to accept asylum.

This chaos, despair and anger will be shared by any staff attempting to work with the individual experiencing such a breakdown. A major therapeutic task, therefore, is identifying, accepting and using such feelings positively. This includes careful examination of ones own feelings, as well as those of other staff. Having acknowledged these feelings, the psychotherapist is better prepared for the painful struggle which lies ahead for any staff team coping with the disturbing process.

In claiming a positive value for entering an institution I assume that in some cases one-to-one, group or family therapy approaches would not be enough to enable the individual to grow. I see the institution as a place for that person to be whilst living through a psychological process that distances her or him from ordinary human relationships and functioning in usual roles. The institution has a positive meaning and function for the individual, which has to be found and used.

In considering the disturbing process itself, I personally see much similarity between psychotic and creative thinking. Boundaries are loosened and reality and imagination merge. Adopting an holistic or homoeopathic model (Vithoulkas, 1980) of health could lead us to conceptualise the psychotic breakdown as an attempt to heal which needs assistance, understanding and an appropriate response, in other words, guidance along a hazardous path. Viewed in this light, a psychotic process is positive and has a potentially beneficial outcome. The task for the person within the process and for those who wish to assist, is to learn how to use the opportunity, and to provide a safe and adequate environment for the person to grow and a gradual meaning to the chaos and apparent destruction involved.

It seems to me that much of the difficulty in caring for the acutely disturbed person stems from our lack of understanding of the disturbing experience itself and its function for the individual. Whichever institution houses the person during a severe crisis or breakdown, be it the family home, community mental health centre or psychiatric hospital, a particular relationship or series of relationships is set up between that individual and the institution. Using psychotherapeutic skills and methods we can examine these relationships, attempt to understand the process in operation and, hopefully enable the institution and the individual to work cooperatively and productively in a therapeutic alliance.

REFERENCES

Douglas, A., (1986), Psychotherpay in an institutional setting: Another look, _Changes_, Vol. 4, No. 1.

Kernberg, O., (1984), _Object Relations Theory and Clinical Psycho-analysis_, Aronson, New York.

Vithoulkas, G., (1980), _The Science of Homoeopathy_, Grove Press, New York.

How can the feminine be introduced into our institutions?

J. GOMERSALL

INTRODUCTION

There is an increasing awareness of the demoralisation and dampening of enthusiasm which can take place for everyone involved in institutions. This can occur not only in prisons and psychiatric hospitals but in all the many organisations which society creates in order to fulfil certain of its functions. The functions which are of special interest here are those which isolate or care for those individuals who deviate from the standards of behaviour agreed by a majority in a particular society.

The dictionary defines 'institution' in two principal ways. Firstly as an organisation or establishment founded for a specific purpose and secondly as an established custom, law or relationship in a society or community.

Both of these definitions contain the term 'establishment' or 'established', indicating one of the main characteristics of institutions which is their resistance to change. In practise this is expressed as an ineptitude in managing change, and also as difficulties in coping with ayone, whether outside or inside the institution, who is the potential harbinger of such change.

POWER

Sụch definitions also imply the existence of some power

within an institution which acts to enable its functions to be fulfilled. Goffman (1968) defined and described the 'total institution' where such power is operated by one group of individuals who have close control over the behaviour and welfare of others. The problems and inflexibility of such institutions are well known. It is not always appreciated however that a similar mode of operation of power, which will here by denoted as 'masculine', is evident in a more covert form in those institutions classified under the second definition. These latter organisations are not as easily recognised nor are they as stable as total institutions. The power within them is however similar, although it operates through such characteristics as the attitudes of those involved. These are often based on the past experience of certain individuals which is projected onto other people who surround them in their present environment. The power also operates through the upholding of ideals. These may be orchestrated by special charismatic leaders who have the facility to gather individual energy and mobilise it into concerted group energy.

This paper is an attempt to study some of the ways in which this power operates. It views some of the problems of institutions as being simply a destructive misuse of what is to be termed a 'masculine' operation of power. It is proposed that what is required is to balance such a mode of operation by being increasingly aware of the possibility of a less objective one which will be termed 'feminine' (whilst not denying that this can also operate in an unbalanced way). Jungian philosophy holds that such forms of power do not exclusively exist in the individual personal psyche but stem from the operation of a collective unconscious. Difficult as it is to prove the existence of such an entity, some individuals and groups appear able to tap a powerful force, although this is often done with great deviation to one side or the other of a feminine/masculine dichotomy. More than this is needed for a creative balance and as creatures, each with specific gender, no individual man or woman has a monopoly of what lies on each side of this dichotomy. Male and female chauvenism each battling to distance the other may now have little more to teach us.

The existence of masculine and feminine attributes within every individual is something which is often ignored by many philosophers and sociologists. This is hardly surprising when one sees some types of group influence surging through institutions and societies. Whether such power is orchestrated and directed by archetypal or by more tangible political or social forces, the ability of individuals to block or facilitate them is worthy of careful consideration. Psychotherapeutic studies may give valuable insights here.

An inability to act or make influential choices is often put down by an individual to the place which they occupy in some hierarchy of status or responsibility within the institution. Although such a place may seem insignificant, it is never one from which power cannot be influenced. Once a position of professional powerlessness is abandoned, it is possible for any person to begin to study the complicated network of power which surrounds them. Eventually such study may lead to an effective pulling of one or two relevant strings in the network. However it will always be important to remain aware of all the forces, both outside and within the individual (which can indeed be powerful if they work together) in order to achieve what are judged to be legitimate aims of an institution, with preservation of the autonomy, happiness and creativity of all who are involved in its functioning.

Masculine power and its excesses

Rycroft (1977) describes the classical Freudian position as associating the term 'masculine' with the human attributes of activity, aggressiveness, sadism and competitiveness. It is probably reasonable to add to these the capacity for objectivity. Writers in many fields and disciplines have reiterated similar attributes and if one simply takes the opposite of each of these terms and labels the resulting collection of characteristics as 'feminine' one can clearly see how the vehement condemnation of Freud as being diminishing of women has come about. Terms which imply much more positive force and value will be introduced for the feminine, but first a brief mention will be made of studies of the way in which masculine power has operated and the work of some pioneers who have attempted to modify it.

At the present time, when there is increasing pressure to close residential institutions and for welfare agencies to work in the community, there must be a certain caution that the benefits provided by the old established institutions do not disappear. Henry VIII in closing the monasteries, robbed the community of their caring functions and paved the way for the far more depriving total institutions of the poor law. It is noteworthy that within large total institutions, however disturbing the exploitation may be, it is often at least observable in contrast to the more covert exploitation which can take place in smaller and less definably located institutions. It is just these latter institutions which often blame the larger residential institutions for their shortcomings whilst remaining blind to their own limitations. The climate of blame and clash of ideologies which can result is not likely to produce a balance of a feminine with a masculine mode of operation of power. It is usually merely a meeting of two antagonistic masculine modes.

Of the many authors who have described the problems of what are here being broadly defined as 'masculine' attributes four are worthy of special mention. Martin Heidegger and Michael Foucault are notable for their attempts to discover basic mechanisms which affect the function of human societies and institutions. They consider both aspects of the definition of institution being used here. The writings of Maxwell Jones and Franco Basaglia are considered for their practical and political attempts to overcome the excesses of masculine domination upon those who are unfortunate in health or status. These are the members of a society who can be so easily isolated by a more priviledged section of that society. It is the latter who can in turn cause isolating institutions to be set up. These are ostensibly established for care and welfare but there are additional motives which remain hidden until challenged, and when such challenge is made it tends to be met with vigorous defensive reactions.

THE IMPORTANCE OF LOOKING BENEATH THE ORDINARY PRACTICES OF SOCIETY

Martin Heidegger (1962) is perhaps one of the most notable writers to look at the way in which the ordinary, simple day to day practices of living of individuals and groups form a background to the way they give meaning to the world around them. This is in many ways separate from systems of belief which often seem more definable and direct in their influence. Heidegger points out how the meaning of such practices in ordinary living is difficult to make explicit but it is often possible to make what he calls 'an interpretation' of the background to these practices. He calls his method 'hermeneutics' (although it must be pointed out that other authors have used this same term to imply rather different methods of interpretation). It would seem that Heidegger is describing an experience and a mode of operation of power which comes under the broad term of 'feminine' as it is being used here. Its meaning is to be distinguished from a direct interpretation such as happens when selfish motivation is suggested as underlying an apparently altruistic action or even when a more sophisticated psychotherapeutic interpretation is made. These are not so difficult to make explicit but can so easily re-enmesh one's thinking in the culture, rather than give the opportunity of looking at a meaning which allows the culture and its everyday practices to be used as a means of transcendence.

For Heidegger, hermeneutics involves understanding and interpretation at a higher level of abstraction than more simple interpretations of why a particular action or practice takes place. It is an interpretation of an interpretation. This is reminiscent of the observation that one way of getting out of a double bind situation is to make a meta communication, a communication about a communication, For example, if a person says to one 'Hallo! how nice to see you, when will you be leaving?' it is reasonable to point out the possible contradiction behind the statement and ask for clarification of their honest sentiments about the desirability of one's continued presence.

The problems of making explicit such a way of seeing things are obvious. However, it is evident as a process in such situations as: that type of psychotherapeutic interaction which facilitates an individual in the art of looking at their own behaviour (developing an observing ego); in the 'peak experience' described by Maslow (1968); and in the care which is taken as the Buddhist monk moves towards enlightenment but is still involved in scrubbing the temple floor. In each of these there is an element of what existential writers would refer to as 'being' rather than 'doing'.

The main problem in such situations, where there is the operation of a balancing force (here referred to as 'feminine'), is that of language and the means of communication. The language of many of the arts such as poetry may be what needs to be utilised and as far as welfare institutions are concerned, a first step may be being made in the advent of such things as occupational and art therapy and in many of the projective techniques now used in group and other approaches.

THE IMPORTANCE OF LOOKING AT THE TECHNIQUES BY WHICH POWER OPERATES

In one of his latest writings Michel Foucault (1986) points out that in freeing ourselves and the institutions within which we work to be truly individual it is necessary to look at techniques by which power operates rather than simply attacking one group or institution.

Such a technique or form of power:

> applies itself to immediate everyday life which categorises the individual, marks him by his own individuality, attaches him to his own identity, imposes a law of truth on him which he must recognise and which others have to recognise in him. It is a form of power which makes individuals subjects. There are two meanings of subject: subject to someone else by control and dependence, and tied to his own identity by a concscience or self knowledge. Both meanings suggest a form of power which subjugates and makes subject to.

He goes on to point out that our present institutions, and this must apply especially to helping institutions, operate through a mixture of the easily recognisable authoritarian (what he calls 'totalising') power techniques, combined with what he calls the technique of 'pastoral power'. This latter form of power operates through assurance of personal salvation and through sacrifice of all individuals, including those who operate the power, by looking after people in every aspect of their lives and knowing an individual intimately.

The analogy here is obvious between what Foucault is describing and with the Jungian concept of the archetype of the 'old wise man' or 'earth mother', also with the therapist who operates in an interpretive and omniscient way and fails to return autonomy to the patient. Just the same failure is seen in any coercive charismatic leader who uses those whom he leads for the inflation of his own egoic power.

It is often only too easy to see the destructiveness of such charisma when it is situated at the opposite pole to that into which our own upbringing has forced us. However as Deikman (1976) points out, we can become fixed in either

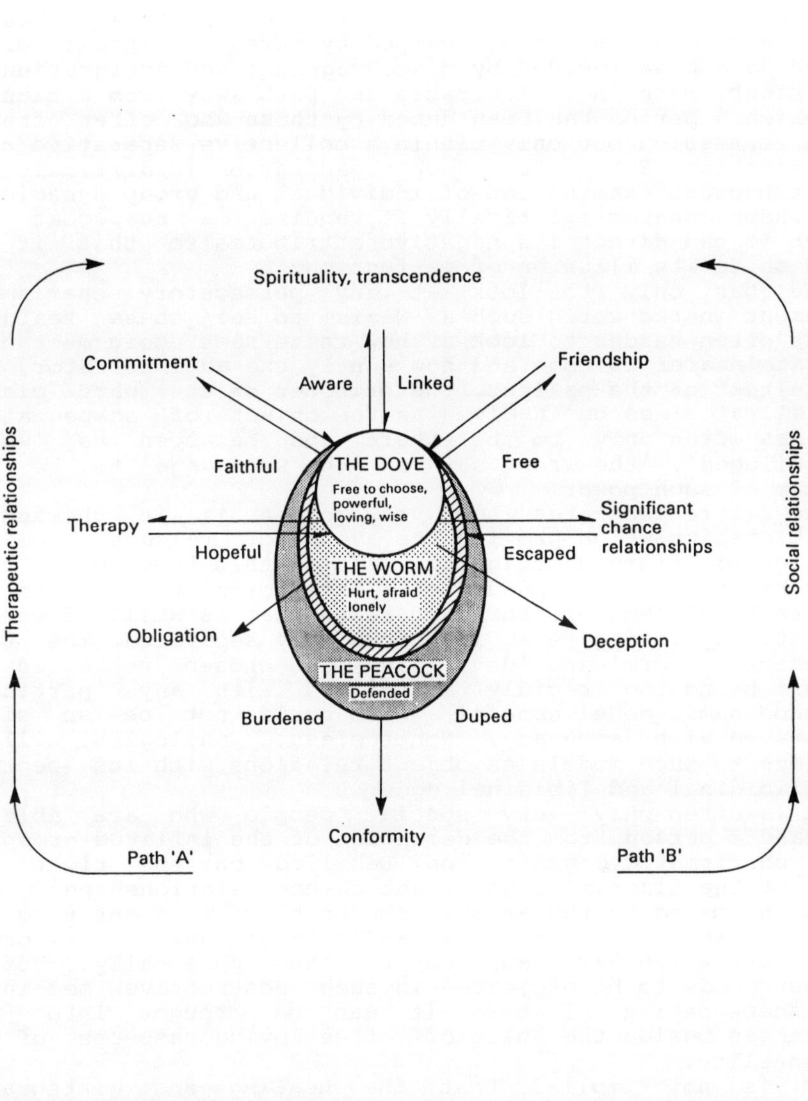

Figure 1. The integrative potential of various underlying phenomena in relationships.

rebellion or conformity, and each of these are still indicative of bondage to the repressive parent.

Figure 1 represents two paths which can lead towards a non egoic relationship, something that most people have at least glimpsed. Path 'A' shown on the left, represents a situation where a person has become swamped by parts of their psyche which have been invaded by discouragement and denigration. On the right, Path 'B' illustrates the path away from a sitution in which a person has been duped by those who offer freedom from repression but only within a collective separative egoic organisation. Escape from such organisation is difficult not least because examination of individual and group dynamics is forbidden. Characteristically it requires a scapegoat onto which it can direct its negative attributes so that it can hold on to its illusion of perfection.

One has only to look at any persecutory charismatic movement in the world such as Nazism to see these features. It is often harder to look at how these same egoic mechanisms operate nearer to home and how subtly the administrator, the consultant or the patient, the prisoner or the ward cleaner can all at times be involved as the object of scapegoating. One has often only to be there and be seen as 'weak', 'privileged', 'the wrong sex' or 'the wrong age' to be the victim of such power.

The figure indicates how very often it is therapeutic relationships which provide the avenue of release from the bondage of enforced obligation. To do this they must first look beneath the defended social exterior of the psyche and interact with what is hurt and reach what is still free and potentially loving, even if defensively separated. The terms 'peacock', 'worm' and 'dove' have been chosen to avoid the figure being too rigidly associated with any particular psychodynamic model none of which could not be so simply portrayed with accuracy. Nonetheless, analogies will be obvious to such models as object relations with its central, antilibidinal and libidinal egos.

It is often only very special people who are able to release a person from the deception of the inflated group ego of a charismatic organisation. Labelled on the right hand side of the diagram 'significant chance relationships'.

As indicated by the arrows, the problem is of entering what is hurt within the individual and helping them to accept it as a hurt which has happened to them personally, but no longer needs to be projected in such destructive mechanisms as scapegoating. Instead it can be brought into full awareness beside the split off, free loving aspects of the personality.

It is not implied that the healing and integrating processes represented on each side of the diagram do not occur in both therapeutic and other significant relationships. However, persons caught in charismatic movements, who are often quite ego-syntonic and satisfied with their life situation, do not present very frequently for therapy.

THE IMPORTANCE OF CONSIDERING THE USE OF ENERGY

What is helpful about such writings as those of Heidegger and Foucault is that they free one from the urge to be an iconoclast and destroy every institution without even recognising that the problem is in the operation of power rather than the institution itself, the purpose or service of which may still be both needed and legitimate. Foucault cleverly never gives finite answers to what one must do, but armed with his insights one can work at producing the most effective use of human energy considering both the collective and individual blocks.

Robert de Board in his book, 'The Psychoanalysis of Organisations' (1978), puts it quite simply:

> Many work practices are really defence mechanisms and drain vital energy away from productive work.

A model based on psychotherapeutic principles can be of value in studying how energy is expended and conserved. Figure 2, at its centre represents the individual or institution as a car battery! This provides a simple plan for studying those activities and influences which can be classed as 'irradiators' (depicted top right) and those which can be considered 'drains' (depicted bottom left). It is also recognised on the left of the diagram that some activities to which energy is directed may in fact be creative and have free flowing interaction with 'irradiator' sources. Others, which are termed 'acceptable duties', are neutral, neither draining nor irradiating. The diagram also indicates how internal destructive forces can inhibit everything creative both externally and internally and it is to the recognition of these forces that much psychodynamic, philosophical, sociological and other studies address themselves.

The term 'integrative overself' has been coined to represent such studies and to avoid the precise terminology of any particular discipline. It need not be left to informed academics to pursue such study. Any insightful person can view the balance of input and output both in themselves and in any organisation around them. They would do well however to look quite deeply into both the individual psyche and the hidden subcultures of human groups. The more subtle internal creative and destructive activities may then be revealed.

The function of the special type of external irradiator, in the form of the facilitating therapist, is indicated down the right hand side of the figure. Once some insight is gained into the internal conflicts of the person or institution such a facilitator may be able to help reduce the effect of internal destrutive activity by initiating some form of therapeutic discharge rather than having it constantly mediating pathological drainage or inhibiting what is creative and restorative.

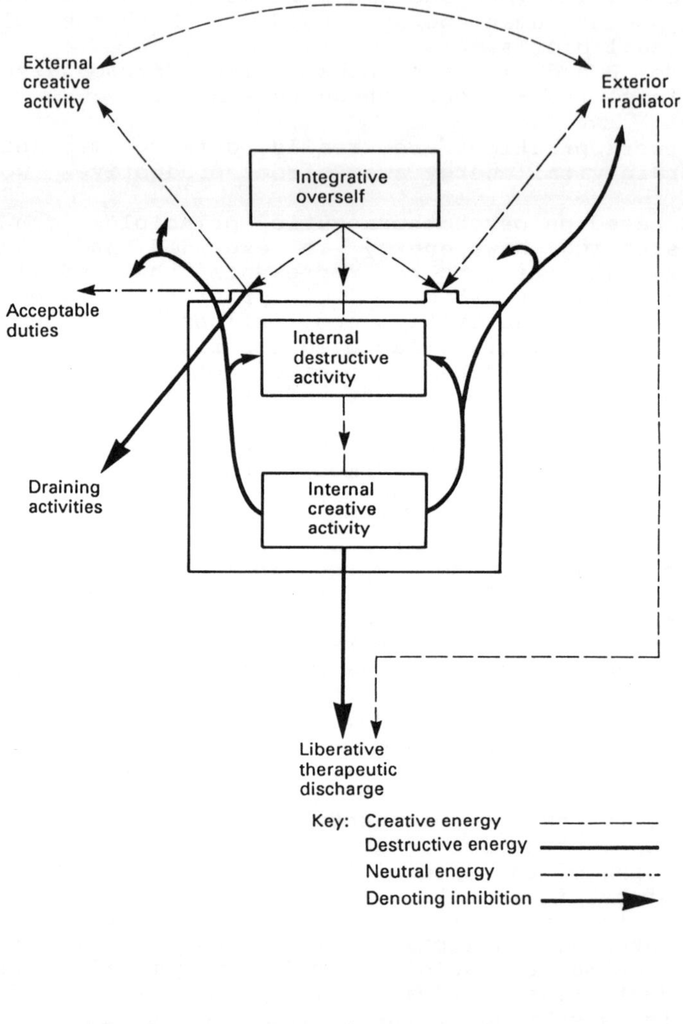

Figure 2. Balance of creative and destructive energies.

DIRECT REFORMERS OF INSTITUTIONS AND SOCIETIES

Foucault (1973) points out how such reformers of total psychiatric institutions as Tuke and Pinel substituted for external persecution a type of moral management which made the individual responsible for their behaviour, and then tried to resubjugate the person to some acceptable code of behaviour.

In his writings on social psychiatry and the therapeutic community, Maxwell Jones (1968) put forward major reforming ideas which enabled individuals to find and develop their creative potential. Progress within the therapeutic community movement has continued and it is undoubtedly of value to many individuals who have never found a place in society.

Franco Basaglia (1968) recognised however, after considerable experience of therapeutic communities, that the democratisation which such communities developed and upheld was directed much more at the community itself rather than confronting the society without, from which its clients came. Fundamental problems may exist within the client but one must be wary that the use of the term 'adjustment' when applied to an individual is not clouding the much more difficult task of confronting society with the adjustment which _it_ may need to effect.

DEFINING THE FEMININE

Like many terms the concept feminine has been grossly over used and expanded. Freud implied connotations of helplessness, passivity and receptiveness, and his so-called phallocentricity has been much criticised (Rycroft, 1977), Surprisingly, Jung does not use the term 'feminine' specifically but focusses on the importance of cultural influences on gender on the often repressed 'anima' in a man's personality (Samuels et al, 1986).

Seifert (1986) in an interesting commentary on the story of Snow White, mentions four criteria which correspond to those of many other authors. These can be expanded to give rather more precise and practical indications to assist workers in the helping professions and in institutions to obtain a greater degree of balance, both in their place of work and in their personal lives. This can give that sense of meaning to life and non-competitive zeal for which so many people seem to be yearning, yet failing to achieve.

Seifert identified these feminine attributes as: (i) a sense of tenderness, (ii) the capacity for devotion, (iii) the recognition of feminine creativity and (iv) the courage to look at rational and intellectual deliberations form the viewpooint of feeling and value.

The sense of tenderness

On the radio recently, a well known poet was visiting a school and the children had been asked to give their ideas about what a poet was. The reactions which emerged included such replies as 'Someone who ponces around amongst daffodils all day making up sloppy rhymes'. Such a tendency to defend vehemently against the expression of tenderness is common. For many people this defence often seems to be restricted to their work, and they may be quite aware of the existence of another, tender side and able to share it in their home life and with children and animals. Extreme examples of this phenomenon are the concentration camp guards whose personality at home changed completely from that which they showed in the institution.

A reason for such resistance to tenderness is not just a fear of what might be seen as unmanly, un-British or namby-pamby, but also a fear of blame and retaliation. Lindebergh (1979) points out how it is difficult to be involved with individuals and share what she terms those 'one and only' moments and then recognise that these must end.

Whilst such a tender exchange takes place, others are likely to become jealous and try to sabotage it. Also, when such an exchange ends, the person with whom one has shared it is likely to feel bereft. Such creative moments are 'present' orientated phenomena, they cannot be held onto and often they can be evoked only by the most general and casual planning of the milieu in which they will emerge, rather than the forceful and detailed orchestration of a whole event. It is hardly surprising that with the inevitable climate of blame which surrounds such feminine exchanges of 'one and only moments' the concentration in so many institutions is to defend against them. This is done via a series of rules and guidelines about professional conduct which looks at blame as a phenomenon which exists outside individuals and one which can be objectified in terms of deviation from various professional practices and which can be defended against by rules and ceremonies in which tenderness has little place (Gomersall, 1987).

There is no evidence that efficiency and task effectiveness are diminished in a tender institution, indeed, when studying America's best run and most efficient and profitable companies, Peters and Waterman (1982) found that attention to individual needs for such things as aesthetically pleasing surroundings was a notable feature.

The capacity for devotion

Commitment is an essential part of both management and therapy, and authors such as Assagioli (1974) have pointed to the importance of recognising a 'personally operating will' (which is so different from one which is directed by an external demanding force as represented at the bottom left hand corner of figure 1). It is also different, as previously mentioned, from one which is operative under the force of charismatic leadership (represented at the bottom right hand corner of figure 1). C. S. Lewis (1971) indicates in what he calls 'friendship' the feminine force which is required to balance those aspects of a relationship in which there is need for a more defined commitment. In the special way in which Lewis defines this friendship, there are no goals or aims other than the sharng of personal and life experience. Apter (1982) distinguishes a similar mode of experience, which he terms 'metamotivational', in his description of the 'paratelic state'.

What is evident, as indicated in figure 1, is the need for the entities 'friendship' and 'commitment' to come together and for individuals to be able to negotiate changes between such pairs of different but potentially balancing phenomena. Such a balance is required both within the individual psyche and with relationships in the society around. Such devotion produces neither a smothered dependency nor a distancing, objectifying independence.

The recognition of feminine creativity

Seifert points out that what is referred to as feminine creativity is much more an attitude, an involvement with a feminine way of being. It may need to be married with more definable functions as planning the steps to a goal, assessing costs in money, time and effort, and in measuring what is produced. Such phenomena are so obvious in modern management skills, flow diagrams, outcome studies and assessment of cost-effectiveness. However, marrying such phenomena is not the same as being swamped by them. Feminine creativity is much more analogous to the process of conception, giving birth and nurturing the growing child. It involves the sacrifice of self to a natural process in which the strong separative ego is laid aside, at least momentarily, as is so artfully described by Alan Watts (1958) in his description of human sexuality. It is being fully present and part of a process as it evolves, it is not having to justify or define one's part in that process.

The ability to look at the intellectual and rational from the point of view of feeling and value.

This feminine attribute is most pertinent when applied science offers something to society, for example nuclear power or the kidney machine. The danger is that only its advantages are seen without a full interactive evaluation of where it is able to be truly of benefit to human beings, where its likely effects are dubious and where they are likely to be disturbing or even dangerous.

BALANCING FEMININE AND MASCULINE

What is advocated is not an inflation of either that feminine or masculine power which only feeds the separative aspect of individual or collective egos (Jones, 1973). What is being looked at are the attitudes and practices within institutions which make for open communication, breaking down barriers which separate individuals. Foucault (1979) describes Jeremy Bentham's 'Panopticon', where a tower at the centre can operate its observing power on peripheral cells but no reverse means is available for the periphery to observe the centre or to influence it. It is most important to be aware of the need to reverse this tendency.

Interesting attempts to recognise the need for such reversal of observing power is seen in the current interest of the media in the personal lives of Royal and other famous people. However, this is little more than tokenism and has not resulted in facilitating genuine two way communication. The power of control and observation still flows almost uninterruptedly from centre to periphery. In such a situation, an excellent way to initiate change is to deliberately question established ceremonies, especially those such as documenting and recording, or establish new ones which deliberately reverse or block the flow of power, rather like Gandhi advocated in a political arena and workers like Erickson and Rossi (1979) demonstrate in their unusually effective therapeutic approaches. Gandhi in a famous letter to Nehru advised that the guide to anyone in power should be to ask how any decision one makes is going to affect the poorest and most disadvantaged person in the system.

It is possible to see a healthy irrationality in some of these maneuvers. As J. B. Priestley (1979) described in defending the woolly mind:

> It combines scepticism of everything with credulity about everything. Being woolly it has no hard edges. It is easily pliant yet it has its own toughness. Because it bends it does not break.

In Ancient Greece, during the 'heiros gamos' or sacred union between high priest and high priestess, unconscious forces were allowed full reign. However lustful, they were to be fully experienced, accepted and transcended. Esther Harding (1971) a Jungian writer describes how this was an attempt to release primitive instincts from the unconscious and integrate them into the conscious personality.

Although the ceremonies must have varied from time to time and place to place, what is fascinating about the descriptions is that even then it was recognised that there could be dire effects on the sanity of the individual participants if they did not make a sacrifice of those attributes which could invade and inflate their masculine and feminine egos. The high priest was required to renounce reason, control and domination. The priestess had to sacrifice the needs of her unconscious to possess that which she loves. One way of helping to ensure this was the general rule that after the ceremony was over the participants were not permitted to see each other again. It is easy to imagine how difficult it must have been to keep this rule.

Much excellent writing has used such accounts of ancient ceremonies and stories from mythology to underline the importance of being aware of the problems of allowing either the masculine or feminine to inflate and dominate, and also the need to recognise their destructive and creative sides. The importance of the Jungian approach is that health, integration and individuation is not generated via the idealisation of any one aspect of human personality which can so easily lead to repression of its opposite. Instead, it is a process of recognising and bringing into balance all the elements, whether conscious or hidden. This requires a toleration of the inconsistency and paradox which at first it presents.

John Rowan (1987) excellently reviews the writings which emphasise the basic androgenous nature of humankind and explodes the patriarchal myth that qualities still traditionally labelled 'feminine' and 'masculine' are separated so radically between the two sexes. Yet he does this without robbing them of their vibrant relationship potential.

He recognises how important it is for each of us to look into our own nature and see there the vulnerability of what Franklin Jones (1973) calls 'the separative human ego'. Ken Wilber (1983) demonstrates how throughout humankind's development one can see beneath the turmoils of history the needs of this ego to preserve itself from feared extinction. Some of the resulting struggles have simple mortal preservation as their motivating force. Others, perhaps far more devastating in their potential for causing the mass murder of war, have the motive of striving for immortality at their root. Such striving is not in the context of a recognition of authentic relationship as taught by many of the greatest teachers. Instead it is the attempt to achieve immortal glory by 'proving', often in bloodiness, that 'my god is better than yours'.

Even if on a much lesser scale and involving bloodless battles, the tensions which separate the various factions within our institutions have a similar basis in the separative ego's need for confirmation and preservation.

Learning to be accepting and considerate towards the possible hurt which could be caused to the vulnerable separative ego of another, may be a first step. Unfortunately however such 'live and let live' philosophies only result in an increase in defensive rituals and in an ignoring of Gandhi's concept of considering the poorest person in the system who, as Foucalt and others have pointed out, is always the major victim of such procedures. Rowan (1987), quoting Hills (1983), points to the problem of the 'spuriously gentle man of our time whose softness protects a core of anger'.

Hills goes on to look at a new masculinity which is emerging. His work is based on what is also emerging as new femininity once the feminist/chauvenist battles are able to still their conflict. It is unfortunate that in such writing the term 'hero' is associated more with the male than the female since it is evident that neither the gentle man nor gentle woman are totally aware of all their potential, even though gentleness can still be a valuable asset on appropriate occasions.

What Hills points out is required of the hero however, (and I assume that this applies to both feminine and masculine heroes) is that if hurt it will not result in panic stricken or depressive flight nor in angry destructive retaliation but that first there will be a looking within to discover that aspect which is 'so hidden that it still has power to sneak up'.

CONCLUSION

Whether for individuals, families or institutions the procedural implications seem very obvious. They have been preached by effective organisations, businesses and therapeutic communities for many years even if what they advocate still falls on the deaf ears of so many who are bound by the seductive competitiveness of egoic battles.

If there are problems or tensions then the need for all involved to meet together and look both outside and within is vital. Only then can forces operating via entrenched attitudes, factional interests and tensions within individual personalities be recognised.

Philosophical works such as those of Heidegger and Foucault can prove excellent insights into general orientation and appropriate milieu for such discussion. The works of Maxwell Jones, Franco Basaglia and many other authors can give a guide as to the practicalities of facilitating organisational change.

So often, however, the core problem lies in those individuals who instead of seeing the need identified by Hills to 'look within', immediately fly into despairing defeated nihilism inflated by deference to the organisational gods (and remember, as Foucault (1979) points out, the central tower in the panoptical can be empty, just as the emperor in the fairy story had no clothes on). Alternatively, they vehemently protest, thrashing around them for the nearest group of people, however inappropriate the bedfellows they may be joining, who will support their immediate needs for security rather than challenge their needs for insight and growth.

ACKNOWLEDGEMENTS

I wish to thank Mrs. Helen Ives for suggesting the idea of introducing a feminine balance within institutions and Dr. Tim Kendall for his insightful discussions on the philosophy of Michel Foucault and access to his library of his writings.

REFERENCES

Apter, M.J., (1982), The Experience of Motivation: The Theory of Psychological Reversals, Academic Press, London.

Assagioli, R.,(1974), The Act of Will, Wildwood House, London.

Basaglia, F., (ed), (1968), Le Instituzione, Negata Einaudi, Turin.

de Board, Robert, (1978), The Psychoanalysis of Organisations, Tavistock Publications, London.

Deikman, A., (1976), Finding Your Way to the Real World Souvenir Press, London.
Erickson, M., H. and Rossi, E. L. (1979), Hypnotherapy: An Exploratory Case Book, Irvington Publishers Inc., New York.
Foucault, M., (1973), A History of Insanity in an Age of Reason, Vintage/Random House, New York.
Foucault, M., (1979), Discipline and Punishment: The Birth of the Prison, Vintage/Random House, New York.
Foucault, M., (1986) in Dreyfus, H. and Rabinow, P. Michael Foucault: Beyond Structeralism and Hemeneutics, The Harvester Press, Brighton.
Goffman, E., (1968), Asylums: Essays on the Social Situation of Mental Patients and Other Inmates, Penguin Books, Harmondsowrth.
Gomersall, J. D., (1987), Defensive caring, Changes, 5, 308-311.
Harding, M.E., (1971), Women's Mysteries, Ancient and Modern, Rider, London.
Heidegger, M., (1962), Being and Time, Harper and Row, New York.
Hills, V., (1983), The courage to let go, Soluna, 4, 25-27.
Jones, F. A. (1973), The Method of the Siddhas, The Dawn Horse Press, Los Angeles.
Jones, M., (1968), Social Psychiatry in Practice, Penguin Books Ltd., Harmondsworth.
Lewis, C.S., (1971), The Four Loves, Fontana, Collins, London.
Lindebergh, A. M., (1979), Gift From the Sea, Chatto and Windus, London.
Maslow, A. H., (1968), Toward a Psychology of Being, Van Nostrand, New York.
Peters, T. J. and Waterman, R. H. Jr., (1982), In Search of Excellence: Lessons from America's Best Run Companies, Harper and Row, New York.
Priestly, J.B., (1979), Over the Long High Wall: Some Reflections on Life, Death and Time, Heineman, London.
Rowan, J., (1987), The Horned God: Feminism and Men as Wounding and Healing, Routledge and Kegan Paul, London.
Rycroft, C., (1977), A Critical Dictionary of Psychoanalysis Penguin, Harmondsworth.
Samuels, A., Shorter, B. and Plaut, F., (1986), A Critical Dictionary of Jungian Analysis, Routledge and Kegan Paul, London.
Seifert, T., (1986), Snow White: Life Almost Lost, Chiron Publications, Wilmette, Illinois.
Watts, A. W., (1958), Nature and Women: A New Approach to Sexual Experience, Thames and Hudson, London.
Wiber, K., (1983), Up From Eden: A Transpersonal View of Human Evolution, Routledge and Kegan Paul, London.

Beating your head against a sponge: the therapeutic community that is Grendon

R. WOODWARD

INTRODUCTION

H.M.P. Grendon is a category B prison near Aylesbury that has a population of approximately 250 inmates. This year sees it celebrate its silver jubilee. Given that many of the prisons in this country can boast a grand Victorian heritage, achieving twenty five years of existence seems a puny summit to scale until it is realised that H.M.P. Grendon is a therapeutic community; or to be more precise, a cooperative of therapeutic communities. For the last twenty five years inmates and staff have fought to make some sense out of why people have done the things they have and how to induce desired changes.

Officially Grendon is a psychiatric prison the history of which starts in a report written by Dr. de Hubert and Dr. East in 1939. Dr. East was Medical Commissioner for prisons and Dr. Hubert a psychotherapist who worked at H.M.P. Wormwood Scrubs. They suggested that:

> psychotherapy as an adjunct to an ordinary prison sentence appears to be effective in preventing or in reducing the chance of future antisocial behaviour.

They suggested that the most satisfactory way of dealing with abnormal and unusual types of criminal would be by the creation of a penal institution of a special kind. Grendon was conceived. It is notable that they saw:

> the main object of psychotherapy in criminal work as being to prevent crime being committed or repeated by the individual.

At this point war created a situation in which the country was able to utilise it's stock of psychopaths, maniacs and ne'er do wells so Grendon's birth was a little delayed. Initially the plan had been to build Grendon in London, however, finding a site was claimed to have been a problem. Many suspect that this was a euphemism for public disquiet at the proximity of such an institution. Those entertaining such a suspicion are not slow to point to the many possible building sites available at that time, a result of the blitz. Eventually the site near Aylesbury was found, and to this day some people who work there are paid an 'inconvenience of location' allowance (perhaps more evidence that it was 'meant to be' in London).

Following its conception in 1939, Grendon was born in 1962. However, during its long pregnancy certain interuterine processes had taken place and the institution that appeared had acquired modified purposes. It appears that a reduction of criminal activity as a result of psychological treatment was not expected. Rather,

> Grendon's three primary objectives will be: to investigate and treat mental disorders generally recognised as responsive to treatment, to investigate offenders whose offences in themselves suggest mental morbidity and to explore the problems of dealing with the psychopath. The prisoners...selected will be those whose mental disorder is not of such nature or degree to qualify for...transfer to a hospital under Section 72 of the Mental Health Act (enacted only three years before) but who require psychiatric treatment and management.
>
> (Commissioner's Report, 1962)

The basic change in emphasis between Grendon's conception and birth, i.e. to change criminal behaviour or investigate, treat and manage difficult criminals, remains to this day a constant source of argument amongst those who try to plan its future development. It also persistently runs through the vast majority of research generated by or about Grendon.

In bringing Grendon up to be a healthy twenty five year old adult, many phases of development have been gone through. Some have been little more than colic or acne however some have been more traumatic. Over the years the regime appears to have moved away from a medical model to a social psychological model (discussed further below). This is reflected, though not attributable to, the fact that the institution is now headed by a prison service Governor whereas before it was headed by a doctor in the role of Medical Superintendent. It would appear that the tinge of schizophrenia is persisting into Grendon's adulthood.

GRENDON AS IT IS TODAY

It is quite possible that by the time this is published, the following description of Grendon may have been rendered inaccurate by decisions made as a result of the latest crisis with chronically overcrowded prisons currently holding a population of around 50,000. The system often makes decisions on numerical grounds at the expense of qualitative considerations. Grendon is particularly vulnerable to these.

Currently Grendon has five treatment wings (four adult and one young offender), an assessment unit and a hospital. Because of the national problem mentioned above Grendon is also housing over fifty Rule 43 prisoners who were transferred in order to alleviate overcrowding elsewhere. This meant that the young offenders were moved into accommodation above two of the adult wings. This unfortunate situation along with the introduction of the much publicised 'Fresh Start' reorganisation of the Prison System (a national reworking of staff hours which will include reduction of overtime) are the current crises with which Grendon as an institution is struggling.

Traditionally the adult units have been more or less autonomous. Each has a regime which, more or less, follows therapeutic community principles, although there are some individual differences in the way these are interpreted and put into operation.

Each wing holds up to forty prisoners and each unit is staffed by one Hospital Principal Officer, one Hospital Senior Officer and ten basic grade staff. Additionally each has a psychiatrist, possibly a psychologist and a probation officer. In some cases lay therapists and professional visitors on placement are common, so it is not unusual to find additional non-uniformed staff on the wings.

The assessment unit, although comparatively new, is in fact a resurrection of an earlier component of the institution. Like all institutions Grendon goes through phases of doing things in different ways, some of which get repeated according to need, changing philosophy and it must be admitted, fashion. The function of the unit is to assess new inmates and to either send them onto the treatment wings or, to return them to the sending institution.

The hospital has recently expanded its functions. It now provides a service to other prisons by taking those inmates who experience a psychiatric breakdown. Apart from this function it provides medical services to the main body of Grendon.

Considerable organisational changes are about to be implemented. The adult units are to be 'paired' in terms of staffing. One Principal officer will be responsible for two of the wings and will be joined by four Senior Hospital Officers and twenty basic grade staff. A psychiatrist and a psychologist will share the responsibility for one pair of wings. On top of this a new attendance system is to be introduced that eliminates overtime. Whilst this appears to represent major change, the main business of Grendon, therapy, is likely to continue without changing stride at all. The strength of the institution is in its population's desire to change themselves through Grendon therapy, a theme which is passed on from generation to generation on each of the wings.

THE INMATES

The inmates are all convicted criminals who have been referred to Grendon, usually by a doctor, as possibly being suitable for therapy. They are a highly recidivist population, and as Marcus (1979) notes, they are a very downwardly mobile population, with a high incidence of people holding an occupational status lower than their fathers. In general they have poor work records, a high incidence of marital breakdown, alcoholism and other difficulties. They exhibit high levels of socially deviant behaviour both inside and outside of the prison setting. None of them however are diagnosable as psychotic and none of them are on psychiatric medication, therapy at Grendon being drug free. This is a crucial policy, and anyone who whilst at Grendon becomes in need of such medication is rested from therapy.

Psychometric testing also shows the population to be highly disturbed, scoring well away from the statistical average for the general population on maladjustment scales.

It is therefore clear from all sources of information that the population of Grendon is far removed from the average person in the street and is likely also to be different from the general prison population. A current part of the Grendon belief system is the statement 'Our reconviction rate maybe no better than any other prison but we work with the worst of the prison population'. Although this may be a slightly romanticised view, there is clear evidence that many of Grendon's population have spent more time in segregation units or on Rule 43 than the general prison population. In fact, underlying the formal reason outlined above, there is frequently an unspoken reason for referral. Grendon is often asked to take an individual in order to give the system a rest from him.

The Grendon regime

The Grendon regime is based on the treatment philosophy that owes its allegiance to the therapeutic community as described by Maxwell Jones (1953). It attempts to mobilise the entire resources of the institution, staff and inmates, in the interests of treatment. Maxwell Jones set out what this means in terms of running the institution;

a) <u>Active rehabilitation</u> as against custodialism and segregation i.e. inmates participate in each other's treatment, they are not passive in relation to, and socially distant from, the staff.

b) <u>Democratization</u> as against hierarchies and status differentiation i.e. discussion and shared decision making takes the place of 'doctor knows best' attitude; a diminution of difference towards rank or professional status.

c) <u>Permissiveness</u>, as against customary limitations on what maybe said and done i.e. a loosening of the traditional disciplinary structure, an atmosphere in which it is understood to be safe to say what one feels in the presence of people whose role is traditionally associated with control and punishment.

d) <u>Communalism</u>, as opposed to an emphasis upon the specialised role of the doctor i.e. treatment takes place in small or large groups, not in the traditional doctor-patient dyadic situation. Therefore the doctor has to 'share' the therapeutic task with both the inmates, and other non-medical grades of staff.

In practice the regime is designed so that every aspect of a Grendon inmate's life revolves around therapy. The focus of therapy is the small therapy groups that meet three times a week and the two weekly community meetings. These meetings are mandatory for all community members, and missing them places the inmate in a position where, if the community should so decide he could be asked to leave the community.

Every aspect of an individual's life in Grendon is governed by group therapeutic principles. If an individual wants to move cell, have a welfare call, go on home leave, change probation officer or anything else, he must first take it to his group. Only when this has been done can it then be referred to the staff group. For issues such as changing labour, the community members themselves run a labour board which candidates for jobs must convince of their suitability. The labour board makes a selection for a particular job and recommends that person to the staff group.

In order to keep the groups working, each group is allocated a pair of uniformed staff who, whenever possible, will sit in on the group. This dual role of therapist and prison officer is an exceedingly difficult one to perform and raises many issues for the staff involved. The staff of Grendon have become expert in the skills required for this dual role.

The phrase 'Take it to your group' is perhaps the most heard saying within the institution, not only by inmates and unit staff. A well known anecdote in Grendon tells of the great deal of anger that was generated by a doctor telling an inmate to take his back pain to his group. Similarly a Governor telling someone to talk to the group because of his attitude can, and does, produce some very interesting responses. If someone declines the invitation they find themselves answering the next community meeting as to why they failed to do so.

Apart from the day to day business of living together, the groups are used to look at the areas of anxiety that inmates have and the way their 'life story' has or still is influencing this. The most powerful process is when the 'here and now' is perceived and understood in terms of previous formative experience. For example, when a group comes to understand that one of its number is nodding and smiling at it in just the same way that he nodded and smiled at his mother in order to avoid really listening to her, then that behaviour becomes a focus for attention. In this situation the rest of the group refuse to play mother and the nodding, compliant member must either find another way to cope with the situation or do something positive to change his response to that situation.

Each community has its own policies, the basic ones being held in common, for example the 'no violence rule'. Other rules may be a little more idiosyncratic according to the unit. An example of this is that on the author's unit the community voted to have a quiet hour after lunch, thus anyone who plays their radio at too high a level can be asked to turn it down or face the consequences of explaining to his group why not.

Of crucial importance is the 'non-confidence' rule. This states that:

a) anything I say to anyone can be fed back to my group or wing.

b) I am prepared to repeat anything that is said to me or that I see. It is my responsibility to feed things back to my group or the wing. This includes things that I might find difficult to repeat.

c) That I will not engage in gossiping. It is best not to talk about someone when they are not there.

The overall effect of this is that from the moment an inmate's cell is opened anything he says or does in the community is public property and can be challenged and fedback to the community. From 'unlock' to 'bang up', a period of some twelve hours each day, every member of the community is immersed in mutual therapy. The intensity of this makes it almost impossible for people to maintain images, stances and fantasies. Sooner or later the most fundamental behaviour patterns and attitudes become apparent and as a result become susceptible to public scrutiny. This may bring social approval or criticism, but above all it offers the person concerned the opportunity to obtain feedback on how his behaviour affects fellow community members. He then has to decide whether or not he wants to alter his behaviour.

What has been briefly outlined could be called a social psychological model of therapy and embodies many of the features that Maxwell Jones described as distinguishing the therapeutic community model of custody from the containment/punishment model of prison.

In practical terms this means that the individuals, the groups, the communities and the entire institution reacts in the same way to the challenging individual. In almost every other prison, anger produces a defensive response. Faced with an angry man, anxiety levels rise and the major aim is to stop the person from being angry i.e. reduce anxiety for everyone. In many instances the only response to this situation by the institution is to put the angry person somewhere safe. In prison this means the block. This cycle can occur over and over again if the person with anger problems or communication problem cannot produce a more adaptive response. At Grendon the response at all levels is different. The institution says to all people who come to it 'you are a responsible adult who can take responsibility for your actions and you can choose to be violent or not'. The staff confronted with the angry person accept that the person is angry and suggest he talk about it at group or wing level. At that level the community members and staff say in effect 'O.K. you're angry, we accept it, now let's look at it with you, and see if we can sort something out'. The overall effect for the community member is that of banging their head against a sponge and eventually discovering that the decision to move their head in the first place was the problem. It is truly amazing how much of people's anger, pain and distress can be soaked up this way and how effectively it is at teaching people to stop banging their heads against the sponge (that is a wall elsewhere), and helping them to decide that they will try something else. At this point a whole range of hitherto unrealised possibilities becomes available.

Grendon's remarkable ability to absorb so much owes everything to its ethos and the energy of its inmates' desire to change themselves. As long as Grendon remains true to its ethos it will remain an example to the prison system as a whole of what could be achieved with a substantial number of other institutions.

POSTCRIPT

Since this paper was prepared and delivered, once again the wheel of adversity has turned on Grendon and it is faced with the problem of fulfilling the ten percent expenditure cuts that have been imposed on the prison system. The struggle to implement Fresh Start continues, a feat not now expected to happen until 1988. On top of this it has been necessary to close a therapy wing in order to preserve the young offender facilities and to house the assessment unit. The pace at which the situation within the prison system is changing is a test of Grendon's ability to adapt and survive. It is a test that it is determined to survive for the sake of all those inmates who wish to change, and the mentally ill who require specialist intervention.

REFERENCES

Commissioner of Prisons, (1963), Report for 1962, H.M.S.O., London.

East, W.N. and Hubert, W.D. de B., (1939), <u>Report on the Psychological Treatment of Crime</u>, H.M.S.O., London.

Jones, M., (1953), <u>The Therapeutic Community</u>, Basic Books, New York.

Marcus, B., (1979), Small group work in a psychiatric prison in, Babington Smith, B. and Farrell, B.A. (eds.), <u>Training in Small Groups</u>, Pergamon Press, London.

PART II
ISSUES IN CLINICAL TRAINING

Assessment of clinical competence

S. MORLEY

INTRODUCTION

The assessment of clinical competence is the central component in the training of a clinical psychologist. There is also a component of continuing assessment used to determine promotion within the NHS. At present post qualification assessment is relatively informal; no form of public examination is required and the criteria for assessment are not obvious. It is likely that post qualification assessment will become an issue if ideas such as Performance Related Pay are introduced. Although the present paper primarily considers the assessment of clinical competence as it pertains to trainees, I believe that some of the issues raised have a more general scope. The present paper will review a current, representative method of assessment, some of its short falls and measures used to counter them. I will argue that the methods of assessment need to be carefully designed to ensure that trainees learn what is necessary. To do this we must generate a definition of what is expected of a competent clinical psychologist.

THE DEVELOPMENT OF ASSESSMENTS FOR CLINICAL PSYCHOLOGISTS

Most present systems of assessment in the UK have evolved from the academic background provided by the Maudsley Institute of Psychiatry in the 1950's. As a consequence the assessments centre on written work; examinations which test the candidate's knowledge of psychological theory, methods and applications; written case reports and a research dissertation. Taken at face value written performance has little to do with clinical competence. Dictionary definitions of the word 'clinical' have two elements: (i) 'Having to do with the sick bed'; by implication this suggests face to face contact with patients. (ii) 'Observing/judging in a cool unemotional way'.

Whilst one does not need to be knowledgeable to make 'unemotional' judgements, it is not unreasonable to suggest that the core feature of a clinical psychologist's competence must include the ability to use the academic base to inform judgement. In practice this component of clinical training has been assessed primarily through unseen written papers, the traditional way of examining candidates in higher education.

The research dissertation obviously derives from an academic source and the requirement of many higher degrees is that they should incorporate a piece of original research by the candidate. Is research ability a necessary part of a clinical psychologist's competence? If it is, is the conventional dissertation the best way of assessing it?

The assessment of a clinical psychologists's performance in clinical settings has developed fairly recently. In my own training I was subjected to reasonably rigorous scrutiny of my ability to administer and score the WAIS, WISC and one or two other tests without error. In contrast to the assessment of testing abilities the assessment of my ability to interview (in various styles) and manage treatment cases was virtually minimal. One of my supervisors insisted that I produced audiotapes to which he listened and gave valuable feedback. Formal assessment by supervisors' ratings was in its infancy. With hindsight one must express surprise at this situation, given that the sophisticated psychologists who trained me were aware of the poor predictive performance of indirect measures of abilities. The importance of assessing criterion variables has been known for many years. This of course is the core of the problem. Whereas performance criterion for the WAIS are unambiguous, criteria for other aspects of clinical competence are less clearly defined and subject to debate. Nevertheless, it would be surprising if clinical psychologists could not reach some degree of agreement on them. Current attempts to assess clinical competence represent a marked improvement on the method of fifteen to twenty years ago but they have problems which are just beginning to be addressed.

It is clear that the assessment of clinical psychologists in training has been dominated by the examination methods demanded by Universities, most of which are understandably conservative in the methods of examinations they regard as acceptable. There are strong points to these methods but they may not be appropriate for the assessment of professional competence.

CURRENT ASSESSMENT

About one third of clinical psychologists in training take the BPS Diploma in Clinical Psychology as their entry qualification to the profession. The Diploma shares many characteristics with University and Polytechnic courses retaining a tri-partite division of examination by written papers, case reports and a research dissertation. All sections are marked by two independent examiners and case reports and dissertations are also orally examined. The classical method of evaluating an assessment method is to estimate reliability and validity coefficients.

Reliability of examinations

Analysis indicates that the BPS examinations are reliably marked. Agreement coefficients between examiners are usually greater than 0.85. This figure is conservative if one considers that candidates on the borderline, i.e. one mark either side of the pass mark, will be assigned to a non-agreement cell. When the marks of these candidates are moderated and differences between markers are resolved agreement is even higher. It is rare for two markers to disagree to such an extent that one awards a clear pass and the other a clear fail.

Validity

The crux of the matter is the external validity of the assessment procedures. Information on this is slight and not reduceable to numerical coefficients. The predictive validity of the assessments is unknown. As far as I can determine no one has investigated whether the marks on the examinations predict whether the candidate will become a 'good clinical psychologist'. The central problem is the definition of a good clinical psychologist. Contemporary clinical psychologists are required to perform many roles from assessing and treating individual patients to carrying out managerial duties. These roles develop as the psychologist gains promotion and the content of clinical practice changes. Psychologists trained twenty years ago were unlikely to be faced with either major managerial issues, involvement in medical psychology, child abuse or cognitive therapy. These aspects of health care delivery were simply not perceived. This point may seem tangential to the issues of assessment but I suggest that one feature of a 'good clinical psychologist' is the capacity to develop psychological solutions to new problems as they arise.

The concurrent validity of the present assessment is high. Marks from all parts of the examination inter-correlate well. One explanation for this is that it represents nothing more than method variance. Each part of the examination relies heavily on written material and general writing and expressive abilities might be over emphasised at the expense of other more central components of clinical performance. At present the inter-relationship between examinations must be treated with caution.

What do the written papers assess?

The <u>content validity</u> of the written papers is extremely high but only because the syllabus supplied in the BPS Regulations is general and exhaustive. For example, listed below is the content of the material which can legitimately appear on the written paper examining developmental psychology. (From the BPS Regulations for the Diploma in Clinical Psychology, 1987/1988).

> The impact of genetic, biographical, sexual, cultural, educational and socioeconomic factors on clinical problems. Clinical applications of normal development from conception to death (e.g. developmental milestones, socialisation, education, personal and sexual relationships, marriage and family, pregnancy and childbirth, work and leisure, unemployment and retirement, ageing, death and dying. Clinical problems characteristic of particular social contexts and stages of the life span, and clinical measurement of age differences and age changes. Implications of the social and development contexts of clinical problems for assessment, treatment and prevention.

One consequence of the syllabus is that it encourages candidates to acquire a wide range of knowledge but little of this knowledge will be in depth. How then do candidates manage the examinations? One strategy which seems to be used is 'question spotting'. Candidates inspect past papers and the current contents of relevant journals and by some heuristic decide which topics are most likely to appear in the examination. This is a very sensible strategy because it mimics the one used by examiners who set the paper. Inspection of past papers suggests that there are core issues which appear in a semi-random order time after time, e.g. performance decrements with ageing. These issues provide the basis of the papers which are leavened with questions on current topical issues and one or two oddities. Given that candidates can only revise a fixed number of topics for exams one might predict that the frequency with which a set question is attempted will be non-random and determined by the match between the examiners' judgements about what ought to be examined and the candidates' estimations of the most likely questions. This survival mechanism is very effective, most candidates pass, and, as predicted, the choice of questions is non-random, see Table 1. The distribution for each paper deviates from that expected by chance (p0.007) indicating that the questions are attempted in a non-random manner. Candidates are very selective in their choices of questions. A number of points arise from this analysis.

Table 1.
The frequency with which questions were attempted on four written examination papers.

Question Number	1	2	3	4	5	6	7	8	9	10	11	12
Paper A	3	17	2	28	1	18	9	3	11	17	9	10
Paper B	25	39	3	5	21	11	5	16	11	1		
Paper C	33	14	8	14	24	15	17	28	7	20		
Paper D	15	2	24	35	2	4	9	33	9			

First it is clear that the process of assessment determines what is learned and how it is learned. There is considerable evidence from education to support this statement (Coles, 1981). Once this is recognised one must ask whether the assessment device properly samples what it is supposed to measure. The rationale for the written examination is that competent clinical psychologists must have a knowledge of psychological theory and method. This is axiomatic as it distinguishes a psychologist from other groups of health care workers. Moreover, it anticipated that clinical psychologists can use their psychological knowledge in clinical settings. It seems unlikely that swotting up for a written examination of the type outlined is an accurate sample of how the trainees use their psychological knowledge. It would be more appropriate to present candidates with a limited range of topics so that they could demonstrate the depth of their psychological knowledge in core areas. This is actually what happens now, but in an indirect and inefficient way. It would surely be more rational to acknowledge this publicly and design an assessment strategy which is less wasteful of the candidates' time and efforts.

Secondly, it behoves us to think about what type of psychological knowledge should be assessed. Berger (1987) argues that there is a body of psychological knowledge which psychologists ought to possess at the end of their training. There are facts about disorders and methods of treating them, technical issues about measurement and basic legal, ethical and procedural details which are encountered in everyday practice. This factual knowledge could be validly tested by unseen written examinations of a short answer nature. Some of this is already tested in written papers but it is intermingled with knowledge which requires a more considered response, which is unlikely to be forthcoming under the time pressured conditions of unseen papers. For example, the candidates are sometimes asked to evaluate the impact of a new treatment for a given set of clients, e.g. memory retraining procedures for head-injured patients.

Until sufficient research is completed there are no answers which might be regarded as unassailable, received wisdom of a factual type. What is required is a careful evaluation of the evidence. The ability to conduct this type of analysis is required by clinical psychologists who, after their training, are likely to be required to evaluate information to guide the development of their work, or to argue for the development of clinical services to an emerging client group. In training, clinical psychologists have countless opportunities to learn how to acquire and apply psychological knowledge in this way. For example, patients present problems which trainees have not encountered previously and time should be allocated for them to research the background literature. There should be opportunities for them to learn to integrate their clinical experience with the academic knowledge base of clinical psychology.

Why do we insist on trainees trying to acquire a wide knowledge base which we cannot test, they do not use and is impossible to learn? Surely we need to determine whether trainees know how to use the body of psychological literature in a critical and constructive manner to further their understanding of clinical problems. Once we accept this we should be able to devise a method (or methods) of assessment which facilitate appropriate learning. Obvious assessment methods available are seen questions and clinical projects. Both methods allow candidates time to research the topic. Objections to these methods are that they may not necessarily represent the candidates' own individual work. Groups of candidates can prepare answers, which, it is argued, obscures important individual differences between candidates and provides protection for the weaker ones. There are counter arguments to this. Firstly, consultation between colleagues over difficult cases and clinical problems does happen and should be encouraged. Building this into the assessment method might encourage good practice among weaker colleagues. Secondly, with the relatively small number of candidates attempting the Diploma examination at the same time it would be possible to devise a set of questions which could be distributed to candidates who do not know each other. This should discourage the preparation of model answers by each training course. Thirdly, a clinical project approach will encourage uniqueness as each candidate would produce a project arising from a clinical problem facing them.

Case reports and supervisors' assessment

Case Reports: The Case Report component of the examination has face validity as a way of assessing clinical competence. The cases are drawn from the three mandatory placements and the specialist placement and can include accounts of work with groups, families and with other professionals. The aim of the case reports is to assess the range of the trainee's clinical competence, reflecting the requirement that clinical psychologists should be generically trained. There is a format for presenting case reports which includes description of initial client presentation, client history, provisional hypotheses, investigations, formulation, intervention and evaluation. All this material must be conveyed within 3,000 words; which requires careful editing and presentation. In recent years the report of the examinations made by the Chief Examiner (e.g. 1986) has reflected the main features considered by the case report examiners. Three major themes appear in these reports; the necessity of a good formulation of the clinical problem, the desirability of evaluating outcomes and the need to relate clinical activity to the body of psychological knowledge. All these elements are reflected in a scientist-practitioner model of clinical work (Barlow, Nelson and Hayes, 1984). I recognise that there are genuine differences within the profession about the suitability of this model but I believe that it is an appropriate stance to take for two reasons. Firstly, it explicitly emphasises the application of psychological knowledge, which is the one thing that sets psychologists apart from other health care workers. Secondly, it ensures that practitioners evaluate their work continuously in a publically accountable manner. To this end I suggest that this aspect of the case reports is valid. The extent to which case reports can be fabricated or doctored to present only the facts that candidates believe the examiners wish to see remains uncertain. It is, however, notable that candidates tend to present only successful cases. Perhaps we would gain more information if 'failed cases' or insoluble problems were reported.

Supervisors' evaluation of clinical competence: Examiners also consider reports from clinical supervisors about the trainee's competence. This information should reflect the observations of experienced psychologists about the performance of the trainee in face to face encounters with clients; a sample of criterion behaviour. Additional aspects of the trainee's competence are rated and it should be possible to build up a picture of the development of competence over the years of training. At the end of clinical placements supervisors are asked to declare whether the candidate is satisfactory (has passed the placement) or unsatisfactory (failed). Almost all supervisors' reports are 'satisfactory'. It may be that all trainees are competent but there are other possible explanations for this blanket satisfaction.

Marzillier (1987) has described the 'cult of the positive' which ensures that supervisors evaluate trainees positively for reasons of social pressure. To overcome this problem he has developed a procedure for evaluating clinical placements which separates the assessment (gatekeeping) element from the feedback component. In the ideal setting feedback should occur continuously as the supervisor interacts with the trainee and provides commentary and advice about the trainee's competence. Assessment at the end of placement provides a gatekeeping function. Here the supervisor is asked to determine whether the trainee will pass or fail the placement. Marzillier has outlined a model of supervision and evaluation which pays attention to both feedback and assessment. One innovation currently being developed by the Oxford course is to assign the assessment gatekeeping component to a third party the Regional or Clinical Tutor. This system seems promising and its evaluation is eagerly awaited.

A different approach to the problems of assessment by clinical supervisors is being piloted in South Wales (Griffiths, 1987). Street (undated) notes that although supervisors are asked to state whether a trainee passes or fails a placement there are no explicit criteria on what constitutes a pass or fail. This reflects the professions' reluctance to specify clinical competence. Street also points out that different placements require different ranges of skills and competencies so that assessments made in specific placements may not have relevance for general clinical competence. Furthermore, when difficulties arise in placements it is often due to interpersonal differences between the two parties which will cloud relatively objective judgement about clinical competence. The South Wales course has introduced two procedures in an attempt to ameliorate these problems. Firstly, trainees are monitored across placements, which emphasises the continuity of training. Briefly, aims (goals) which are negotiated at the beginning of each placement are monitored. If these are not achieved there is a procedure for carrying them forward into future placements. Moreover, each unachieved aim is clarified and the action required to achieve it is specified. Secondly, each trainee attends a review meeting on three occasions interspersed throughout training. The meeting comprises the relevant supervisors together with the tutor and course organiser. This meeting identifies the trainee's strengths and positively acknowledges them. It also determines the areas to which the trainee must pay further attention; once again specific remedial actions are developed. As in the Oxford scheme these procedures have the merit of separating feedback and assessment (gatekeeping). The South Wales course has also developed a procedure for placement failure and appeals. These innovations are just being made and two or three years will be necessary to appraise their impact.

The development of procedures such as those described should lead to more comprehensive assessments of clinical competence. Clinical skills and abilities should be more closely defined and monitored. One consequence of these procedures will be the greater accountability of the supervisors whose role as a primary teacher of clinical psychologists should be emphasised. This must be acknowledged and the profession should pay special attention to staff development in order to meet this role in the training of future colleagues.

Research dissertations

Research has always been seen as one of the components of clinical training and it was enshrined as part and parcel of clinical practice by the Trethowan Report (HMSO, 1977).

Undoubtedly some trainees flounder during their research projects and current information suggests that for many this will be the only and last time in their lives that research is undertaken. There are several analyses of this phenomenon and recommendations for overcoming the shortfall (Heller, 1984; Watts, 1984). It is unfortunate that the presence of a separate dissertaion component seems to emphasise the remoteness of research activities from clinical practice. (In the same way the written papers seem to be hived off from case reports and clinical work). Is it possible that trainees view research as a single enterprise remote from their clinical concerns? If this is true it is a great tragedy. Most trainees are curious about their work and show considerable critical ability at times. Curiosity and critical awareness are components of research which should be fostered and developed through training. Just as clinical skills (i.e. direct client management skills) require breaking down into manageable chunks and careful rehearsal so do research skills. It should be possible to develop clinical research training and assess it over the course of training. For example it might begin with the trainee completing clinical projects, continuing through attempts to monitor ongoing cases and conduct single case experiments, carrying out a small scale survey on one placement, until finally a small project is prepared and completed. All this activity should build up research skills over training rather than expecting them to be achieved as a lump at the end of training. A scheme such as the one described would also have the merit of tying research to the clinical context.

CONCLUSION

In reviewing an example of how clinical psychology trainees' competence is assessed, I have argued that the form of assessment used, its content and timing, determine what is learned. There is evidence that what is learned for assessment purposes is not necessarily beneficial to the trainees. The present system appears to fragment the trainees' knowledge so that material learned for the different parts of the examination is not integrated. In summary the assessment system is reactive and its by-products probably interfere with appropriate learning.

It is important to design assessment systems so that they facilitate appropriate learning as well as being reliable and free from unwanted bias. A number of suggestions have been made about restructuring written assessments and research training so that they are more closely aligned with the trainees' everyday clinical work and facilitate the integration of academic knowledge with clinical work. The problems of assessing clinical performance in placements are beginning to be recognised and tackled. This approach has implications for the role of clinical supervisors and academic tutors which will require clarification. It is important to note that a good assessment procedure cannot be divorced from the structure of academic and clinical learning. Assessment must be driven by the curriculum rather than tacked on as an afterthought. The curriculum should be determined by our conception of a competent clinical psychologist. This paper has hinted at the issues which I consider to be definitive of a clinical psychologist and I conclude by offering an outline definition.

The central task of a clinical psychologist is to use psychological knowledge to facilitate the solution of problems presented by people in distress or who are socially disadvantaged. To do this the clinical psychologist must demonstrate an approach to problem solving which incorporates access to psychological knowlege and ability to evaluate and use it, and an understanding of the social and developmental context of the person's distress.

This rather broad and tentative definition contains two main elements:

1. Active problem solving. Psychologists should not be mere technicians. Although technical knowledge is needed, they must be capable of solving and evaluating solutions of novel problems; this requires research skills.

2. Psychological Knowledge. Psychologists must be able to use formal psychological knowledge in solving the problems they face.

ACKNOWLEDGEMENTS

This paper was prepared while the author was a member of a working party convened under the auspices of the BPS Board of Examiners for the Diploma in Clinical Psychology. I wish to acknowledge my colleagues (Colin Coles, Joan Kirk, Tony Lavender, John Marzillier, John Revell and Fraser Watts) and to state that the final content of this paper represents my personal views and not those of the working party or the official view of the BPS. I also wish to thank David Griffiths and his colleagues in South Wales for giving me access to unpublished documents detailing the development of the 'Policy for Placement and Course Failure'.

REFERENCES

Barlow, D.H., Nelson, R.O. and Hayes, S.C., (1984), The Scientist Practitioner: Research and Accountability in Clinical and Educational Settings, Pergamon Press, New York.

Berger, M., (1987), What a psychologist needs to know. Paper presented at the British Psychological Society Annual Conference, Brighton.

Coles, C.R., (1981), The influence of examinations on the curriculum in Metz, J.C.M., Moll, J. and Walton, H.J. (eds.), Examinations in Medical Education: A Necessary Evil?, Proceedings of the 1980 Conference of the

Association for Medical Education in Europe.
D.H.S.S., (1977), The Role of Psychologists in the Health Service: Report of the Subcommittee, HMSO, London.
Griffiths, D., (1987), Personal Communication. Documents on the South Wales In Service Training Course.
Heller, M.B., (1984), PROCRAST: Why don't clinical psychologists do more research, _BPS Division of Clinical Psychology Newsletter_, No. 45, 35-40.
Marzillier, J.S., (1987), The evaluation of clinical competence. Paper presented at the British Psychological Society Annual Conference, Brighton.
Report of the Chief Examiner, (1986), _Bulletin of the British Psychological Society_, 39, 108-109.
Street, E., (undated), Failed placements. Unpublished Ms.
Watts, F.N., (1984), Applicable psychological research in the NHS, _Bulletin of the British Psychological Society_, 37,41-42

Minimal and ideal standards of a clinical training course

G. PARRY

INTRODUCTION

A clinical psychologist applies psychological knowledge and skills to clinical problems. These skills include psychological assessment and treatment, where the psychologist is in direct contact with the client. Equally important is a wide range of applications which do not involve face to face client contact; research, teaching, staff management, consultation and service planning. The clinical problems to which they are applied are already very diverse, and becoming more so. Treating depression, problems in family relationships, eating disorders, memory problems; helping parents solve their child's behaviour problem or helping staff cope with severely challenging behaviours; planning interventions to reduce pain suffered by burned children during dressing procedures or to stop head banging in a person with a severe mental handicap - these are a small sample of the range of problems addressed. There are other clinical problems to which psychologists could make a contribution and only custom, practice and lack of funding prevents them.

Training achieves many purposes. It allows graduates to build up the knowledge and skills base needed to begin to work in clinical psychology. It has other latent functions, for example, socialisation into the profession's system of values and beliefs and provision of support during the trainee's role transition.

STANDARDS OF TRAINING

What constitutes minimum and ideal standards of training is neither immutable nor uncontroversial. It is arrived at by discussion and debate, based on the experience of the trainers, members of the profession, the employers and those responsible for accreditation. What is an acceptable minimum training and what would be ideal depends on the roles clinical psychologists occupy (e.g. researcher, clinician, manager, service planner), the knowledge base they draw on, the client groups they serve and the career structures, including opportunities for post qualification training, available to them. These things are changing all the time.

Our clinical role was at one time almost exclusively concerned with formal psychometric assessment. Other people, mainly doctors, provided treatments and called for a psychological opinion as an aid to that treatment. In a similar way the physician may ask a radiologist or a haematologist for information. The clinician's role now includes taking responsibility for psychological assessment, formulation, treatment and evaluation of outcome, and training must reflect this changing practice. This evolutionary process continues and new roles develop all the time, a recent example of this being the increasing acknowledgment of the contribution which may be made by psychologists to service planning.

The psychological knowledge base does not remain static. For example, psychological models of stress and coping processes were not available two decades ago, yet are now widely applicable to many clinical problems. Other topics are dropped from the curriculum and therefore a minimum standard for a syllabus must alter accordingly.

Traditional client groups have been the 'mentally ill', the handicapped and children. More posts are now becoming available working with the elderly, physically handicapped, physically ill people and those misusing drugs. Although a competent applied psychologist has skills and knowledge which can be used in all these contexts, if we are committed to generic training, the acceptable minimum exposure to these groups during training will vary. An optimum training in the different clinical skills involved is crucially dependent on the range of client groups psychologists serve.

Those responsible for basic training must also take account of future career structures and the following two questions should be asked. What will the post-qualification career development of the psychologist be? Will there be opportunities for continued specialisation, training and updating of skills? In particular, the minimum standard crucially depends on how much support or supervision is available in the first years after qualifying or how independently the new professional is required to practise.

Over the years clinical psychologists have become more professional. One form this has taken is that they have much more control over who shall be admitted to their ranks. In the early years it was, in effect, the employer who determined this. At present, the profession defines minimum training standards through a process of internal debate and emerging consensus, rather than these being decided by, for example, NHS management or an external 'Clinical Psychology Accreditation Board'. Having said that, since the NHS (in the majority of cases) funds our training courses in order to meet its recruitment needs, it is able to exert pressure, through the control of funding. Current policy within the NHS is that managers should be allowed to manage NHS resources and that services should not be influenced by professional aspiration. This will lead to funding being used and withdrawn far more deliberately as a political weapon. Our internal debates about standards must always take account of the wider political climate and financial pressures on training.

Minimum standards

The group within the British Psychological Society which upholds minimum standards is the Committee on Training in Clinical Psychology. The current minimum requirements for training courses are enshrined in its document 'Criteria for the assessment of postgraduate training courses in clinical psychology'. This is a public document available through the BPS. Although decided by the Committee and ratified by the Professional Affairs Board, these criteria are subject to revision in consultation with trainers and consumers. The 'minimum' criteria are very modest. They specify that courses should be organised by experienced clinicians with academic standing who have the time to devote themselves to the task. They stress that a course is a collaborative enterprise between the educators and the NHS staff, that the entrance procedures should be fair and that selection should not be influenced by candidates' ability to fund themselves. The current minimum standards emphasise measurable quantities of supervised clinical experience, such as a minimum of 250 days clinical work and compulsory experience with mental handicap, child and adolescent problems and adult psychological problems. A range of other placements should be available. Trainees should also have experience of work with high priority groups in the health service, such as elderly and long term patients. Supervision should not be undertaken by newly qualified staff, and should be monitored by the course officers. Supervisors should be aware of the responsibility they are undertaking. There should be a coherent academic curriculum and teaching plan. Trainees should have at least half a day a week for private study. There should be formal teaching of research methods, critical appraisal of published research and trainees should undertake and formally report a significant piece of research . Academic knowledge, research ability and clinical competence should be evaluated thoroughly and trainees who are professionally incompetent should not qualify.

In one sense these minimal criteria for evaluating training do not take us very far. They have evolved to prevent undesirable practices, rather than serving as a model for desirable ones. Although one of the fundamental aspects of the committee's work is to police minimum standards, it also aims to influence the quality of training. This is much more difficult to specify.

Ideal standards

We can (and do) discuss ideal training standards indefinitely . The Committee on Training, in travelling from course to course and examining each in detail, is in a unique position to observe the problems common to all. Over recent years, a number of issues have emerged as central to the quality of training. I should like to focus on three, which seem important when characterising an ideal course. First, clinical skills should be taught and assessed properly. Secondly, courses should adopt an explicit model of training, that is each course should address the issue 'What does a clinical psychologist need to know'. (There is of course room for pluralism here). Finally, the trainees' central task of integrating theoretical knowledge and clinical know-how should be fostered not hindered.

The first two of these have been discussed recently by John Marzillier and Michael Berger respectively in an excellent symposium at the 1987 BPS conference (Morley and Parry, 1988). John Marzillier describes the 'cult of the positive' where, because of the friendly relationship which almost invariably develops between the trainee and the supervisor, a searching and objective assessment of the trainee's clinical skill is made very difficult. He details a number of proposals which would ensure that the assessment of clinical skill becomes more independent of the goodwill between supervisor and trainee. These have, incidentally, been implemented in the Oxford course. Mike Berger emphasises the importance of thinking psychologically, of working from a psychological formulation. This analysis of the problem, apart from being one activity which identifies us as psychologists, ensures that procedures can be implemented and monitored in a way which avoids the 'mindless technology' of 'off the shelf' techniques.

The third issue is linked to this. It will not be possible for trainees to think a problem through from first principles or to make a psychological formulation unless they are able to integrate their theoretical and clinical knowledge. The problem of how to achieve this integration engages many courses up and down the country. I have recently been wrestling with it myself, as we have been planning and implementing a new curriculum for the Wessex course. How do we ensure that we train clinical psychologists who can have access to their psychological knowledge when faced with clinical problems? Part of the problem lies in the split between undergraduate and postgraduate training. We sometimes forget that new trainees arrive as adult psychologists with much theoretical knowledge which is in principle applicable to the clinical problems they address. Yet how difficult it is for them to use this knowledge effectively. Teaching third year undergraduate students has taught me the difference between being able to manipulate concepts and being able to understand what they mean when applied in the real world. It's the difference between knowing about something and knowing something.

There is a danger that trainees will inhabit two worlds, two parallel training courses, one of academic learning and another of clinical practicalities. The former is concerned with what the examiners (often referred to as 'They') require, and at times can bear little relationship to the latter. If the links are not properly made, there is a danger of a 'craft' or 'clinical management' approach to psychological problems. The process becomes one of diagnosis and prescription. For example, this is depression so the treatment is cognitive behaviour therapy, this is obsessional disorder so the treatment is response prevention, and so on. The very basis of our profession is lost and the consequences of that in the long term are, I believe, very dire. Apart from anything else, we would have a job convincing the funding authorities that up to three years' full time postgraduate study is necessary in order to become competent at this kind of prescribing. In the end, I think it would be a great loss to the scientific community as well.

POT FILLING AND JIGSAW PUZZLING

Colin Coles, a psychologist at the University of Southampton Faculty of Medicine, applies cognitive psychology to the problems of medical education, and is interested in the wider issues of professional training. He encourages us to consider the models of training we adopt. One way of exploring this is to examine the metaphors of the learning process which underlie our courses.

'Pot filling' is one such metaphor, and assumes that the clinical psychology trainee is an empty, rather leaky vessel, into which knowledge is poured. Some splashes out, some drains away, but over a period of time, the level of knowledge in the pot gradually rises, and can later be tapped, either in a clinical situation or in an examination. In one aspect or another, much of our academic teaching is based on this metaphor. The problem is that everything we know about human learning suggests that it is unhelpful and misleading.

We know, for example, that the learner is not a passive recipient of information, but is very active. Nor are trainees empty vessels, but have already been studying psychology, not to mention life, for a number of years. Information is processed and becomes meaningful to the learner insofar as it can be linked to existing knowledge in a schematic form. A metaphor which captures this activity is of the trainee completing a jigsaw puzzle. Pieces are scanned to become part of a wider picture, and the learner is engaged in an act of construction in fitting these pieces together. The cognitive task is to encode theoretical information in such a way that it can be recruited in a later clinical context. This is made easier if theoretical information is encoded with regard to concrete clinical exemplars.

Once we take seriously that our job is to facilitate not hinder the trainees' task of integrating theoretical and practical knowledge, a number of questions arise. These are best addressed explicitly as part of a curriculum planning exercise rather than left to sort themselves out. For example, how can we organise clinical and academic teaching so that the trainee does not inhabit two separate worlds? Is it best to present theory first (prior to placement experience) or theory after (when it might make more sense)? Is academic material best taught in blocks of time or 'drip fed' over a number of separate days? When the curriculum is implemented, how can we build in evaluation and feedback, so that we check whether we are reaching our objectives and what should be done if we are not?

THE WESSEX 'SANDWICH'

There are probably as many answers to these questions as there are courses. In the Wessex course we have recently planned and implemented a new curriculum which attempts one solution, in the context of a small course for a large Region. Our goal is an integrated training course, where the trainee has complementary and mutually illuminating experiences in the academic and clinical placement phases.

The educational difficulty with our previous curriculum was that trainees from first and second years of the course were taught together and that there was a mixture of placements undertaken. This made it impossible to relate the content of the academic programme to the experience of the trainees directly, despite a 'day release' system.

The curriculum redesign involved a number of steps. We (that means the course officers, the supervisors, the academic teachers and the trainees) discussed and agreed a 'course philosophy' which made our objectives explicit. This was very valuable, since it forced us to discuss, and reach a consensus on, what we thought a clinical psychologist needed to know and how we thought it should be taught. Specifying objectives also makes it more possible to evaluate the outcome. We then moved to a biennial intake and synchronised the first two placements so that all trainees would be having their mental health and handicap placements simultaneously. One obvious limitation is that such an arrangement is only possible because of a low ratio of trainees to placements.

These steps solved several problems, in that the syllabus could now be covered in a temporal sequence. We then decided, after consultation with other courses, to move to a block teaching system for most of the syllabus rather than stay with 'drip feed'. This left us with the conundrum of whether to have the block before the relevant placement (when it could 'prepare' the trainees, but they would not have any concrete clinical experiences to relate the theory to) or after the placement (when they would have a great deal of experience to make sense of the theory but would have had no prior preparation). We decided to precede the block with a two week period in the placement where the trainees' role is to develop their observational skills, so that each one brings to the academic block personal experiences of talking to staff and patients and observing the work of the staff. This structured observation period includes both quantitative and qualitative assignments.

We then turned our attention to the content of the teaching blocks. There are four blocks in the first two years of the course, and in each one we aimed to foster theory-practice links, by explicitly relating the teaching to the trainees' observations, by bringing in supervisors to relate 'clinician's tales', by including skills teaching and by trainee-based seminars. Exemplars of clinical problems are therefore emphasised at the time that the theory is presented. The corollary of this is that the placement experience should continue to make the links. For this reason, as well as conventional supervision and clinical skills teaching, we have organised individual tutorials in the placement by someone explicitly assigned to discuss academic reading in relation to the clinical work being undertaken. In addition, trainees complete an academic assignment which relates to their clinical work for each placement. The final feature of the placement is that professional practice teaching and case discussions continue to be on a 'day release' system, rotating around our ten Districts.

Apart from the observation-theory-experience sandwich, there is nothing particularly innovative about this design. However, it serves as an example of a planning and implementation process which tries to address explicitly the problems of integrating academic knowledge and clinical applications. Of course any design has strengths and weaknesses, and undoubtedly we shall find out the problems of this one, given time.

REFERENCES

Morley, S. and Parry, G., (eds.), (1988), _Professional Issues in Clinical Psychology Training_, Division of Clinical Psychology, BPS.

The fit between training and clinical practice

A. DABBS

Those of us directly concerned with clinical postgraduate training and ultimately responsible for the content and structure of courses are constantly faced with the question 'training to do what'. It is not simply a matter of organising a training programme for today but rather the provision of an adequate preparation for five years hence, when today's trainees become independent practitioners in the senior grade. I must admit that in my own region of Yorkshire the task is made much easier by the existence of a well organised post-qualification training committee equipped with a small budget which is used to arrange a regular programme of training events. This enables those of us concerned with basic training to decide what might be safely omitted or curtailed within the already overcrowded curriculum, in the knowledge that matters can be taken up at a later time when the direct clinical relevance is more immediately apparent.

With regard to entry to clinical training there has been no lack of applications from excellent graduates for the past twenty years and it has been something of a mystery to me how one applicant has been preferred over another with an apparently equivalent academic background. It has to be recognised that there are very obvious differences between undergraduate courses and that is how it should be. Some university departments of psychology have a strong social science base to their undergraduate courses, while others have a more biological emphasis. The task facing courses is to try to identify which kind of background produces the better clinician (although this presumes it is possible to define a 'good' clinician). What matters to me is that the potential trainee demonstrates a curiosity about human behaviour that has been nurtured during undergraduate years and made sharper by an understanding of experimental method and measurement as relevant to Psychology, which includes a basic grasp of statistical numeracy. I have not been impressed by graduates who are fluent in their expositions of other peoples' models and theories and see everything from a particular standpoint, whether it is Skinnerian learning theory or neo-Freudian dynamics.

Selection of aspiring clinical trainees is achieved by one means or another and over recent years it has become more apparent that the agencies which control the purse strings of financial sponsorship exercise their interest by selecting candidates relevant to the expectations of that particular organisation. They choose candidates who they believe are likely to make a contribution to the clinical services of the Region, District, Unit or Special Hospital. Similarly, the award of an MRC studentship is based on the belief that the individual has clinical research potential. These are very evidently highly unreliable criteria, theoretically open to a deal of argument but in practice such arguments tend not to take place. What I have also observed over the years has been a tendency to avoid the seemingly 'difficult' or 'idiosyncratic' applicant in favour of the middle-of-the-road, compliant future basic grade clinical psychologist who is rather like themselves. One wonders if the likes of Monte Shapiro, Vic Meyer or Don Bannister would have succeeded in obtaining NHS sponsorship today.

The most difficult task for any head of course is to balance current pressures to include matters of contemporary interest, against what is perceived to be the likely future of the profession. All courses are faced with attempting to 'fit a quart into a pint pot' and this task has not been facilitated by a series of poorly thought through recommendations emanating from the Training Sub-Committee of the Clinical Division of the British Psychological Society (BPS). Doubtless we all feel a vague positive regard for our own original clinical training and it so happens that over the past decade the recommendations of the Training Sub-Committee have revealed an emphasis on the acquisition of time spent gaining clinical experience thus reflecting the background of committee's membership. A similar state of affairs was evident in medical undergraduate education twenty years ago when attempts were made to reduce the time spent in learning anatomy by rote. The prevailing attitude was 'it did me no harm, and if I had to endure it, so can they'. Personally I see no merit in requiring a trainee to spend a specified number of days occupied in a particular area of clinical work that may be of no personal interest. On the other hand, I do appreciate the relevance of requiring trainees to complete a defined number of detailed and properly supervised case studies drawn from different areas of clinical sub-specialties. To put it bluntly, it is likely that the university based clinical training programme will be the one opportunity that most psychologists ever have for post-graduate academic study, access to libraries and discussions with tutors, while they will have another thirty years and more to spend acquiring clinical experience of greater or lesser relevance.

What, then, might a prospective clinical psychologist be likely to be doing four or five years from today? Perhaps the question should be restated along the lines, 'what are the professional strengths of a clinical psychologist that are likely to remain in demand over the next twenty years such as to enable an income to be earned and a contribution made to the general welfare of society?'. The evidence that clinical psychology is a valued profession can be seen by its rapid increase in numbers and its ready infiltration into a wide range of clinical specialties which had not previously considered seeking the services of clinical psychologists. In West Yorkshire we have clinical psychologists working in Pain Clinics, Physical Rehabilitation Units, Secure Forensic Units, Children's Dialysis Units, Child Abuse Centres, Community Units for the Elderly, Diabetic Clinics and the more usual Neurosurgery/Neurological Clinics. I only trust we don't over-reach ourselves and eventually make the kind of outrageously unrealistic claims for our profession as did Psychiatry in the 1960's. Personally, I regret the apparent withdrawal of clinical services from the traditional psychiatric hospitals where clinical psychologists have a great deal to offer to the chronically ill and psychiatrically disabled.

What we have seen happening over the past decade has been a re-run of the difficulties that affected clinical psychology training in the United States during the 1950's and 60's and continues to rumble on. Postgraduate clinical training in the USA was originally defined by the American Psychological Association (APA) in 1924 and comprised the acquisition of a Ph.D. in the general abnormal field, plus one year as a supervised clinical intern/trainee working in a hospital or clinic. State licensing began in 1946 broadly following the APA recommendations and this rapidly spread down the eastern seaboard. In 1949 complaints about the adequacy of professional training obtained a forum at the Boulder Conference and this question was reconsidered at further meetings in Chicago, 1965 and Colorado, 1973. The essence of the argument was between those who advocated the acquisition of particular clinical skills and experience against the traditionalists who stressed the need to develop basic scientist-practitioner attributes of a more academic kind. What happened was that the more senior members of the profession, in particular, those directly concerned with graduate training in the universities, won the argument at conference after conference. In well prepared presentations they demonstrated that for the profession to continue to develop and expand, the applied scientist-practitioner model was the essential pathway to follow. The average practical clinician working in provisional centres did not simply remain acquiescent with the more eminent members of the profession but began to consider the employment of less academically qualified assistants as routine testers or behaviour therapists (psychology department technicians if you like) and in addition they set up what became known as 'Professional Schools'. This alternative form of clinical training led to a Psy.D. or D.Clin.Psychol. which was recognised by the individual state in which the school was based but had no wider recognition. The California School of Professional Psychology was one of the first of these organisations to be established and reading about it is very reminiscent of the kind of messages emanating from the Clinical Division when referring to the argument for the establishment of the Diploma in Clinical Psychology of the BPS (Kubie, 1970). In 1980 the APA began to swing back to its more conservative approach to clinical training, and was more openly critical of these Professional Schools. It began with an attempt to define the content of basic undergraduate degree programmes in terms of acceptability for postgraduate clinical training. This threatened the Professional Schools which had been much more broadminded regarding who they would accept for training as therapists of a particular orientation or approach. The APA went on to define the qualifications of those who might legitimately use the terms 'Professional Psychologist', 'School Psychologist' or 'Industrial Psychologist' in such a manner that the Professional Schools would be hard put to fulfill them. The argument of the provincial psychologists remains along the lines of querying who is to provide the treatments or assessments that are currently in vogue. The Reagan era has cut back significantly on public services such that there are few clinical psychologists in established posts and consequently greater demands are made upon them. There has been a rush into private practice, not suprisingly mostly from the products of Professional Schools, and there is a legitimate case to be made for the production of a grade of personnel prepared to carry out fairly routine assessments and treatments in public service. The analogy with the state of affairs prevailing here in the UK is too obvious to spell out. The one significant difference has been the lack of a clear policy stated by the BPS.

I would agree that a valid case can be made for the scientist practitioner model of training and that this training contains within it certain core areas of study which would enable a trainee to make a useful contribution to any area of clinical work. It does presume, however, that programmes of postqualification training are available in the locality to permit the average basic grade psychologist to extend levels of expertise in a particular clinical area of personal choice, e.g. psychotherapy, neuropsychology etc. When considering the definition and implementation of the scientist-practitioner model of training and the question whether it can be defined and implemented, one might do well to reiterate the statement of the APA in 1947 produced at a time when State licensing was the dominant contemporary issue:

> This (training) would involve an acquaintance with the primary body of psychological theory, research and methods on which further training and interdisciplinary relationships can be built. Preparation should be broad; it should be directed to research and professional goals. Participants should receive training in three functions: assessments, research and therapy with the special contribution of the psychologist as a research worker emphasised throughout.
>
> APA (1947)

From this standpoint it can be appreciated that the location of specialty in which a trainee is engaged is of only secondary importance. The core issue of training is the acquisition of the knowledge and skills to enable the aspiring clinical psychologist to bring his or her psychological awareness to bear on problems of ill health in a scientific manner. It is not simply a matter of equipping trainees with an armoury of techniques, though that comes into it, but rather an understanding of the application of scientific method to human problems covering the whole life span from childhood to old age.

In retrospect one becomes better able to appreciate the amount of time spent in redundant activities. On a personal level I arguably wasted many hours engaged in the niceties of Rorshach administration and scoring during the 1950's. In the 1960's computers became the predomianting fascination and like many others, I must have spent hours fiddling away producing rather simple statistical packages of minimal value that were instantly superseded by much more sophisticated programmes produced by professional statisticians. This led to an interest in Personal Construct Psychology and contemplation of the method and the results obtained from individual patient grids. I must have consumed as much time as I had devoted to Rorschach in the past. No doubt I was a poor judge of contemporary relevance. The current preoccupation of the higher echelons of the profession with 'Management' appears to me to be yet another of these topics of almost immediate redundancy. It does not require a gifted prophet to foresee that the administration and management of the Health Service is in a state of flux heading towards an end result in the 1990's which is going to be very different from what we see around us at the present time. It is a safe bet to assume that clinical psychology services will become unit based and be subject to a kind of 'privatisation'. My personal guess is that it is likely to become some form of a 'contracted' service along the lines of General Practice but what happens to physiotherapy will provide some guidelines for the future. It may well be that independent practitioners are employed on a fee earning basis to provide a service to specified clinical units.

I raise this matter because clinical courses are under a certain amount of pressure to include 'management' topics in the curriculum. This could prove to be an area of instant obsolescence. The recent BPS document (1986) prepared for the

National Health Services Training Authority: 'Management Training Needs of Clinical Psychologists', is impressive in its total failure to grasp what is actually happening in the NHS as more financial control and responsibility is delegated to the District and Unit Managers. On the positive side the document does succeed in making a case for self-selected clinical psychologists to acquire management training at a postqualification level in order to enable them to widen their career opportunities. Personally I feel it is a desirable aim to facilitate the transfer of the clinically incompetent and those of our colleagues who have suffered 'burn out' to a less personally demanding occupation. It is a phenomenon well recognised in medical circles and regarded as a form of early retirement for those who have suffered many years of increasing demand for their clinical services. The tradition was to seek management opportunities within professional organisations but the current turmoil within the administration of the NHS has opened up a new field of opportunity for these people. The question is, how much, if any, of this Management Training should occupy scarce time in already packed postgraduate clinical courses? Perhaps it is too early to respond with any certainty as the prevailing political/economic reorganisation of the NHS is as yet unresolved and more important topics have priority.

The crux of my argument is that clinical courses must focus on the core skills and knowledge that will enable a clinical psychologist of the 1990's to contribute to patient welfare in any health setting, and secondly to continue to emphasise those characteristics of the profession that have been demonstrated to have made a well trained clinical psychologist a highly sought after clinical scientist confident of contributing to the investigation of ill health and psychological dysfunction. If, after a couple of years in the basic grade (which incidentally might have been called 'internship' or 'pre-chartering') the individual psychologist should seek to become an analytical psychotherapist or a radical behaviour modifier, so much the better. I would hope that they would remain in clinical practice with a continuing scientific curiosity until such time as they felt they had no more to offer and might then contemplate a new career, perhaps in administration or management. My one regret is that so many of the trainees who have passed through excellent postgraduate courses have failed to make their personal contributions to public scientific knowledge. When I speak to them later in their careers and ask why they did not communicate their experience to others, I am given the excuses of shortage of time or a mistaken belief that their contribution would be too modest or insignificant and be largely irrelevant. Perhaps it should become a formal requirement of clinical psychologists that they pass on their knowledge to others, particularly to the newer generations of the profession but the matter of professional morality is far too large a question to consider at this time.

In conclusion one may only state that postgraduate clinical

training courses have met with modest success. Many of our products have sunk without trace into routine clinical practice but a significant few have continued to make advances in knowledge and techniques to the benefit of all of us. Those responsible for training programmes must always look to the future and are required to balance current interests and topics of fashionable concern, e.g. child abuse, against the likely demands to be made of the profession five to ten years hence. From my personal appreciation of the current literature I would prognosticate that the most significant advances are likely to be made in the general area of cognitive processing. This will lead to a re-awakening of interest in topics like thought disorder, ruminations, memory disturbances , various forms of cognitive impairment and, dare I say it, psychometric assessments. Time will prove how mistaken I am and I trust there will be another 'Current Issues in Clinical Psychoogy' Conference in five years time at which a speaker might refer back to this address to report that it was not all fantasy.

REFERENCES

B.P.S. (1986), Management Training Needs of Clinical Psychologists. Report of Working Party.

Garfield, S.L., (1974), Clinical Psychology: The Study of Personality and Behaviour, Edward Arnold/J.W.Arrowsmith.

Kubie, L.S., (1970) in Holt, R.R (ed.) New Horizons for Psychotherapy, Int.Univ.Press, New York.

Reisman, J.M., (1981) in Walker, C.E. (ed.) Clinical Practice of Psychology, Pergammon Press.

Watts, F.N., (1985), Clinical Psychology:Health Trends Vol. 17.

PART III
THE RELEVANCE OF COGNITIVE THEORY, RESEARCH AND PRACTICE

Introduction

I. MILLS

INTRODUCTION: COGNITIVE THERAPY

Cognitive therapy was developed from the cognitive theory of emotional disorders formulated by Beck (1967, 1976) and suggests, firstly that faulty information processing leads to a maladaptive disturbance in feelings and behaviour, and secondly, that correction of this disturbance will relieve the emotional distress.

The framework for this information processing resembles work in experimental psychology on current theories of cognitive networks. The description by Clark (1988), although describing cognitive theory of anxiety, succinctly demonstrates the generality of the basic principles of cognitive theory. According to Clark, dysfunctional beliefs and rules which have related contents are said to be associated together within memory to form higher order cognitive structures called schemas, which can vary from being situation specific ('If I don't pass the exam, I'm a failure as a person') to a more global domain of reference ('I must not fail at anything I do or I'm a failure as a person'). Once activated, schemas facilitate the processing of information consistent with the content of the schema and inhibit the processing of information inconsistent with the schema.

These basic principles can apply across a range of emotional disorders with the content or theme of the dysfunctional network varying according to the nature of the disorder.

To begin with, cognitive therapy concentrated on depression (Beck, 1967, 1976). Three areas of psychological functioning were identified as being instrumental in the development and maintenance of depression and were described as the cognitive triad, logical errors and schemas.

The cognitive triad is a constellation of beliefs forming a negatively distorted view of the self and of the world and the future as it relates to the self. It occurs as a consequence of logical errors in cognitive processing which in turn are a function of the 'schemas' (rules or assumptions which define the principles for selecting and encoding information). In depression the main theme of the distorted cognitions emphasises perceptions of loss and deprivation.

In cognitive theory of anxiety, which was developed later, the cognitions relate mainly to the perception of threat or danger. The distortions being manifested in overestimation of the degree of threat or danger and underestimation of the individual's ability to cope with it effectively. This perception of threat, together with the individual's perceived inability to deal with it, triggers off the anxiety response which in turn can become a source of threat, thereby creating a self-perpetuating vicious circle of anxiety.

The application of cognitive theory is being further extended to provide cognitive models for the understanding and treatment of panic disorder (Clark, 1986; Clark and Salkovskis) where the important cognitions centre on misinterpretations of bodily changes as signs of impending self-related disaster or catastrophe such as hear t attack, impending insanity, etc.. Accounts of obsessional disorder have also benefited from cognitive therapy where the theme of the cognitions relates to the extent to which an individual's action or lack of action will result in harm to others for which they will be responsible.

More recently cognitive theory has been applied to personality disorder (Young, in Press) and to borderline personality disorder (Pretzner, 1983).

COMPARISON WITH OTHER THERAPIES

The central notion of cognitive theory is that an individual's interpretation of the available information from internal and external environments, determines emotional responses. In other words, it is the meaning that an individual attaches to events that influences the emotional and behavioural response. Cognitive therapy concentrates its activity, therefore, on correcting these interpretations and enabling the individual to attribute more realistic and less dysfunctional meanings to these events, thereby reducing emotional distress.

Cognitive therapy differs from both behavioural and psychodynamic approaches, its general philosophy probably being best described as 'collective-empiricism' (Young and Beck, 1983) which emphasises the joint role of therapist and patient in testing out dysfunctional cognitions and allows the patient to reach his/her own conclusions instead of relying on the interpretation of the therapist. It is not, as is generally thought, confined solely to the application of a series of cognitive techniques, the style and structure of therapy and the quality of the patient-therapist relationship are also important.

As mentioned above, the style of cognitive therapy is collaborative, structured and directive. It is a problem solving approach that utilises the socratic method of inductive questioning and concentrates on the individual's current state of functioning. It is time limited (approximately fifteen to twenty sessions for depressive disorders but frequently less for anxiety disorders such as panic attacks). Education and homework are important features of therapy. The therapist needs to demonstrate sufficient empathy, warmth and concern towards the individual but not to allow these qualities to become too intrusive. They are seen as necessary but not sufficient conditions for successful outcome.

Emphasis is placed on actively enabling the individual to recognise dysfunctional beliefs, to test their validity and to replace them with less dysfunctional beliefs. During this process the operation of underlying schemas is often revealed and these too can be subjected to cognitive therapy techniques aimed at identifying rigid rules, all or nothing thinking etc..

Cognitive techniques include eliciting dysfunctional thoughts through the use of, for example, imagery, inductive questioning, the daily record of dysfunctional thoughts and taking advantage of changes in mood during the session. The validity of these thoughts can be put to the test in therapy or during homework sessions designed as small experiments, by using procedures such as examining the available evidence or reattribution of the possible cause (for example lack of concentration, loss of energy, can be a function of the emotional state and not an enduring negative feature of the individual's personality). Identification of schemas can be achieved by, for example, asking the individual to try and identify the pattern or common rule that is shared by a list of dysfunctional beliefs. These rules can then be subjected to reality testing in the same way as beliefs, although frequently the nature of the schemas is gradually revealed to both therapist and patient during the process of identifying and discrediting irrational thoughts.

In the earlier stages of therapy behavioural strategies such as scheduling of activities, graded task assignment, ratings of mastery and pleasure and cognitive rehearsal are often used to overcome such problems as the low activity level of the depressed patient or the avoidance behaviour of the anxious patient, before progressing to the use of cognitive strategies. At all times it is important that the individual understands the rationale for the particular activity he/she is being asked to engage in, therefore the therapist needs to continually check that this is the case.

THE VALIDITY OF COGNITIVE THERAPY

Cognitive theory: experimental studies

The observation that the thoughts of depressed individuals have negative themes led to the development of cognitive theory. Since then the relationship between mood and negative thinking has been examined experimentally, with each of the two variables, mood and cognition, being manipulated independently. Teasdale (1983) reviews the available research and concludes that there is evidence for the existence of a reciprocal relationship between mood and cognition, in which negative cognitions appear to produce depression and conversely depressed mood appears to increase the accessibility of negative cognitions. This creates a vicious circle which perpetuates and possibly intensifies depression. He goes on to say that there is a clear need for psychological treatment, such as cognitive therapy, which aims at breaking the vicious circle by which cognitions and depression maintain each other.

The premise that modification of cognitions by cognitive therapy could relieve depressed mood was tested and supported by Teasdale and Fennell (1982), who compared cognitive therapy techniques with exploratory techniques when addressing identified, negative thoughts of depressed patients currently receiving cognitive therapy. The greater change in belief resulting from cognitive therapy techniques was accompanied by a greater reduction in self-rated depressed mood than was obtained in the thought exploration condition.

Cognitive therapy: clinical trials

As cognitive therapy was first introduced as a treatment for depression, the majority of clinical trials of cognitive therapy have been carried out with depressed subjects. Studies have demonstrated that cognitive therapy is effective and compares favourably with the use of the antidepressant imipramine hydrochloride (Rush et al, 1977), behaviour therapy and non-directive therapy (Shaw, 1977) and supportive psychotherapy (Shipley and Fazio, 1973). Most studies have been carried out in the USA and on depressed students but in 1981, Ivy Blackburn and her colleagues in Edinburgh carried out a well designed large scale study using general hospital out patients and general practice patients, comparing cognitive therapy alone, antidepressant medication alone and combined cognitive therapy and medication. The effectiveness of tricyclic antidepressants as a treatment for depression has been well established (e.g. Morris and Beck, 1974). For hospital outpatients the combination treatment was most effective with cognitive therapy alone being more effective than antidepressant medication alone. For general practice patients, cognitive therapy alone was the most effective treatment. The presence of endogenous features appeared to have no significant effect on the efficacy of cognitive therapy. Weismann (1978) reported a similar additive effect of cognitive therapy and medication whereas Rush et al (1977) found cognitive therapy to be more effective in the treatment of depressed outpatients than tricyclic antidepressants.

COGNITIVE THERAPY: THE WAY AHEAD

Although it has been argued that cognitive theory of depression has an inadequate conceptual basis for a model of cognitive processing (Power and Champion, 1986), Beck's theory of the nature of emotional disorders is a theory insofar as it generates hypotheses that can both be tested experimentally and also can generate new models of treatment. The cognitive model of panic disorder recently developed by Clark (in press) is a good example of an experimentally based psychological treatment. As mentioned above cognitive models of treatment for obsessional disorder (Salkovskis, 1985;1988 current volume) and personality disorder (Young, in press) are currently being developed. It would appear that cognitive theory and treatment approaches based upon it has a valuable contribution to make in the treatment of affective disorder, which has yet to be fully developed.

Although specific contraindications to the use of cognitive therapy have yet to be identified, clinical observation suggests that individuals with impaired reality testing ability or cognitive impairment will not be able to cooperate with treatment. Cognitive therapy is unlikely to be successful with people experiencing severe personality disturbances or psychotic disorders (Rush and Giles, 1982). However, contrary to the received thinking regarding psychotherapy in general, social factors such as socio-economic status or educational attainment appear to have no significant adverse effect, although some modification of the technique may be necessary; operating at a more concrete than abstract level for example.

The therapeutic skills of the therapist are also important. Cognitive therapy is complex and it can be difficult at times to avoid appearing confrontational. Fennell and Teasdale (1982) caution against novice therapists carrying out cognitive therapy with chronically depressed patients.

CONCLUSION

Beck's cognitive theory of depression has led to the development of a treatment of depression that has proved to be effective in clinical trials. The reciprocal relationship between cognitions and mood has been demonstrated experimentally providng support for the basic premise that dysfunctional thoughts lead to emotional distress. Cognitive therapy is a complex and skilled activity which is in the process of being extended from its original area of depression, to anxiety and more recently to panic disorder, obsessional disorder and personality disorder.

REFERENCES

Beck, A.T., (1967), Depression: Clinical, Experimental and Theoretical Aspects, Harper and Row, New York. Republished as Depression: Causes and Treatment, Philadelphia, University of Pennsylvania Press, 1972.

Beck, A.T., (1976), Cognitive Therapy and the Emotional Disorders, International Universities Press, New York.

Beck. A.T. Rush, A.J., Shaw, B.F. and Emery, G., (1979), Cognitive Therapy of Depression, Guildford Press, New York

Blackburn, I.M., Bishop, S., Glen, A.I.M., Whalley, L.J. and Christie, J.E., (1981), The efficacy of cognitive therapy in depression using cognitive therapy and pharmacotherapy each alone and in combination, British Journal of Psychiatry, 139, 181-189.

Clark, D.M., (1986), A cognitive approach to panic, Behaviour Research and Therapy, 24, 461-470.

Clark, D.M. (1988), A cognitive model of panic attacks in Rachman, S. and Maser, J.D. (eds.), Panic: Psychological Views, Lawrence Erlbaum, Hillsdale, New Jersey.

Clark, D.M. (in press), Cognitive therapy for anxiety, Behavioural Psychotherapy.

Clark, D.M. and Salkovskis, P.M. (in press), A cognitive behavioural treatment for panic attacks in Huber, W. (ed.), Proceedings of the 2nd European Conference on Psychotherapy Research, University of Louvain Press, Belgium.

Fennell, M. and Teasdale, J., (1982), Cognitive therapy with chronic drug refractory, depressed outpatients: A note of caution, Cognitive Therapy and Research, 6, 4 455-460.

Morris, J.B. and Beck, A.T., (1974), The efficacy of anti-depressant drugs: A review of research (1958-1972), Archives of General Psychiatry, 30, 667-674.

Power, M.J. and Champion, L.A., (1986), Cognitive approaches to depression: A theoretical critique, British Journal of Clinical Psychology, 25, 201-212.

Pretzner J.L., (1983), Borderline Personality Disorder: Too Complex for Cognitive Therapy? Presented at 91st Annual Convention of the American Psychological Association at Anaheim, L.A.

Rush, A.J., Beck, A.T., Kovacs, M. and Hollon, S.D., (1977), Comparative efficacy of cognitive therapy and pharmacotherapy in the treatment of depressed outpatients, Cognitive Therapy and Research, 1, 17-37.

Rush, A. and Giles, D., (1982), Cognitive therapy: Theory and research in Rush, A.J. (ed.) Short Term Psychotherapies for Depression, Guildford Press, New York.

Salkovskis, P.M., (1985), Obsessional-compulsive problems: A cognitive behavioural analysis, Behavioural Research and Therapy, 25, 571-583.

Shaw, B.F., (1977), A comparison of cognitive therapy and behaviour therapy in the treatment of depression, Journal of Consulting and Clinical Psychology, 45, 549-551.

Shipley, C.R. and Fazio, A.F., (1973), Pilot study of a

treatment for psychologicl depression, Journal of Abnormal Psychology, 82, 372-376.

Teasdale, J.D., (1983), Negative thinking in depression: Cause, effect or reciprocal relationship?, Advances in Behaviour Research and Therapy, 5, 3-26.

Young, J.E. and Beck, A.T., (1982), Cognitive therapy: Clinical applications in Rush, A.J. (ed.), Short Term Psychotherapies for Depression, Guildford Press, New York.

Young, J.E. (in press) Scheme-focussed cognitive therapy for personality disorders, in Beck, A.T. and Freeman, A.A. (eds.), Cognitive Therapy for Personality Disorders, Guildford Press, New York.

Weissman, M.M., (1978), Psychotherapy and its relevance to the pharmacotherapy of affective disorders: From ideology to evidence in, Damascio, A. and Killam, K. (eds.), Psychopharmacology: A Generation of Progres Lipton, Raven Press, New York.

Negative thinking and depression

S. CARR

INTRODUCTION

In the area of depression, cognitive theory and research has been aimed at elucidating the way in which moods affect thinking processes (and vice versa) both in non-clinical subjects and in people prone to depression. The aim is to understand more about the involvement of cognitive processes in depression, and ultimately to improve treatment approaches. In this paper I will concentrate on the question of whether there are enduring differences between people prone to depression and those who are less prone to depression in terms of cognitive structures or processes. In other words, is there such a thing as 'cognitive vulnerability' to depression?

BECK'S THEORY OF COGNITIVE VULNERABILITY

Work on cognition in depression has received much of its impetus from the cognitive theory of depression proposed by Aaron T. Beck (1972). Beck posits a central role for negative thinking in maintaining depressive symptoms and has developed a therapy package based on this, which aims to reduce depression by intervention at the cognitive level. Cognitive therapy clients are encouraged to recognise the role of thinking in mood processes, to gain distance from thoughts (i.e. view them as thoughts rather than expressions of fact) and to challenge the validity of the thoughts through examination of currently available evidence, or by collecting further evidence in behavioural experiments. Controlled trials of cognitive therapy have thus far provided very promising results, outcome being as good as, or better than, drug treatments (Rush et al, 1977; Blackburn et al, 1981; Murphy et al, 1984). However, if therapy aimed only to reduce current negative thinking and depressive symptoms. Beck would see this as incomplete:

> Changing his erroneous or dysfunctional assumptions has a direct effect upon the patient's ability to avoid future depressions...the therapist may tell the patient that even when the symptoms of depression have abated, he will remain vulnerable to future depressions until these beliefs are identified and changed.

As this quote implies, Beck's theory proposes that vulnerability to depression consists in the possession of depressogenic schemata, which can be conceived of as a set of dysfunctional assumptions such as: 'If I am not a success, life has no meaning', 'If I am not loved by everyone, I cannot go on living' (Kovacs and Beck, 1978, p.528). Part of the attraction of this theory lies in the fact that it would clearly be possible to hold such beliefs and yet not be depressed as long as you believe you are a success, or are loved. Nevertheless, these assumptions would render you vulnerable to the development of negative thoughts about yourself and depression, given that events occurred in the relevant domains.

Beck's theory, if correct, has important implications for clinical practice, which are summed up in the quotation above. It is therefore of some importance to try to establish whether depression prone persons are indeed characterised by such dysfunctional assumptions.

Research on dysfunctional assumptions and their persistence

A questionnaire has been developed which is intended to measure dysfunctional assumptions (Weissman and Beck, 1978). This is called the Dysfunctional Attitude Scale (DAS), and consists of a collection of statements exemplifying the kind of assumptions described above. Respondents are asked to indicate the degree to which they agree or disagree with each one, and scoring is such that agreement with dysfunctional attitudes results in higher scores. The DAS has been shown to relate to current depression, for example, Weissman found a correlation of + 0.58 between DAS score and level of depression in a study of depressed psychiatric patients (Kovacs and Beck, 1978). However, for the purpose of this paper, the more interesting question is whether or not people prone to depression, but not currently depressed, differ on the DAS from those who are not so prone to depression.

Because depression typically has a high rate of relapse and recurrence, it is reasonable to assume that people who have experienced an episode of depression are vulnerable to further episodes. Thus it is of interest to see whether the elevated DAS scores of depressed patients persist, even when the person has recovered from the depressive episode, and several studies have examined this question. Of these, one (Eaves and Rush, 1984) found that DAS scores, although lower following recovery than during the depressive episode, were still elevated compared to nondepressive controls. However, three other studies (Silverman et al, 1984; Simons et al, 1984; Hollon et al, 1986) found no difference between the scores of recovered depressives and those of people who had not been depressed. Since in the Eaves and Rush study recovered depressives were retested within a month following recovery, it has been suggested that the results may indicate that dysfunctional attitudes may take some time to normalise following recovery.

Thus the evidence to date suggests that depressive vulnerability is not manifested in the endorsement of more dysfunctional assumptions on a questionnaire measure. Although this would seem to be inconsistent with Beck's theory, it is possible that what is really being encountered is a measurement problem. Many studies (reviewed by Nisbett and Wilson, 1977) have shown that people may not be able to give accurate reports of their own internal processes. It is possible that depression prone people may respond as if they hold such assumptions, should the appropriate conditions arise, and yet still be unwilling to endorse such attitudes on a questionnaire. Beck is not always clear in his writings as to whether the maladaptive cognitive structures are expected to be always evident, or whether they are latent, and become evident once activated by an appropriate event.

This being said, it leaves two problems: firstly a theoretical one of how to proceed with research if the concept is unmeasureable, and secondly a clinical problem, in that it is very difficult to ask someone to work on challenging a dysfunctional assumption which they deny holding.

At this point, it may be useful to turn to a related theory of cognitive vulnerability, one which predicts that under normal circumstances people vulnerable to depression will not show evidence of abnormal cognitive processes, and yet which offers the possibility of being able to test for vulnerability. This is the theory put forward by Teasdale (1983).

'VICIOUS CIRCLE' MODEL OF VULNERABILITY TO DEPRESSION

In order to present this model, it is necessary to take a step backwards and first describe some of the research performed on the relationship between mood and cognitive processes in non-clinical subjects. The starting point of Beck's theory was the observation that depressed people think in negative ways. However, as has been pointed out many times, this association could result from either an effect of negative thinking on mood, or an effect of mood on negative thinking. In order to clarify the causal nature of the relationship between depression and negative thinking, research has aimed at systematically manipulating one or other of these. This research has been thoroughly reviewed by Teasdale (1983), and only the essentials will be reiterated here.

The effects of thinking on mood

Relatively little research has been performed on this causal direction. However, the studies which have been undertaken suggest that thinking does indeed affect mood. This has been shown in two ways, firstly, by showing that experimental increases in negative thinking tend to lead to increased depression (Teasdale and Bancroft, 1977), and secondly, that experimentally decreasing negative thinking leads to decreased depression (Teasdale and Rezin, 1978; Teasdale and Fennell, 1982; Fennell and Teasdale, 1984).

The effect of mood on thinking

Experimental manipulation of mood has been shown to affect cognition. A variety of mood induction techniques have been used for this purpose, but probably the most popular of these has been a technique described by Velten, (1968). This consists of reading a series of mood suggestive statements, while actively trying to achieve the required mood. Research reviewed by Clark (1983) has indicated that the effects of this procedure cannot be accounted for by subjects' efforts to act as if they were in the requested mood, and that the effects of the depression induction tend to parallel effects seen in mild natural depression.

A very large number of studies have been performed, looking at the effects of inducted moods on cognition, for example, Blaney (1986) found twenty nine studies of effects of mood on memory. In general, results have suggested that depressed mood increases the accessibility of negative information compared with happy mood. A typical result is that demonstrated by Teasdale and Russell (1982). Subjects (who were student volunteers) were asked to learn a list of words, which included positive and negative trait adjectives (such as 'kind', 'helpful', 'cruel', 'mean') and were then put into either a happy or a depressed mood using Velten's technique. They then were asked to recall as many adjectives as possible. After returning to normal mood they learned a second list of words, including a new set of positive and negative adjectives, then were put into the opposite mood and again asked to recall as many words as possible. Figure 1 shows the number of positive and negative adjectives recalled in each mood.

As can be seen, there was a strong interaction between mood at recall and pleasantness of word, with more pleasant than unpleasant words recalled in happy mood, and more unpleasant than pleasant words recalled in despondent mood.

There might be concern as to whether such mood effects on recall are confined to the artifical manipulation of mood. It is therefore reassuring that Clark and Teasdale (1982)

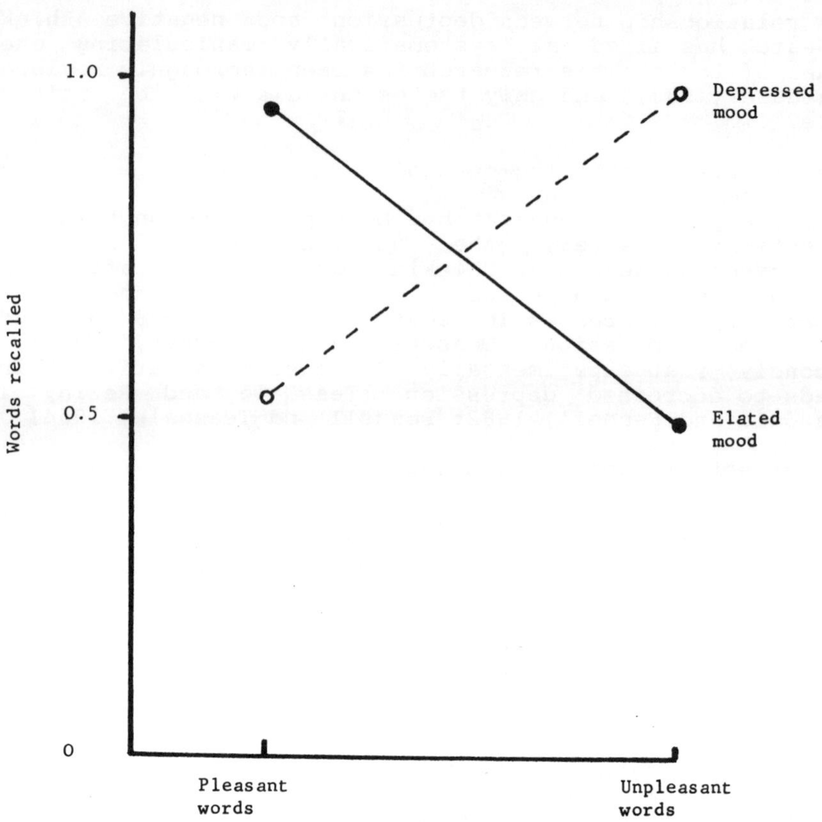

Figure 1. Mean number of positive and negative personality trait words recalled in elated and depressed mood (after Teasdale and Russell, 1982, redrawn with author's permission.)

found a similar effect, using natural mood variation. Their subjects were depressed people who showed strong diurnal variation in their degree of depression, and so they were able to test them on two occasions, once during the time of day when they were regularly more depressed, and once during the time when they were less depressed. In this study, the dependent variable was the number of pleasant and unpleasant memories produced in response to neutral cue words on the two occasions. The results are shown in Figure 2.

Again, there is an interaction between mood and pleasantness of memories, more happy than unhappy memories being produced on the less depressed occasion, and more unhappy than happy on the more depressed occasion.

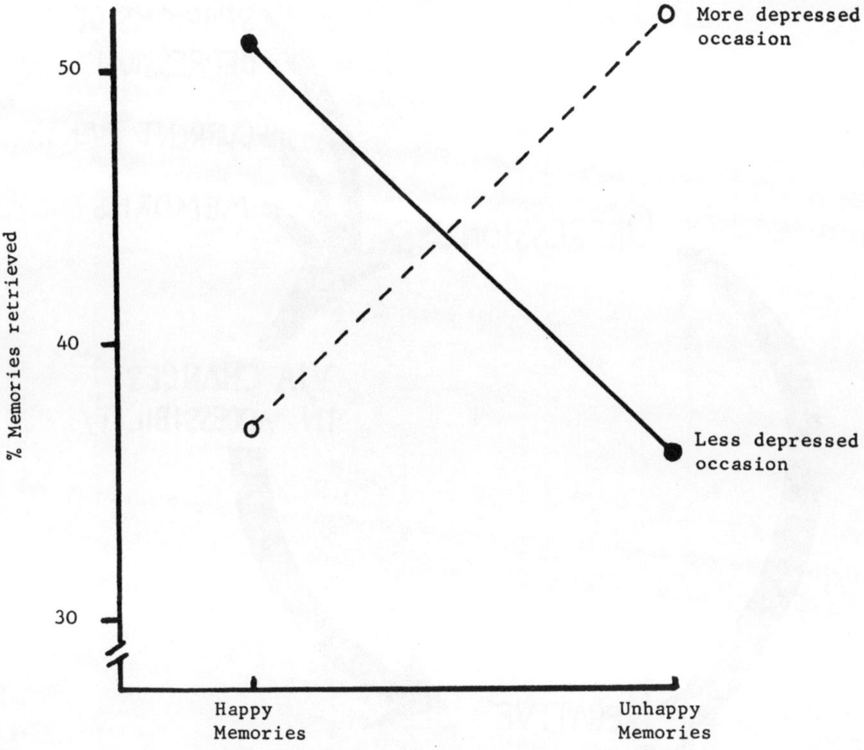

Figure 2. Mean percentage of memories retrieved (after Clark and Teasdale, 1982, redrawn with author's permission).

The reciprocal relationship between mood and cognition.

The most likely answer to the question of causality is that both causal directions are operative, i.e. that:

> negative cognitions appear to produce depression, and conversely, depression increased the probability of just those cognitions which will cause further depression
>
> (Teasdale, 1983, p.3).

This reciprocal relationship is summed up in Figure 3, taken from Teasdale (1983).

Teasdale's model describes the effects which are found on average, among subject groups. However, he goes on to suggest that there may be differences between people in the links between mood and cognition. In particular, he suggests that an important individual difference factor may be the kinds of cognitions activated by depressed mood. If these are of the globally self-devaluative type, these cognitions are in turn likely to cause further depression, and hence the

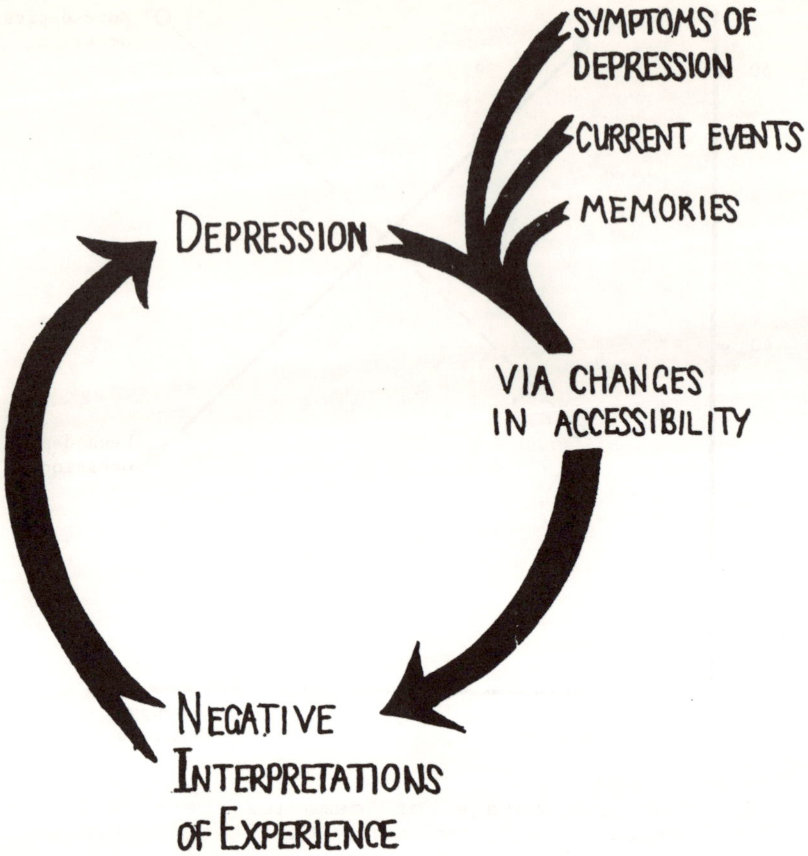

Figure 3. Reciprocal relationship between mood and cognition (after Teasdale, 1983, redrawn with author's permission.)

person will become tied into the vicious circle shown in Figure 3.

This is important, because it implies that, firstly, people vulnerable to depression will not under normal circumstances think particularly negatively, but secondly, that when in depressed mood it may be possible to detect differences between vulnerable and less vulnerable individuals with respect to the kinds of thoughts which are activated. It follows that induction of temporary depressed mood could be used as a kind of probe to detect such differences.

The effects of mood on cognition in individuals vulnerable to depression.

Research using mood induction as a tool to demonstrate differences between those who are vulnerable to depression and those who are not is just beginning. Returning to Beck's theory of vulnerability, one question of interest would be whether recovered depressives would show elevated scores on the DAS compared with non-depressives, when all are put into depressed mood. Such a study was attempted by Blackburn and Smyth (1985), using the Velten mood induction procedure, and a variety of questionnaire measures, including the DAS, as dependent variables. Unfortunately, the experiment was unsuccessful in that the Velten depression induction proved ineffective for the recovered depressives. Quite why that occurred was unclear, but at any rate, the failure to induce a significant mood change meant that no test of the experimental hypothesis could take place.

More successful was a recent study by Teasdale and Dent (1987). Rather than using a questionnaire measure, they used an information processing approach to demonstrate differential activation of positive and negative self-referent concepts. Thirty two women who had recovered from an episode of depression were compared with twenty one women who had never experienced significant depression. These subjects were asked to perform a self rating task, saying whether or not each of a list of positive and negative trait words described them. Following this they were asked to recall as many words as possible. The self rating and recall task was performed twice, once in normal mood, and once in induced depressed mood. In this experiment, the mood was induced using the musical induction procedure, in which mood suggestive music is played to the subject, who is also asked to try to 'get into' the mood. The mood induction was successful, producing a mildly depressed mood for the majority of subjects.

Results were quite complex and in fact differences were found between recovered depressives and never depressed women while in normal mood; the recovered depressives were more likely to endorse one or more negative word as self descriptive, and showed poorer recall of self referrred positive words. In addition, however, some support for Teasdale's model was obtained, in that recovered depressives in the induced mood showed better recall of negative trait words which had been endorsed as self descriptive than the never depressed subjects. The two groups did not differ on this measure in normal mood. The results therefore suggested that there may be cognitive differences between more and less vulnerable individuals in normal mood, which can be demonstrated using more subtle measures than questionnaires, but also that vulnerable individuals may tend to show greater activation of negative self-referent concepts by depressed mood.

These results indicate the heuristic value of Teasdale's model. Another experiment to be interpreted in the light of this model was that of Clark and Teasdale (1985). They found a sex difference in the effect of mood on recall of positive and negative trait adjectives, with females showing a strong mood biasing in recall while men did not. The results are shown in Figure 4.

These results were discussed with reference to their possible relevance to vulnerability to depression, starting

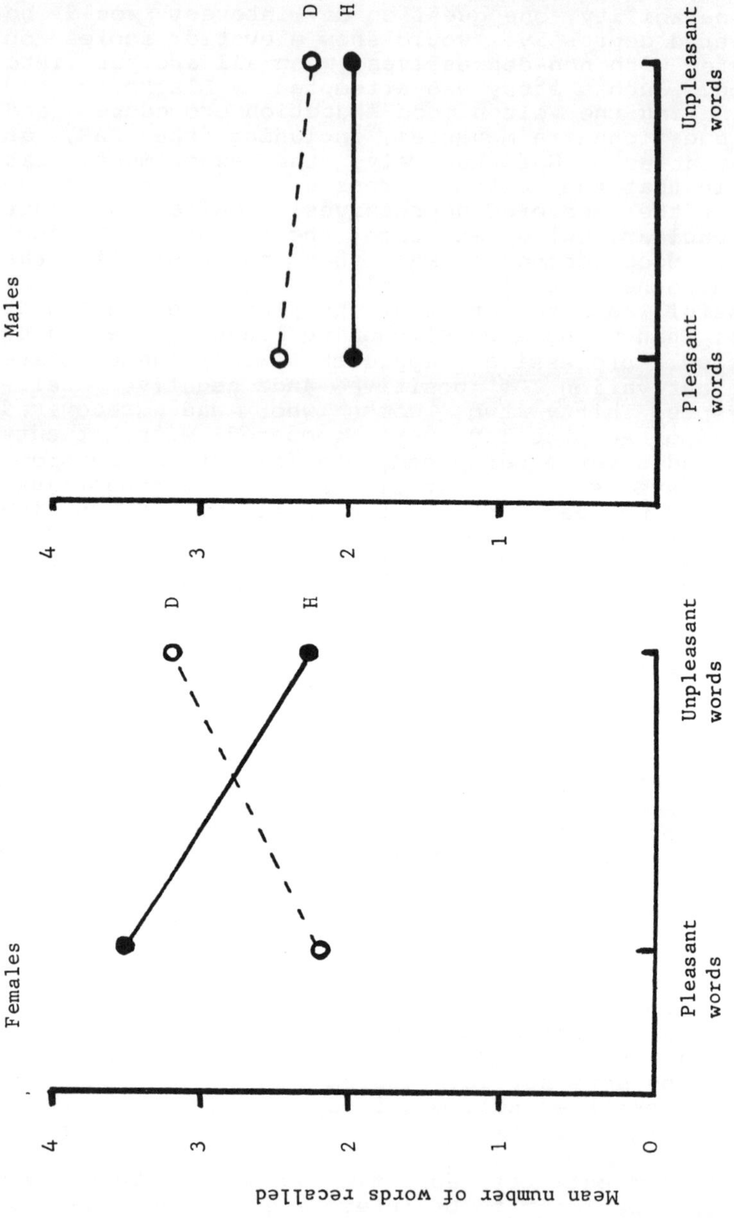

Figure 4. Mean number of pleasant and unpleasant trait words recalled by female and male subjects in happy and despondent moods. (After Clark and Teasdale, 1985, redrawn with author's permission).

from the premise that females can be seen as vulnerable to depression, because of the greater prevalence of depression among women (Weissman and Klerman, 1977).

> The observed sex difference in the effects of mood on accessibility suggests that a given level of depression is more likely to selectively prime negative cognitions in women than in men. Women are therefore more likely to be strongly tied into the vicious circle...and so are more likely to move from a mild dysphoric reaction to a more severe one, and also take longer to recover.
>
> Clark and Teasdale, 1985, p.1606

However, before it can be taken as demonstrated that women are more likely to be depressed because they are more likely to think negatively when in depressed mood, it is important that the generality of the sex difference finding be established. In fact the sex difference finding has <u>not</u> proved consistently replicable, in experiments by myself and also by Williams (1986). Whilst one experiment produced weakly supportive results, it did not reach statistical significance. In two further samples, using extremely similar methods and materials to those of Clark and Teasdale (1985), I found no suggestion of a sex difference, both male and female subjects showed mood-biasing in recall of trait words. Williams (1986) tested a very large sample of men and women (150 in all) and found a significant mood congruency effect in recall for both sexes, but absolutely no interaction with sex.

Thus it would seem that in this case caution is in order: there are many other possible factors (including social and environmental factors, see Jenkins and Clare, 1985) which may account for a greater prevalence of depression among women, and it is important that these should not be neglected as possible causes.

Finally, the larger purpose of Williams' study deserves a mention. As described, she has tested a large group of subjects (university students), to see to what extent they show biasing in recall of information as a result of depressed mood induction. These subjects are now being followed up prospectively, periodically reporting on their experiences of depression during the follow up period. Thus it will be possible to test whether mood-biasing of self referent concepts can serve as a predictor of subsequent depressive experiences. This, therefore will provide a stronger test of the usefulness of Teasdale's (1983) model, and will provide some indication of the potential of the mood induction-information processing paradigm in identifying people who are vulnerable to depression.

REFERENCES

Beck, A.T., (1972), <u>Depression: Causes and Treatment</u>, University of Pennsylvania Press, Pennsylvania.

Beck, A.T., Rush, A.J., Shaw, B.F. and Emery, G., (1979), Cognitive Therapy of Depression, Guildford Press, New York.

Blackburn, I.M., Bishop, S., Glen, A.I.M., Whalley, L.J. and Christie, J.E., (1981), The efficacy of cognitive therapy in depression: A treatment trial using cognitive therapy and pharmacotherapy, each alone and in combination, British J. of Psychiatry, 139, 181-189.

Blackburn, I.M. and Smyth, P., (1985), A test of cognitive vulnerability in individuals prone to depression, British J. Clinical Psychology, 24, 61-62.

Blaney, P.H., (1986), Affect and Memory: A review, Psychological Bulletin, 99, 229-246.

Clark, D.M., (1983), On the induction of depressed mood in the laboratory: Evaluation and comparison of the Velten and musical procedures, Advances in Behaviour Research and Therapy, 5, 27-49.

Clark. D.M. and Teasdale, J.D., (1982), Diurnal variation in clinical depression and accessibility of memories of positive and negative experiences, J. Abnormal Psychology, 91. 87-95.

Clark, D.M. and Teasdale, J.D., (1985), Constraints on the effects of mood on memory, J. Personality and Social Psychology, 48, 11595-1608.

Eaves, G. and Rush, A.J., (1984), Cognitive patterns in symptomatic and remitted unipolar major depression, J. Abnormal Psychology, 93, 31-40.

Fennell, M.J.V. and Teasdale, J.D., (1984), Effects of distraction on thinking and affect in depressed patients, British J. Clinical Psychology, 23, 65-66.

Hollon, S.D., Kendall, P.C. and Lumry, A., (1986), Specificity of depressotypic cognitions in clinical depression, J. Abnormal Psychology, 95, 52-59.

Jenkins, R. and Clare, A., (1985) Women and mental illness, British Medical J., 291, 1521-1522.

Kovacs, M. and Beck, A.T., (1978), Maladaptive cognitive structures in depression, Am. J. Psychiatry, 135, 525-533.

Murphy, G.E., Simons, A.D., Wetzel, R.D. and Lustman, P.J., (1984), Cognitive therapy and pharmacotherapy. Singly and together in the treatment of depression, Archives of General Psychiatry, 41, 33-41.

Nisbett, R.E. and Wilson, T.D., (1977), Telling more than we know. Verbal reports on mental processes, Psychological Review, 84, 231-259.

Rush, A.J., Beck, A.T., Kovacs, M. and Hollon, S., (1977), Comparative efficacy of cognitive therapy and pharmacotherapy in the treatment of depressed outpatients, Cognitive Therapy and Research, 1, 17-37.

Silverman, J.S., Silverman, J.A. and Eardley, D.A., (1984), Do maladaptive attitudes cause depression?, Archives of General Psychiatry, 41, 28-30.

Simons, A.D., Garfield, S.L. and Murphy, G.E., (1984), The process of change in cognitive therapy and pharmacotherapy for depression. Changes in mood and cognition, Archives of General Psychiatry, 41, 45-51.

Teasdale, J.D., (1983), Negative thinking in depression: Cause, effect or reciprocal relationship?, Advances in Behaviour Research and Therapy, 5, 3-26.
Teasdale, J.D. and Bancroft, J., (1977), Manipulation of thought content as a determinant of mood and corrugator electromyographic activity in depressed patients, J. Abnormal Psychology, 86, 235-241.
Teasdale, J.D. and Dent, J., (1987), Cognitive vulnerability to depression: an investigation of two hypotheses, British J. Clinical Psychology, 26, 113-126.
Teasdale, J.D. and Fennell, M.J.V., (1982), Immediate effects on depression of cognitive therapy interventions, Cognitive Therapy and Research, 6, 343-352.
Teasdale., J.D. and Rezin, V., (1978), The effects of reducing frequency of negaqtive thoughts on the model of depressed patients - tests of a cognitive model of depression, British J. Social and Clinical Psychology, 17, 65-74.
Teasdale, J.D. and Russell, M.L., (1982), Differential effects of induced mood on the recall of positive, negative and neutral words, British J. Social and Clinical Psychology, 22, 163-171.
Velten, E., (1968), A laboratory task for induction of mood states, Behaviour Research and Therapy, 6, 473-482.
Weissman, A. and Beck, A.T., (1978), The Dysfunctional Attitude Scale, Paper presented at the meeting of the Association for the Advancement of Behaviour Therapy, Chicago.
Weissman, M.M. and Klerman, G.L., (1977), Sex differences and the epidemiology of depression, Archives of General Psychiatry, 34, 98-111.
Williams, R., (1986), Personal communication.

Intrusive thoughts and obsessional disorders

P. SALKOVSKIS

INTRODUCTION: JUST HOW SUCCESSFUL IS BEHAVIOUR THERAPY?

The treatment of obsessive compulsive disorder is commonly believed to represent the most successful application of behaviour therapy, in a disorder which was previously regarded as intractable and likely to follow a deteriorating course. More specifically, average success rates of seventy five percent have been reported (e.g. Foa and Goldstein, 1978; Kirk, 1983). Furthermore, treatment efforts can be more efficiently directed, because those patients who are unlikely to respond to the usual behavioural interventions have been identified (Foa, Steketee, Grayson and Doppelt, 1983; Rachman, 1983). These are patients with overvalued ideation, with severe concurrent depression, ruminators (obsessions without compulsions), and patients not complying with treatment.

Although it is undoubtably true that behaviour therapy has indeed been outstandingly successful, there are important reservations. Firstly, 'treatment failures' are at least as distressed as other patients, and no behavioural strategies have yet been developed to make treatment effective for this group. Secondly, treatment of obsessional patients is often lengthy, distressing (to both patient <u>and</u> therapist) and sometimes incomplete. The success of behaviour therapy is less impressive still when other factors are taken into account. Published reports of seventy five percent success do not include twenty five percent treatment refusers, and twelve percent dropouts. (Note also that published reports from research centres do not always accurately reflect the situation in routine clinical practice). These figures mean that at least fifty percent of patients suitable for and seeking treatment for obsessions do not resolve their problems and this is before relapse rates are taken into consideration.

These results suggest that the application of behavioural treatment to obsessional problems needs to be extended in order to encompass those patients who do not currently benefit from the treatment offered. In order to consider possible extensions of behaviour therapy, we need to refer to the theoretical principles upon which treatment is based. Theoretical accounts of behavioural approaches to obsessive compulsive disorder either suggest that ritualistic behaviour is part of the mechanism serving to maintain obsessional thoughts (e.g. Rachman and Hodgson, 1980), or that it at least inhibits habituation by shortening the period during which exposure to the thoughts occurs (e.g. Marks, 1981). Thus, the generally accepted psychological model of obsessive-compulsive behaviour gives ritualising a crucial role in preventing the natural occurrence of habituation. The most widely accepted psychological model is summarised in table 1.

Table 1

Psychological model of obsessive-compulsive disorder

1. Obsessions are conditioned anxiety stimuli which have failed to habituate.

2. Responses which terminate the anxiety or discomfort associated with such stimuli (i.e. compulsions) are reinforced by the reduction of discomfort, so that escape behaviours are reinforced and become increasingly likely to follow obsessions.

3. There are a variety of behaviours which patients develop over the longer term and are intended to avoid the occurrence of obsessional thoughts; these avoidance behaviours can become pervasive in the same way as agoraphobic avoidance.

In summary:
Compulsions function to terminate exposure to feared stimuli, producing short term relief but preventing full exposure and habituation.

This formulation highlights the importance of prolonged exposure with response prevention as the primary mechanism of change. Note, however, that this view of the maintenance of obsessional problems has not changed since the early or even mid 1970's (Rachman, 1971; 1976). This probably explains why, while this model is supported by some experimental data, a number of important findings are not accounted for, whilst other data is actually inconsistent.

FINDINGS WHICH ARE NOT ACCOUNTED FOR BY, OR ARE INCONSISTENT WITH, THE PSYCHOLOGICAL MODEL

The model predicts that obsessional ruminations (usually defined as obsessions without overt compulsive behaviour) should be extremely easy to treat because of the absence of any compulsive behaviour which might otherwise terminate exposure. However, progress in the treatment of compulsions has not generalised to the treatment of obsessional ruminations. The problem is succinctly summarised by Rachman (1983), who wrote that:

> The main obstacle to the successful treatment of obsessions is the absence of effective treatments.

Clearly, this state of affairs is clinically problematic (because patients with ruminations are distressed and require treatment) and makes little sense theoretically. Thus, if compulsive behaviour is a key variable in the maintainance of obsessions as suggested by work such as that of Rachman and his associates, then ruminations should spontaneously remit or be readily treatable by simple habituation methods (Rachman, de Silva and Roper, 1976; Roper and Rachman 1975; Roper and Rachman, 1973). This is not true, as demonstrated by several outcome studies which show that ruminations are highly resistant to treatment (see Salkovskis and Westbrook, 1988).

However, this particular problem can be dealt with in a relatively simple way, if it is assumed that ruminations are not simply obsessional thoughts, but can be divided into intrusive thoughts (as occur in obsessional compulsive disorder) and neutralising thoughts (the mental equivalent of compulsive behaviour). Neutralising thoughts can be regarded as fulfilling the same function as compulsive behaviour (i.e. they terminate exposure to the obsessional stimuli and therefore prevent habituation taking place). The defining characteristic of covert neutralising is not the content, but rather that the neutralising thought is deliberate (voluntary) as opposed to an intrusion, which is uncontrolled and involuntary. If this is so, then the problem becomes one of the proper application of the existing model with this modification so that neutralising requires attention in treatment. The implication of this is that exposure <u>and covert response prevention</u> are both required. There are a number of other implications of this conceptualisation which can explain why ruminations are, in fact, more difficult to treat than obsessive-compulsive disorder. A full account of these can be found in Salkovskis and Westbrook (1988), and Salkovskis and Kirk (1988).
(1988).

A variety of important but unexpected findings have been reported which are not accounted for by the simple psychological formulation. These include the fact that some patients show increased anxiety when they ritualise (e.g. Beech and Liddell, 1974; Rachman and Hodgson, 1980, chapter 13). Discomfort experienced when an obsession is provoked can be decreased by the presence of the therapist in patients with checking rituals, but not patients with contamination and washing rituals (Rachman, de Silva and Roper, 1976; Roper and Rachman 1975; Roper and Rachman, 1973). It is a common clinical observation that reassurance seeking is prevalent and problematic in washers, checkers and ruminators; this behaviour occurs with similar intensity and characteristics as ritualising behaviours. A sensitivity to criticism has been identified; this differentiates phobics and obsessive-compulsives (Rachman and Hodgson, 1980).

Several writers have been puzzled as to the adaptive significance of intrusive and obsessional phenomena. For instance, Rachman and Hodgson (1980) ask:

> Why do obsessions persist despite their obnoxious and self defeating properties? Are obsessions mere flotsam or do they serve some psychological function.

This question has become more interesting as it has become clear that unpleasant and unwanted intrusive thoughts are very common amongst normal subjects (Salkovskis and Harrison, 1984; Rachman and de Silva, 1978). This led Rachman (1981) to identify the questions of greatest interest as concerning the nature of intrusive thoughts, their origin, the reasons for persistence and the cause of their uncontrollability. Furthermore, Rachman (1981) suggests that the solution to the puzzle of intrusive thoughts might:

> lead to advances in our understanding of thinking in general. Are not most of our thoughts intrusive?.

The problems identified above suggest that an extension of the existing theoretical framework is required if further advances in the psychological treatment of obsessional problems are to be made (c.f. Teasdale, 1982), but offer the hope that progress may advance our understanding of thought processes in general. In the rest of this paper, the cognitive-behavioural approach to obsessions is described, together with an outline of the broader implications of such an approach. Finally, some experimental work currently under way will be described.

THE THEORETICAL CASE FOR TREATMENT: A COGNITIVE-BEHAVIOURAL HYPOTHESIS OF THE NATURE AND MAINTENANCE OF UPSETTING INTRUSIVE THOUGHTS

A recently outlined cognitive-behavioural formulation of obsessional problems and their treatment (Salkovskis, 1985; Salkovskis and Warwick, 1988) can account for the findings discussed above, whilst retaining the basic structure of the behavioural model which has been so useful in the development of effective treatment for obsessions.

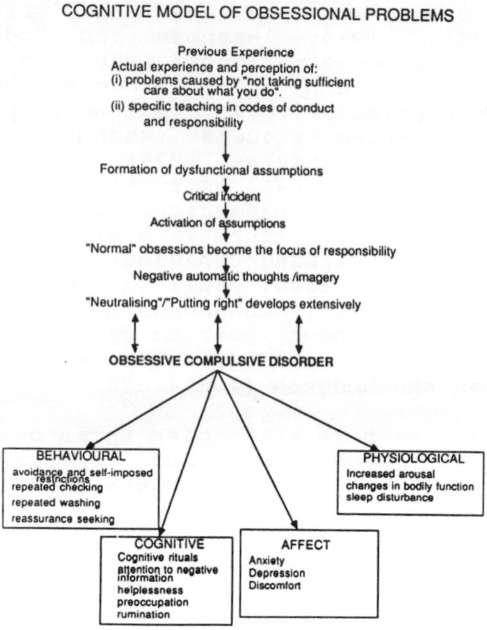

Figure 1. Cognitive model of the development of obsessive-compulsive disorder

This model suggests that normal intrusive thoughts play a key role in the development of obsessional problems, interacting with assumptions about responsibility and neutralising thoughts/behaviour, as shown in figure 1.

Thus, intrusive thoughts are a normal phenomenon which can become problematic as a result of particular beliefs about the nature and content of the thoughts themselves. In particular, the beliefs which are problematic are those which concern responsibility. What happens is that an intrusive thought with implications for responsibility occurs in an individual who believes that having this thought makes them responsible for the prevention of harm. When the thought is evaluated in this way, the individual feels compelled to act to prevent harm. Although such an action relieves the initial feeling of being responsible, it strengthens the assumption that responsibility was truly involved ('washing my hands prevented my family from being contaminated'). Someone may have been having intrusive thoughts concerning violence for some considerable time without these thoughts causing more than transient distress. However, when he or she has a baby, a combination of the stress of new responsibility and these thoughts can lead to the belief that they may act upon their intrusive thoughts, thus becoming responsible for harm to their helpless child. This belief can result in the development of both <u>avoidance</u> (e.g. trying not to be left alone with the child, locking away knives) and <u>neutralising</u> (compulsive) thoughts and behaviours associated with the intrusions (e.g. fighting the intrusion by thinking how much he or she loves the child). Neutralising and the associated transient relief it brings, has two effects, firstly, it reinforces the compulsive behaviour, which is learned as an habitual response to intrusive thoughts. Secondly, it prevents changes in the beliefs which resulted in the neutralising. For instance, the patient described above might respond to the thought 'I might stab my baby' by locking up knives and getting their spouse to keep the key, and may believe that these behaviours actually prevented them from stabbing the baby. This belief making future similar actions more likely, particularly because the patient did not have any chance to discover that they would not act on these thoughts. Thus, neutralising can have the effect of changing their belief about responsibility with respect to thoughts. Figure 2 shows the way in which this model accounts for the various phenomena associated with obsessive problems. Notice that intrusive thoughts do not produce discomfort; it is the negative automatic thoughts, in which the intrusion is evaluated, which do this. In the example above, the intrusion might be 'I will hit my baby'. If the person experiencing this responds by thinking 'that's a funny thought', or simply ignores it, no discomfort will be experienced. However, if the person thinks 'I must not have that thought or I might act on it' or 'How can I be sure I am not going to hit my baby?', then intense discomfort and the urge to attempt to keep the thought at bay will follow.

IMPLICATIONS OF THE MODEL: NOT GOOD IDEAS AND BAD IDEAS, JUST IDEAS AND COMPELLING ONES

There are a number of implications of this cognitive model. Interestingly, one of these may help clarify the function of unwanted intrusive thoughts. The model suggests that the initial occurrence of intrusive thoughts is unconnected with the unacceptability or discomfort associated with these, but that discomfort arises as part of a secondary evaluation. Thus, the occurrence of intrusive thoughts reflects areas of current concern, and these intrusive thoughts can be positively, negatively or neutrally valenced, depending on the evaluation made by the individual experiencing them. <u>Why</u> should intrusive thoughts occur? The most obvious explanation of this is that <u>ideas</u> occur constantly, and in ways which are normally helpful. In problem solving, the best results of 'brainstorming' are obtained without censoring; all possible ideas are considered, whether 'good' or bad. If novel approaches to a person's current concerns are being sought, precensorship tends to inhibit the process of generating ideas. Indeed, in order to evaluate an idea as useful or useless, good or bad, it has to be processed in some way before it can be accepted or rejected. In evolutionary terms, the survival value of generating ideas irrespective of their later evaluation is clear in terms of

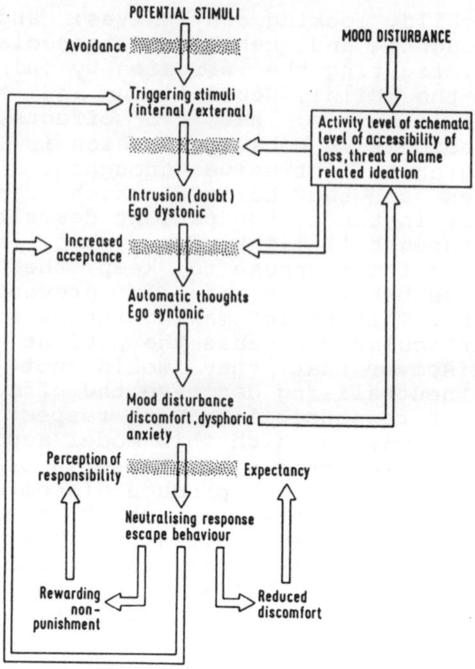

Figure 2. Hypothesised processing influencing the rate of normal and intrusive thoughts

expansion of the scope of ideas considered. Furthermore, normally 'unacceptable' ideas can, under changed conditions, become useful, particularly in extreme circumstances. The same account can be used to explain the intrusiveness of this type of thought; for ideas to be useful they have to be noticed and evaluated hence the compelling nature of these thoughts. If this is true, then the tendency for disturbed mood (anxiety, depression and anger; Rachman and Hodgson, 1980) to worsen intrusions can also be seen as serving a positive psychological function. Ideas are needed most urgently under stress. If this is so, both positive and negative intrusions should increase under stressful circumstances.

Recently, this view received support from an experiment by Edwards and Dickerson (1987), who evaluated the characteristics of both positive and negative intrusions. Edwards and Dickerson found that normal subjects reported both positive and negative intrusions, with positive intrusions being more frequent. The primary characteristics of positive and negative intrusions were found to be very similar as indexed by controllability, relation to external triggers, form, lifespan and duration. The variables which differed were those which would be regarded secondary in the present analysis; that is, subject ratings of congruence with beliefs, general acceptability, and harmfulness. Also consistent with the present hypothesis, tendency to neutralise was similar in positive and negative intrusions. High scores on the depression subscale of the profile of mood states were associated with decreased controllability in both negative _and_ positive intrusions.

The other important question is why neutralising and compulsive behaviour should be associated with the persistence of upsetting and unpleasant intrusions? Referring to the concept of an 'idea generator' producing thoughts which are competing for limited attention, it seems that many ideas (good and bad) do _not_ persist. Those which do are usually thoughts which have a degree of _salience_, that is, ideas which persist are those with important implications for what one is doing or will do in the immediate future, regardless of the acceptability of the initial idea. Figure 3 shows the way these factors may operate to determine aspects of the priority of processing of intrusive thoughts.

The model has implications for therapy. Similar to the behavioural model, therapy should be directed at preventing behaviours related to the obsession (note that these can be either overt _or_ covert). The other area where change could be implemented is in the appraisal of thoughts once they occur. Cognitive therapy is particularly suitable, because the approach concentrates on methods designed to change the evaluation of thoughts and events as a means of bringing about clinical improvement. The foregoing analysis pinpoints those characteristics which should be the target for cognitive treatment; these are evaluative thoughts (negative automatic thoughts) rather than characteristics such as controllability, intrusiveness and other primary characteristics. This leads to the consideration of general issues in the clinical application of cognitive therapy in obsessive-compulsive disorder.

APPLYING TREATMENT PROCEDURES IN CLINICAL PRACTICE THE CLINICAL CASE FOR COGNITIVE THERAPY

Recently, much has been written about the relative merits of cognitive and behavioural approaches to anxiety disorders. This has sometimes led to an undesirable and unnecessary degree of polarisation (e.g. Gurnani and Wang, 1987; Warwick and Salkovskis, 1987). Whilst it is important to identify mechanisms involved in clinical improvement, it is premature to draw any firm conclusions about the relative merits and demerits of the cognitive procedures which are increasingly being used alone or in combination with behaviour therapy. Whilst the onus is on those developing such approaches to define their position within an empirical framework, new techniques often require development. Cognitive therapy can be usefully regarded as a new paradigm which adds to and enhances behavioural procedures, without losing the benefits of the behavioural approach (Salkovskis, 1986; Teasdale, 1982).

Much of the early research into cognitive approaches to

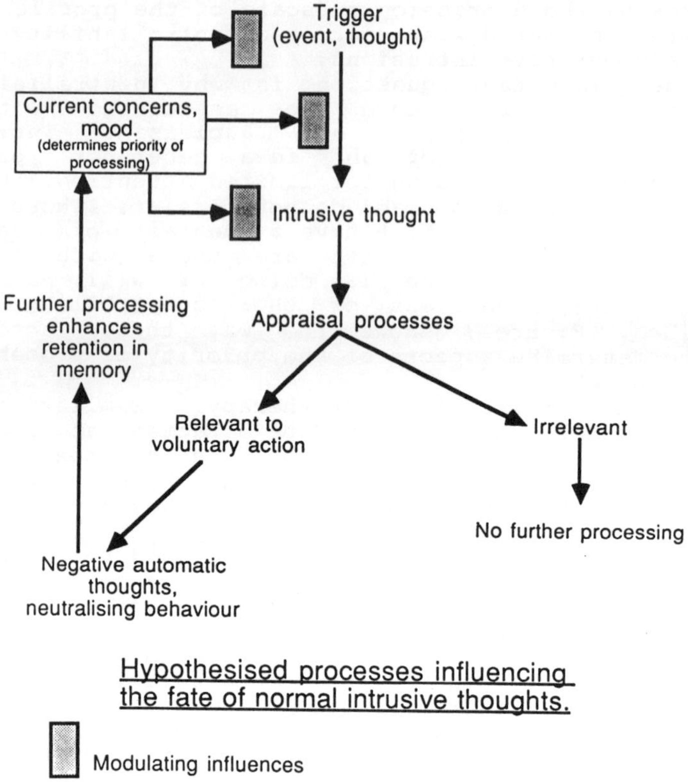

Figure 3. Hypothesised processes influencing the fate of normal intrusive thoughts

anxiety was based on inappropriate cognitive formulations and treatments carried out by inexperienced therapists in an often inappropriate fashion (Salkovskis, 1987). However, cognitive theories of and treatments for anxiety states have more recently been refined to the point where proper investigation has become possible. That the empirical basis of cognitive procedures in obsessions has yet to be fully established is consistent with the stage of development of cognitive theories, the main requirement being for further exploratory studies (Salkovskis and Warwick, in press). The potential for the application of cognitive treatments can be inferred from the success of cognitive therapy with depression, and the obvious cognitive aspects of obsessions. For instance, Marks (1981) comments that:

> obsessives develop a more elaborate set of beliefs around their rituals than phobics develop around their fears. Cognitions seem to play a larger role in obsessive than in phobics. Minor changes in obsessives' perception of a situation can therefore produce a marked change in their behaviour
>
> (Marks, 1981, p.40)

This being so, the use of cognitive procedures in the treatment of ruminations is twofold. Firstly, cognitive approaches are used to enhance or enable compliance in similar ways already used to engage patients in behaviour therapy. For example, informal cognitive strategies are already the mainstay of the approach to total noncompliance. Marks (1981) has highlighted both the unstructured application of 'cognitive' techniques and the limitations of the purely exposure based approach when he argued that

> calm, gentle, yet firm persuasion is helpful, but if the patient resists strongly, little can be done.
>
> (Marks, 1981, p. 97).

Cognitive therapy may change this gloomy outlook, using an approach which involved the identification and modification of thoughts and beliefs which prevent the patient from engaging in treatment (for an example of this application, see Salkovskis and Warwick, 1985). Secondly, more direct modification of the processes involved in the obsessive's perception of situations triggering their obsessions may be helpful. Further details of both approaches are outlined in Salkovskis and Warwick (1988), and are common to the treatment of all obsessional patients. It is also encouraging to note that there are now two reports in which cognitive therapy has been shown to be as effective as exposure and response prevention in the treatment of obsessive-compulsive disorder (Emmelkamp, 1987). Although the therapeutic effectiveness of cognitive approaches to obsessional disorders is welcome, it provides only indirect support for the view proposed here. More direct support requires specific experimental studies testing predictions derived from the hypothesis.

STUDIES OF NORMAL OBSESSIONS

As described above, intrusive thoughts which closely resemble clinical obsessions have been identified in the normal population (Rachman and de Silva, 1978; Salkovskis and Harrison, 1984). These intrusive thoughts have become the focus of research into obsessional phenomena, based on the idea that clinical obsessions represent an extreme form of normal intrusive thoughts. For instance, Parkinson and Rachman (1980) showed that when deliberate provocation of thought was used, the pattern of discomfort observed was closely parallel to that observed in obsessional patients, although only one of the sixty subjects in this study experienced an urge to neutralise. This and other studies have demonstrated sufficient similarity between intrusive thoughts in normal subjects and clinical obsessions to support the use of intrusive thoughts as an analogue (or milder form) of clinical problems. In particular, I have hypothesised (Salkovskis, 1985) that obsessional thoughts are normal intrusions which, in vulnerable individuals, have come to be maintained by compulsive and neutralising behaviours.

I have been investigating these issues, jointly with Julia Davis, Helen Dent and David Westbrook. The cognitive behavioural hypothesis outlined here and elsewhere (Salkovskis, 1985) lead to two specific predictions about the clinical development of obsessional thoughts from intrusive thoughts in normal subjects, and the maintenance of obsessional thoughts once they have developed.

1. Neutralising in normal subjects should be associated with strong beliefs in ideas of responsibility (but not threat or loss, which are associated with anxiety and depression; Beck, 1976).

2. If neutralising in response to intrusive thoughts is increased, then subjects should be less likely to habituate to the repeated occurrence of the intrusive thought than subjects in whom the degree of exposure is equivalent but the neutralising thought does not occur.

In a study testing the first prediction, we surveyed 243 normal subjects, eliciting a range of information about intrusive thoughts (Dent and Salkovskis, 1986; Salkovskis and Dent, 1988). The principal findings relevant to the present discussion were that subjects who reported neutralising behaviour scored higher on the MOCI (Rachman and Hodgson, 1978) than did those not reporting such behaviour. There were no differences on measures of anxiety and depression. As predicted, subjects who neutralised had significantly higher scores on a rating of belief for thoughts of responsibility for harm, but not on thoughts of threat and loss.

In the second study, normal subjects who reported that they neutralised their intrusive thoughts were recruited. Following an interview designed to elicit distressing intrusive thoughts and specific neutralising thoughts, the intrusive thought was taped on a thirty second loop. Half the subjects were instructed to use their neutralising thought after listening to each occurrence of the thought and the other half asked to count quickly backwards from twenty (in order to control for exposure). The tape was played sixteen times, and the subjects rated their discomfort at every third presentation. Following a pause of thirty minutes, the tape and ratings were repeated with instructions to listen only. Discomfort ratings were the principal dependent variable; of particular interest was the effect of the first presentation (when groups differed in required response) on the second presentation, in which requirements were identical. We predicted that pre-exposure to the thought _with_ neutralising would prevent subsequent reduction of discomfort on the second trial as compared to exposure _without_ neutralising. The preliminary results of this experiment showed that (a) despite comparable levels of discomfort at the point when the thought was first elicited, neutralising resulted in significantly more discomfort than counting as rated during the _first_ stage of presentation. (b) This difference was not present during the early stages of the second presentation of the thought, but strongly re-emerged towards the end of the second presentation sequence. Thus, expectation that neutralising will be carried out _increased_ the anxiety associated with an intrusive thought, and increased discomfort evoked by the same intrusive thoughts at a later point when neutralising is no longer being carried out.

CONCLUSIONS

Behavioural treatment of obsessive-compulsive disorder has resulted in a truly dramatic improvement in the prognosis of this condition. It is therefore particularly surprising that little progress has been made in the _understanding_ of the psychological mechanisms involved in obsessions. It now appears that behavioural treatments may have reached the limits of their effectiveness (e.g. twenty four hour exposure and response prevention). Unfortunately, not all patients comply with or respond to behavioural treatment, so that there is a need for new approaches. The cognitive model previously proposed elsewhere (Salkovskis, 1985) may account for findings which are not explained by the traditional behavioural model by incorporating and extending the features which have made behaviour therapy a successful treatment. The cognitive formulation of obsessions has led the author to a more fully integrated hypothesis concerning unpleasant _and_ _pleasant_ intrusive thoughts and their persistence, in which these thoughts are regarded as a part of a normally adaptive mechanism. It is hypothesised that intrusive thoughts _persist_ because of the development of 'neutralising' (compulsive) thoughts and behaviours associated with the intrusions. Upsetting intrusive thoughts become _problematic_ because of specified dysfunctional beliefs about the nature of intrusive thoughts, responsibility for harm to others (and the consequent need to take preventative action); any action taken (overtly or covertly) then increases the tendency to persist. Two experiments testing aspects of this cognitive-behavioural hypothesis have provided some support for this view of intrusive thoughts and obsessions.

The clinical implications of the hypotheses advanced in this paper can be summarised as follows.

(i) Assessment should take into account that neutralising may be a major maintaining factor in obsessional problems. Ruminations should be divided into obsessional thoughts and neutralising thoughts, where obsessions are involuntary intrusions and neutralisers are deliberate, voluntary behaviours intended to reduce anxiety or risk.

(ii) Treatment of obsessive compulsive disorder and ruminations should involve both the exposure and reponse prevention, again considering that neutralising can be overt or covert.

(iii) Cognitive procedures can be helpful in enhancing the compliance with and response to more traditional behaviour therapy.

ACKNOWLEDGEMENTS

I am grateful to Julia Davis, Helen Dent, Anne Jeavons, Joan Kirk, Hilary Warwick and David Westbrook for their assistance with the studies described here. The author would also like to thank the Medical Research Council of the United Kingdom for their support.

REFERENCES

Beck, A.T., (1976), Cognitive Therapy and the Emotional Disorders. International University Press, New York.

Beech, H.R. and Liddel, A., (1974), Decision making, mood states and ritualistic behaviour among obsessional patients In H.R. Beech (ed.), Obsessional States, Methuen, London.

Dent, H.R. and Salkovskis, P.M., (1987), Clinical measures of depression, anxiety and obsessionality in non-clinical populations, Behaviour Research and Therapy, 24, 689-691.

Edwards, S. and Dickerson, M., (1987), On the similarity of positive and negative intrusions, Behaviour Research and Therapy, 25, 207-211.

Emmelkamp, P.M.G., (1982), Phobic and obsessive-compulsive disorders, Plenum, New York.

Emmelkamp, P.M.G., (1987), Chapter in W. Huber (ed.), Progress in psychotherapy research, University of Louvain Press, Louvain.

Foa. E.B. and Goldstein, A., (1978), Continuous exposure and strict response prevention in the treatment of obsessive-compulsive neurosis. Behaviour Therapy, 9, 821-829.

Foa, E.B., Steketee, G., Grayson, J.B. and Doppelt, H.G., (1983), Treatment of obsessive-compulsives: When do we fail?. In Foa, E.B. and Emmelkamp, P.M.G (eds.), Failures in Behaviour Therapy, Wiley, New York.

Gurnani, P. and Wang, M., (1987), Comments on Salkovskis and Warwick: Treating treatment failures, Behavioural Psychotherapy, 15, 101-103.

Hackmann, A. and McLean, C.A., (1975), A Comparison of flooding and thought stopping in the treatment of obsessional neurosis, Behavioural Research and Therapy, 13, 263-269.

Headland and McDonald (1987), Rapid audio-tape treatment of obsessional ruminations: A case report, Behavioural Psychotherapy, 15, 188-192.
Hodgson, R. and Rachman, S.J., (1977), Obsessional-compulsive complaints, Behaviour Research and Therapy, 15, 389-395.
Kirk, J.W., (1983), Behavioural treatment of obsessive-compulsive patients in routine clinical practice, Behaviour-Research and Therapy, 21, 57-62.
Marks, I.M., (1981), Cure and care of neurosis, Wiley, New York.
Nisbett, R.E. and Ross, L., (1980), Human Inference: Strategies and Shortcomings of Social Judgement. NJ, Prentice Hall, Englewood Cliffs.
Parkinson, L. and Rachman, S.J., (1980), Are intrusive thoughts subject to habituation?, Behaviour Research and Therapy, 18, 409-418.
Rachman, S.J., (1971), Obsessional ruminations, Behaviour Research and Therapy, 9, 229-235.
Rachman, S.J., (1976), The modification of obsessions; A new formulation, Behaviour Research and Therapy, 14, 437-443.
Rachman, S.J., (1981), Unwanted intrusive cognitions. Advances in Behaviour Research and Therapy, 3, 89-99.
Rachman, S.J., (1983), Obstacles to the successful treatment of obsessions in Foa, E.B. and Emmelkamp, P.M.G. (eds.), Failures in Behaviour Therapy, Wiley, New York.
Rachman, S.J., de Silva, P. and Roper, G., (1976), The spontaneous decay of compulsive urges, Behaviour Research and Therapy, 14. 445-453.
Rachman, S.J. and Hodgson, R., (1980), Obsessions and compulsions, NJ. Prentice Hall, Englewood Cliffs.
Roper, G. and Rachman, S.J., (1975), Obsessional-compulsive checking, Behaviour Research and Therapy, 13, 25-32.
Roper, G., Rachman, S.J. and Hodgson, R., (1973), An experiment on obsessional checking, Behaviour Research and Therapy, 11, 2271-277.
Salkovskis, P.M., (1983), Treatment of an obsessional patient using habituation to audiotaped ruminations, British Journal of Clinical Psychology, 22, 311-313.
Salkovskis, P.M., (1985), Obsessional-compulsive problems: A cognitive-behavioural analysis, Behaviour Research and Therapy, 25, 571-583.
Salkovskis, P.M., (1986), The cognitive revolution: New way forward, backward somersault or full circle?, Behavioural Psychotherapy, 14, 178-282.
Salkovskis, P.M., (1987), Cognitive therapy: Is it always cognitive, is it always therapy? in, Dent, H.R. (ed.) Clinical Psychology: Research and Development, Croom Helm, London.
Salkovskis, P.M. and Dent, H.R., (1988) Intrusive thoughts, impulses and imagery: Cognitive and behavioural aspects. Manuscript in preparation.
Salkovskis, P.M. and Harrison, J., (1984), Abnormal and Normal obsessions: A replication. Behaviour Research and Therapy, 22, 549-552.
Salkovskis, P.M. and Kirk, J.W., (1988), Obsessional

problems. in Hawton, K., Salkovskis, P.M., Kirk, J.W. and Clark, D.M. (eds.) Cognitive-Behavioural Treatment of Adult Psychological Disorders: A Practical Guide, Oxford University Press, Oxford.

Salkovskis, P.M. and Warwick, H.M.C., (1985), Cognitive therapy of obsessive-compulsive disorder - treating treatment failures, Behavioural Psychotherapy, 13, 243-225.

Salkovskis, P.M. and Warwick, H.M.C., (in press), Cognitive therapy of obsessive-compulsive disorder. In Perris, C., Blackburn, I.M. and Perris, H. (eds.) The Theory and Practice of Cognitive Therapy, Springer, Heidelberg.

Salkovskis, P.M. and Westbrook, D., (1988), Treatment of obsessional ruminations, Manuscript in preparation.

Teasdale, J.D., (1982), What kind of theory will improve psychological treatment? In Boulougouris, J. (ed.) Learning Theory Approaches to Psychiatry, Wiley, New York.

Wolpe, J., (1958), Psychotherapy by Reciprocal Inhibition, Stanford University Press, California.

Warwick, H.M.C. and Salkovskis, P.M., (1987), Reply to Gurnani and Wang, Behavioural Psychotherapy, 15, 280-283.

PART IV
SCHIZOPHRENIA AND WORK WITH FAMILIES

Relatives' expressed emotion and schizophrenia: facts and fallacies

C. VAUGHN

RESEARCH BEGINNINGS

Twenty five years have passed since the early epidemiological studies of George Brown and his colleagues hinted at the importance of family influences on the course of schizophrenia. This work began as a search for environmental explanations of why some schizophrenic patients repeatedly relapsed after hospital discharge, despite regular medication, and others did not. Brown saw himself as a detective trying to make sense of a very complex puzzle. Although it was assumed that schizophrenia had biological origins, the theoretical underpinnings were few. (For a critical evaluation of the illness model of schizophrenia, see Bentall 1987). Indeed, Brown and his fellow investigators at the MRC Social Psychiatry Unit in London took a sceptical view of 'schizophrenogenic' theories concerning the role of the family in the development of schizophrenia. Despite this scepticism, some early findings by Brown et al suggested that family influences might affect the course of the illness (Brown, 1959; Brown et al, 1962). Some patients seemed to be reacting against close ties with relatives, perhaps because of a sensitivity related to the disease process. Brown decided to try to identify aspects of family life which might make a schizophrenic patient better or worse. He was not looking for signs of deeply disturbed relationships. Whatever was going on, he reasoned, was likely to be more ordinary than this. So an attempt was made to develop an instrument which could record the range of feelings and emotions to be found in ordinary families. This standardised, semi-structured research instrument has come to be known as the Camberwell Family Interview (CFI). All judgements of 'Expressed Emotion' (EE) are based on it. In its abbreviated form (Vaughn and Leff, 1976b) it takes between sixty and ninety minutes to administer. Key relatives in the patient's household are interviewed separately at crisis point, shortly after the patient's admission to hospital. All interviews are tape recorded for later analysis.

Using the CFI it was possible to identify aspects of family life which were associated with post-discharge relapse. Of the hundreds of rating scales originally employed, only three showed independent relationships with the course of schizophrenia: relative's critical comments, hostility and emotional overinvolvement. These three scales (the first a frequency count, the second and third global measures) were combined into an index of EE, essentially an indicator of a relative's negative affect or intrusive overconcern towards the patient. The EE index is rated on the basis of both feelings expressed during the interview and reported behaviour outside it.

RELATIVES' EE AND RELAPSE

A considerable body of cross-cultural evidence has accumulated which suggests that the EE index has predictive validity where relapse patterns in schizophrenia are concerned. It also has predictive power for other diagnostic groups, most notably for patients suffering from depression (Vaughn and Leff, 1976a; Hooley, Orley and Teasdale, 1986). However, the focus in this paper is only on schizophrenia. The main results from independent prospective follow up studies carried out in London (Brown, Birley and Wing, 1972; Vaughn and Leff, 1976a) and Los Angeles (Vaughn et al, 1984) were remarkably similar in their respective relapse figures for patients from low EE and high EE homes. In each of the studies, patients returning to high EE homes after hospital discharge were three to four times more likely to relapse during a nine month follow up period than were patients returning to low EE homes. In each of the studies, relative's EE at the time of admission proved to be the best single predictor of symptomatic relapse, more powerful than any clinical feature of the patient's schizophrenia. Two other factors, regular medication and reduced contact with relatives, exerted a protective influence on patients returning to high EE homes, but the link between relative's EE and relapse remained independent of all other variables investigated.

In recent years, Anglo-American findings have been replicated by studies in other cultures, for example in Chandigarh, India (Leff et al, 1987) and in a Mexican-American population in Los Angeles (Karno et al, 1987). Various content and concurrent validity studies (e.g. psychophysiological studies and studies of the direct interaction between family members) offer further proof that EE is conceptually sound (Kuipers et al, 1983; Valone et al, 1983; Miklowitz et al, 1984; Strachan et al, 1986; Szmukler et al, 1987). The research has stimulated psychoeducational approaches to helping families of the mentally ill, as well as more intensive family intervention programmes which have achieved considerable success in meeting their stated goals (Falloon et al, 1982; Leff et al, 1982; Falloon et al, 1985; Leff et al, 1985; Hogarty et al, 1986; Tarrier et al, 1987). Nevertheless, there are a number of unresolved questions and controversial issues raised by the EE investigations which cannot be ignored.

WHAT IS EE?

A recurrent and justified criticism of the Expressed Emotion research is that it has failed to indicate precisely what the concept measures, how it manifests itself, or how it operates to influence the vulnerable individual. While it appears to tap qualities of family life which can either protect patients against relapse or make relapse more likely, the process by which this happens has remained unclear. To an extent EE researchers must take the blame for this state of affairs. For years our main concern was to establish conclusively the predictive value of the EE index by replicating the results of previous investigations. These efforts paid off in one sense, in that it was possible to demonstrate repeatedly that social influences on the schizophrenic patient are very powerful. Indeed, they are so powerful that they can override the effect of prescribed medication for some very vulnerable patients. The price of this single-minded approach, however, has been the neglect until recently of the great mass of qualitative data which has accumulated. The relatives' interviews are rich sources of information concerning patterns of emotional response and family interaction in the months preceding a psychiatric crisis. Only now are these data being explored in depth. Also, until recently there has been a reluctance to assume that a relative's reported reactions or interview behaviour necessarily reflected what went on in the patient's presence, in the absence of more direct evidence. Such evidence now exists: independent investigations of direct interactions between patient and relative have confirmed interview impressions, suggesting that in a majority of cases there is a correspondence between these different sources of information (Kuipers et al., 1983; Valone et al., 1983; Miklowitz et al, 1984; Strachan et al, 1986; Szmukler et al, 1987). This reassuring new evidence suggests that the relatives' accounts can be viewed as valid descriptions of family life at time of interview.

One notable fact about the hundreds of families assessed over the years is that patients from high EE and low EE households are not significantly different in a clinical sense. They cannot be distinguished on measures of premorbid adjustment, severity of psychopathology at admission, or residual symptomatology after discharge. The differences between households lie not in the patients, but in the relatives: low EE and high EE relatives differ markedly in their responses to a patient's objective condition.

RELATIVES' RESPONSE CHARACTERISTICS

Throughout the several decades of EE research, it has been possible to identify a number of characteristics which tend to distinguish relatives who score highly on criticism or emotional overinvolvement from those who do not (Leff and Vaughn, 1985; Vaughn, 1986).

Firstly, there are cognitive differences: for example, differences in attitude towards the legitimacy of the illness which tend to evolve in absence of any professional counselling. Low EE relatives tend to believe that the patient is suffering from a genuine illness. Because the patient is truly ill, it is reasoned, he or she is unlikely to be able to control all or most symptoms experienced, therefore one must make allowances. This view causes the relative to be more tolerant of very disturbed behaviour and to lower expectations for performance. By contrast, many high EE relatives (particularly those who are highly critical) show little understanding of the patient's ordeal. There are doubts about the legitimacy of the disorder. Patients are thought to be able to exercise control over both positive symptoms and deficits in performance. Normal behaviour and a high level of functioning are expected form the patient after an apparent recovery and discharge from hospital.

Secondly, low EE and high EE relatives differ in their emotional reactions to the illness. This may seem a tautological statement. However, if one compares the respective accounts of two parents, one highly critical, one not, it is notable that the same behaviour of the patient will be described in very different ways. The less critical relative will tend to describe even undesirable behaviour in language which is neutral, objective, even detached. Any dissatisfaction which is expressed is likely to be muted; opinions lack the emotional <u>intensity</u> of remarks made by high EE relatives.

Finally, there are marked differences in the ways in which relatives behave towards the ill patient, by their own reports. Low EE relatives are calmer in a crisis and more adaptable generally. Over time, usually by a process of trial and error, they build up repertoires of successful coping techniques for dealing with difficult behaviours. Some setting of limits occurs, i.e. social control <u>is</u> exercised over the patient at times, but in a manner which is not intrusive or confrontational. High EE relatives, by contrast, appear to be less flexible, with few problem-solving skills. They will persevere with the same unsuccessful approaches, nagging, confrontations, shows of intrusive overconcern, even when these tactics clearly fail to achieve their objectives.

The impact of these different response styles on the

schizophrenic patient is predictable. Patients seldom avoid low EE relatives who are calm, non-intrusive, and respect the patient's need for social distance (usual even in good relationships). Conversely, patients in high EE households are more likely both to avoid family members and to show agitated aggression. An irritable or violent outburst from a patient often is provoked by some critical or intrusive action on the part of the relative; high EE relatives freely admit this.

It is commonly assumed that persons prone to episodes of schizophrenia have an underlying psychobiological vulnerability which makes it difficult for them to process complex stimuli and deal with social relationships. If this is true, then the link between a high EE response and patient relapse becomes more understandable. High EE relatives may be more emotionally arousing to the patient, while low EE relatives have a calming effect. Indeed, these interview impressions based on the relatives' accounts are supported by psychophysiological findings (Tarrier et al, 1979; Sturgeon et al, 1981; Sturgeon et al, 1984).

NEW DIRECTIONS IN RESEARCH

There are a number of directions in which researchers might move in the future, following on from our current state of knowledge. It seems increasingly important that we learn to differentiate different types of families within the high EE and low EE categories; explore various family models; and compare a range of strategies for defining family relationships and patterns of interaction. While it is possible to identify distinguishing features of high EE and low EE relatives, there is considerable variation within the dichotomized categories. One relative's intense criticism and reported hostility towards a patient clearly may predate the onset of illness, reflecting a poor relationship of many years' duration. Another relative will claim that family relations were very good prior to the appearance of schizophrenia, and restrict criticism to specific behaviours of the patient which only appeared in the context of an illness episode. Yet another high EE relative may not be critical at all, but rather score highly on the emotional overinvolvement scale, for example, the mother who adopts the role of a concerned caretaker and does everything for her adult child. These are very different response styles, yet each will be labelled 'high EE'.

It also is desirable to distinguish between the majority of relatives (whether high EE or low EE) who seem quite ordinary and normal, and the minority of relatives (less than twenty per cent of those interviewed) who have extreme or bizarre ways of responding to the patient and the illness. The latter group, who display characteristics sometimes described as 'schizophrenogenic', will make great demands on any clinician hoping to influence the course of the illness by family intervention. But many other relatives may derive considerable benefit from simply receiving basic mental health education and a measure of support from the services when it is needed.

Two additional, related research questions are 'What are the determinants of a high or low EE response?' and 'Is EE a state or a trait?' Information bearing on both of these questions exists, although further investigations are required. At a given point in time, the deteriminants of a relative's degree of expressed emotion are likely to include the following:

- the quality of the pre-illness relationship with the patient
- the patient's current behaviour (degree of disturbance and extent of secondary handicap)
- the relative's perceived ability to cope, and related problem solving skills
- idiosyncratic personality factors
- the amount and quality of information available concerning the illness
- external stresses, such as unemployment
- crosscultural differences in societal responses to the illness

Few of these influences on EE have been studied sytematically, but each appears to be of some importance.

In the 'EE as state vs. trait' debate the safest answer would seem to be: sometimes it is the one, sometimes it is the other. In the EE investigations it was always assumed that the EE level at time of key admission represented a potential to respond in a characteristic way, particularly at a time of crisis. However, fluctuations in EE levels over time certainly occur. Changes are most likely in cases where the relative's emotional response seems to be a direct reaction to the patient's behaviour when ill. For about thirty per cent of relatives, a good recovery by the patient results in a lowering of EE at follow up, particularly in the number of critical comments. Changes in the opposite direction, i.e. from low EE at admission to high EE at follow up, are uncommon. They are most likely to occur when a patient fails to make a good recovery from a single episode and the relative becomes increasingly pessimistic about the patient's future, in the absence of appropriate counselling or support.

The fact that the high EE designation is made at a crisis point may help to explain the failure of the EE index to predict relapse in every instance. EE is an 'umbrella' concept, a cross sectional measure which does not discriminate between short term reactions to an illness and more enduring, deep-rooted patterns of response. For families with a history of 'disordered' relationships, temporary improvements in patient functioning are unlikely to alter relatives' attitudes and behaviours very much.

The EE index was devised for research purposes and is best viewed as a risk 'marker'; an indicator of the emotional temperature in a household at a particular point in time. Its continuing usefulness as an isolated indicator of risk is in doubt. Recent findings suggest the value of (i) considering the role of the different components of EE in influencing (ii) different kinds of outcome, and (iii) multi-factorial analyses which examine the interaction of different variables. A combination of risk markers is likely to predict a variety of outcomes more successfully than any single risk marker such as the global EE index. Relevant outcome measures include level of social functioning and the extent to which the patient is troubled by negative symptoms, as well as by the reoccurrence or exacerbation of positive symptoms (the more narrowly defined criterion of relapse in most EE studies to date).

EE AND THE MANAGEMENT OF SCHIZOPHRENIA: CLINICAL IMPLICATIONS

Recently the EE research has been criticised (Hatfield, Spaniol, and Zipple, 1987; Kanter, Lamb and Loeper, 1987) as the latest exercise in blaming the family of the schizophrenic patient, since it appears to place families into dichotomous categories labelled 'good' (low EE) and 'bad' (high EE). This interpretation of the literature subsequently has itself attracted criticism (Leff and Vaughn, 1987; Mintz et al, 1987). I believe it to be a misreading of the EE findings, yet it is an understandable misreading. Frequently I am asked by clinicians 'Is there some quick and easy way of identifying high EE families. The EE findings seem interesting and relevant but we have no time for an hour long interview with assessment time to follow'. My answer is 'Suppose you were able to apply a 'high risk' label to a family? What then? What use would such a label be in the absence of a deeper understanding of the family, how it functions, and its respective assets and needs?'. Such understanding requires individualised behavioural assessment or a similarly sensitive and comprehensive approach. Simplistic, potentially harmful labelling is no substitute. Thus the clinical utility of the global EE index is likely to be quite restricted. This message is appreciated by persons already engaged in EE based research or clinical work, but clearly needs to travel further than it has to date.

Meanwhile relatives' interviews reveal a great need for clinically relevant information to be circulated more widely to the professionals who come into contact with patients and their families. I have been listening to sad tales of schizophrenia and the family (for most relatives' tales <u>are</u> very sad) for many years, and their rather despairing accounts of experiences with professionals do not reassure. Whatever the country, whatever the health care system, the quality of care does not seem to have improved greatly with the passage of time. Certainly it does not reflect the current state of knowledge concerning the management of schizophrenia. Too often relatives cannot obtain help when they first need it, in the early stages of the illness, so that the patient receives attention only when a full blown crisis has occurred. Insensitive management by doctors at this stage can result in loss of confidence in the services and cause lingering recriminations between patient and family. In some cases family relationships are permanently affected. Following hospital admission, few families receive adequate information about the illness, medication and its side effects or other related issues. They are given no guidelines as to what to do, how to cope, when the patient returns home. Problems of management which might benefit from a constructive, problem solving approach are not acknowledged. Such problems include how to 'fill the days' if the patient is not to deteriorate; how to deal with anhedonia and depression (both common post psychosis problems); how to give responsibility to someone who appears not to want it ('I try to let him run his own life, but he doesn't run his own life!'); how to set realistic expectations without exerting too much pressure; how to deal with medication noncompliance. Management problems such as these are experienced by all families, not just high EE families. Persons working in clinical settings need not master the EE rating procedure in order to understand the implications of these statements of need, or the relevance of some relatives' <u>successful</u> coping strategies, for their own clinical practice.

REFERENCES

Brown, G.W., (1959), Experiences of discharged chronic schizophrenic mental hospital patients in various types of living group, <u>Millbank Memorial Fund Quarterly</u>, 37, 105-131.

Brown, G.W., Birley, J.L.T. and Wing, J.K., (1972), Influence of family life on the course of schizophrenic disorders: A replication, <u>British Journal of Psychiatry</u>, 121, 241-258.

Brown, G.W., Monck, E.M., Carstairs, G.M. and Wing, J.K., (1962), Influence of family life on the course of schizophrenic illness. <u>British Journal of Preventive and Social Medicine</u>, 16, 55-68.

Falloon, I.R.H., Boyd, J.L., McGill, C.W. et al (1982), Family management in the prevention of exacerbations of schizophrenia, <u>New England Journal of Medicine</u>, 306, 1437-1440.

Falloon, I.R.H., Boyd, J.L., McGill, C.W. et al., (1985), Family management in the prevention of morbidity of schizophrenia: Clinical outcome of a two-year longitudinal study, <u>Archives of General Psychiatry</u>, 42, 887-896.

Hatfield, A.B., Spaniol, L. and Zipple, A.M., (1987), Expressed emotion: A family perspective, <u>Schizophrenia Bulletin</u>, 13, 221-226.

Hogarty, G.E., Anderson, C.M., Reiss, D.J. et al. (1986), Family psycho-education, social skills training and maintenance chemotherapy in the aftercare treatment of schizophrenia: I. One year effects of a controlled study on relapse and expressed emotion, <u>Archives of General Psychiatry</u>, 43, 633-642.

Hooley, J.M., Orley, J. and Teasdale, J.D., (1986), Levels of expressed emotion and relapse in depressed patients,

British Journal of Psychiatry, 148, 642-647.
Kanter, J., Lamb, H.R. and Loeper, C., (1987), Expressed emotion in families: A critical review, Hospital and Community Psychiatry, 38, 374-380.
Karno, M., Jenkins, J.H., de la Selva, A. et al., (1987), Expressed emotion and schizophrenic outcome among Mexican-American families, Journal of Nervous and Mental Disease, 175, 143-151.
Kuipers, L., Sturgeon, D., Berkowitz, R. and Leff, J., (1983), Characteristics of expressed emotion: Its relationship to speech and looking in schizophrenic patients and their relatives, British Journal of Clinical Psychology, 22, 257-264.
Leff, J.P., Kuipers, L., Berkowitz, R. et al., (1982), A controlled trial of social intervention in the families of schizophrenic patients, British Journal of Psychiatry, 141, 121-234.
Leff, J.P., Kuipers, L., Berkowitz, R. and Sturgeon, D., (1985), A controlled trial of social intervention in the families of schizophrenic patients: Two year follow-up, British Journal of Psychiatry, 146, 594-600.
Leff, J.P. and Vaughn, C.E., (1985), Expressed Emotion in Families: Its Significance for Mental Illness, Guildford Press, New York.
Leff, J.P. and Vaughn, C.E., (1987), Expressed emotion (Correspondence), Hospital and Community Psychiatry, 38, 1117-1118.
Leff, J.P., Wig, N.N., Ghosh, A. et al, (1987), Expressed emotion and schizophrenia in North India: III. Influences of relatives' expressed emotion on the course of schizophrenia in Chandigarh, British Journal of Psychiatry, 151, 166-173.
Miklowitz, D.J., Goldstein, M.J., Falloon, I.R.H. and Doane, J.A., (1984), Interactional correlates of expressed emotion in the families of schizophrenics, British Journal of Psychiatry, 144, 482-487.
Mintz, L.I., Liberman, R.P., Miklowitz, D.J. and Mintz, J., (1987), Expressed emotion: A call for partnership among relatives, patients and professionals, Schizophrenia Bulletin, 13, 227-235.
Strachan, A.M., Leff, J.P., Goldstein, M.J. et al., (1986), Emotional attitudes and direct communication in the families of schizophrenics: A cross-national replication, British Journal of Psychiatry, 149, 279-287.
Sturgeon, D., Kuipers, L., Berkowitz, R., Turpin, G. and Leff, (1981), Psychophysiological responses of schizophrenic patients to high and low expressed emotion relatives, British Journal of Psychiatry, 130, 40-45.
Sturgeon, D., Turpin, G., Kuipers, L., Berkowitz, R. and Leff, J., (1984), Psychophysiological responses of schizophenic patients to high and low expressed emotion relatives: A follow up study, British Journal of Psychiatry, 145, 62-29.
Szmukler, G.I., Berkowitz, R., Eisler, I., Leff, J. and Dare, C., (1987), Expressed emotion in individual and family settings: A comparative study, British Journal of

Psychiatry 151, 174-178.
Tarrier, N., Barrowclough, C., Vaughn, C. et al, (1988), The community management of schizophrenia: A controlled trial of a behavioural intervention with families to reduce relapse, British Journal of Psychiatry, in press.
Tarrier, N., Vaughn, C., Lader, M.H. and Leff, J.P., (1979), Bodily reactions to people and events in schizophrenia, Archives of General Psychiatry, 36, 311-315.
Valone, K., Norton, J.P., Goldstein, M.J. and Doane, J.A., (1983), Parental expressed emotion and affective style in an adolescent sample at risk for schizophrenia spectrum disorders, Journal of Abnormal Psychology, 92, 399-407.
Vaughn, C.E., (1986), Patterns of emotional response in the families of psychiatric patients, in Goldstein, M.J., Hand, I. and Hahlweg, K. (eds.) Treatment of Schizophrenia: Family Assessment and Intervention, Springer-Verlag: Berlin.
Vaughn, C.E. and Leff, J.P., (1976a), The influence of family and social factors on the course of psychiatric illness: A comparison of schizophrenic and depressed neurotic patients, British Journal of Psychiatry, 129, 125-137.
Vaughn, C.E. and Leff, J.P., (1976b), The measurement of expressed emotion in the families of psychiatric patients, British Journal of Social and Clinical Psychology, 15, 157-165.
Vaughn, C.E., Snyder, K.S., Jones, S., Freeman, W.B. and Falloon, I.R.H., (1984), Family factors in schizophrenic relapse: A California replication of the British research on expressed emotion, Archives of General Psychiatry, 41, 1169-1177.

Family therapy where the designated patient is in a psychiatric hospital: pitfalls and potentials

E. JONES

INTRODUCTION

During the period 1981 to 1984 a team of family therapists conducted brief work in an adult psychiatric hospital setting with patients (the word 'patient' is used because the work was done in a medical setting) who had been diagnosed as schizophrenic and their families. The setting up of the team and the negotiations required to find space and permission to work in this way within the therapists' own department requires another paper (Nitsberg et al, 1985). In this paper the focus will be on the approach used with the families, and more particularly with professional collegues in the hospital. This paper is not designed to prove that one may 'cure' schizophrenia by means of family therapy, but rather to share the experiences of one team working successfully with a number of families in which such a diagnosis had been made. Our criteria for 'success' were that the designated patient should be symptom free, should not be re-admitted to hospital or engage in other forms of therapy within the formal or informal follow up period and, more subjectively, that family relationships should have changed and eased to permit family members to get on with the ordinary business of living in a way that seemed satisfactory to them and to us.

The phrase 'designated patient' will be used to indicate that member of the family designated as such by professionals and family. The diagnosis is based in each instance on the hospital case records, compiled from consultants' and ward assessments. The case material is drawn from cases where the designated patient was a young adult (aged nineteen to twenty five) and the author was the primary therapist.

The family therapy team met once a week and had a fluctuating membership with a core of four who were all clinical psychologists in a district psychology department based in a psychiatric hospital in London. Because the author had established the family therapy service in the hospital, team relationships were complex in that we were both a functioning team, and we were also in a trainer/trainee relationship, which levelled out over time as the other team members gained skill and experience in this particular therapeutic approach. While this paper will be on the professional context of, and certain idiosyncratic approaches to, work with schizophrenics and their families; much of the minute by minute detail of therapy with these families will not be discussed, since in my view it does not differ materially from other similar family therapies once the groundwork has been laid properly, and since this type of therapy has been described well elsewhere (Haley, 1980; Selvini Palazzoli et al, 1978). The experiences of the team, especially in the beginning, compel me to sound a cautionary note: while for the purposes of this paper the 'ordinary' therapeutic skills are taken for granted, it is important to stress that this refers to the <u>'ordinary' skills of experienced family therapists</u>. The author does <u>not</u> wish this paper to be considered a 'how to' manual encouraging beginning family therapists to take on work with these difficult cases.

Each of the team members was attached to an acute admission ward as part of their general departmental work. This entailed attendance at ward staff meetings, ward patient groups and other activities which varied form ward to ward. In order to illustrate the professional negotiation process, I will discuss our first family therapy referral in detail.

CREATING A CONTEXT FOR WORK

I was attached to a ward whose prevailing orientation was psychodynamic. This meant that all the patients admitted to the ward were required to participate in a daily psychotherapy group run by different members of staff on different days. The groups were rather difficult, since the patients varied greatly in age, social circumstances, 'realism' etc. One of the consequences of this was that staff greeted the arrival of floridly symptomatic, interesting 'YAVIS' patients (young, attractive, verbal, intelligent, single) with undisguised relief, and such patients would have a considerable amount of attention lavished upon them. However, the ward staff would also become despondent when such patients did not improve after a period in hospital and such a situation led to the first tentative family therapy referral to our team. At this point, I negotiated a set of procedural agreements with the medical and ward staff which became the basis for all our subsequent family work with clients referred while they were still inpatients. Because the consultant psychiatrist and charge nurse were favourably biased towards psychologists in general and interested in my family work, I had some leverage for negotiation.

1) We agreed that we would meet with the family once while the designated patient was still in the hospital. The family members would receive a letter from the therapist asking them to attend a meeting to discuss the difficulties experienced by the designated patient, i.e. <u>not</u> an invitation to family therapy. The purpose of this meeting would be for us to assess whether we could work with the family and for the family to do the same in relation to us. After this, we would not meet the family again until the designated patient had left hospital, no matter how long this took. This was also spelled out to the family during the first meeting. The interval between the first family meeting and discharge was usually between one and three weeks. As time went on and our colleagues' confidence in us grew, we increasingly found that referrers would agree to arrange a discharge date as soon as we had set an appointment date. The rationale of this decision is that experience in other residential settings had convinced me of the absurdity of focusing therapy on the family system when the designated patient's major current system was that constituted by fellow patients and staff within the residential setting. However, focusing therapy only on the residential system seemed equally unlikely to have a significant impact on the 'back-home' system (Haley, 1980).

2) The medical control of the patient's medication would be passed to the general practitioner (GP). This necessitated a letter from (usually) the senior registrar 'in charge' of the case to the GP saying that all psychiatric contact with the patient would now stop and that I and my team would now have sole therapeutic contact with the patient and the family. The GP would be informed of the patient's current medication, and the senior registrar would express the hope that the patient could gradually be weaned off medication. It will be clear that the team had a hand in the composition of this standard letter! This would be followed by a letter from the therapist to the GP indicating the general purpose of the family meetings and inviting contact whenever this seemed necessary.

There are several reasons for this step. In our experience, discharged in-patients are seen regularly by the GP and by psychiatric staff in out patient clinics. Because of the rotating placements of most psychiatrists in training, in practice this often meant that the designated patient would see a different doctor every few appointments. The caseload of these doctors often meant that they did not get the full picture of the patient's situation and therefore would play safe by giving repeat prescriptions, even though the patient might no longer want medication. Conversely, some young doctors with an interest in psychotherapy would find themselves very frustrated by the conveyor belt/despair experience of their duties and would become attached to their intermittent meetings with outpatients (particularly 'YAVISes') thus often producing a situation in which parallel therapies negated each other. Although we benefitted greatly from the Milan group's idea on including the referring person in the system (Selvini Palazzoli et al, 1980a), we preferred where possible to obtain a clear space in which to work. We knew also that GP's tend to be busy and relieved at the prospect of terminating repetitive visits to their surgery by patients requiring routine continuation of medication. They were therefore often more able to make the decision to stop medication where this seemed relevant. All designated patients in the case examples presented here had come off medication before the end of therapy. In practice, we would usually wait until the designated patient and family started complaining about medication, declare ourselves unable to comment on this because we were psychologists, and offer to write a supportive letter to the GP. This letter would say something like:

> X, and his/her family seem to be doing well (examples), and they are now saying that they would like X's medication stopped. I would be interested to see how X does without medication, since it is at this stage impossible to tell what the apparent improvement is due to, and whether it will last once medication is stopped. When in your judgement the time is right I would be pleased if you would start to reduce his/her medication.

The rationale offered to the ward staff for the transfer of medical control was that it would provide continuity of medical care and help the designated patients to start thinking about themselves as living in the community rather than being attached to the hospital. Therefore, the contact with us would be the only remaining link with the hospital and it would be more easily terminated than the others, given that the family would be participating in the work.

It seems to me essential that the above work must be done so that the family therapists will have the necessary space and leverage to work effectively with the family. An important corollary of negotiating such an agreement with colleagues, and one at which non-medical staff often baulk, is that the family therapist then has to accept full responsibility for the case, including any potential disasters. In our case, our colleagues' willingness to let us take responsibility for our work was a function partly of the Trethowan commission's recommendations regarding the autonomy of clinical psychologists and partly of the long and mutually respectful relationship between our department and the psychiatric consultants.

Achieving agreement for family work.

<u>Professional colleagues</u>. Initially, referrers were under

the impression that the designated patient should have 'settled down' in hospital and be 'well controlled' with medication before our family work could commence. However, repeated reiteration by team members that we preferred to strike while the iron was hot and did not mind if the designated patient was still behaving 'psychotically' finally convinced referrers, who were perhaps in a not wholly charitable mood after being nagged for months to refer cases to us, although or even because the designated patient's behaviour had shown no improvement while in hospital. Improvement in symptomatic behaviour would often follow the first family session while the designated patient was still in hospital; it is open to discussion whether this improvement was due to the session. Initially, patients were referred to us and discharged from hospital because hospital staff saw no improvement from the hospital regime, so that even YAVISes induced a feeling of hoplessness. Later referrals seemed to reflect a conviction on the referrers' part that family work might be the treatment of choice. Our early canvassing for referrals contained several elements: frequent discussion with consultants and other hospital staff on the application and philosophy of family therapy; teaching inputs to various professional groups in the hospital; family work with clients referred from outpatient clinics by consultants; and a declaration on our part that although we were confident about our family therapy skills with the more usual populations referred to us, we were not certain of its applicability to a population with psychotic diagnoses, so that we would be interested, as research minded psychologists, in taking on any and all referrals from the wards to see whether or not we could achieve results. A summary of the team's experience with three different consultant psychiatrists in charge of three admission wards may be helpful:

1) The consultant embraced a theoretical view which differed from ours, but he respected the psychology department, and after a few difficult trial cases he consulted with the team members on the ward about the suitability of referrals and facilitated the implementation by ward staff of the team's conditions (see 'Creating a context for work'). While never convinced that this way of working produced more than superficial symptom relief, he nevertheless ardently hoped that hospitalised patients could return to a full life, and he was prepared to be pragmatic in the pursuit of this goal.

2) The team member working on this ward had a long standing difficult relationship with the consultant, which never improved despite many discussions and consultations. Although the consultant was interested in any new approaches that might offer hope of recovery to patients, it was striking how often miscommunications, lack of communication, forgetfulness, multiple plans of action and confusion (mutually produced) dogged the management of these cases, which on the whole did less well than those from any other source.

3) This consultant was new to the hospital, had a radical anti-institutional point of view and was very pleased with the results of his first few referrals to us, with the result that he became an invaluable ally in the creation of a clear space for working with families. A case illustration follows.

A family consisted of a father who lived for ten months of the year in Pakistan for business reasons, a mother who was a housewife, and four sons, of whom the three oldest had been multiply involved with all the resources of the local helping professions for years, without any sign of positive change, and indeed with increasing indications that these young men were becoming completely institutionally dependent. Dr. C. referred the family to us, saying to them that he considered that the boys were not suffering from an illness (despite previous diagnoses of schziophrenia) and that this was a matter that could best be sorted out by the whole family working together on the problem. He then got in touch with every professional agency which the family had been in the habit of using, and he asked them to respond to any approach from the family by saying, 'I understand from Dr. C. that you have been refereed to...as a family. I would rather wait until you have seen them before discussing what further help I might offer you'. The family cancelled several appointments with us, meanwhile approaching many of their previous helping agencies, where they were met with the above statement. When we saw them about one and a half months after the referral was made, they had already brought about major changes in their lives, which included an abandonment of symptomatic behaviour by the sons, and their mother said to us that the repeated experience of being told that it was a family matter, as orchestrated by Dr. C. had convinced them that it was time they sorted out their problems for themselves. While the sons were 'ill' they needed to be treated and managed by professionals, but now they could make decisions as a family. Thus, it may be assumed that in this case (and probably in many of the others we saw as well) the agreement to limit the work done with the family to one professional group only constituted a major input for change.

<u>The Family</u>. A question often asked is how much 'fascination' does the therapist have to exercise in the first session to achieve agreement to further sessions in a family such as that described above. Discussing her work with the families of schizophrenics, Mara Selvini Palazzoli states, 'during the first session we literally try to fascinate our families with our type of questions, with our competence' (Selvini Palazzoli and Prata, 1983, p.242). The careful preparatory work with professional colleagues creates pressure on the family to accept the option of family work. Obviously, this pressure would be counterproductive if the family experienced it as dumping, blaming or threat, but the experience of a lessening of alternatives and a strongly hopeful recommendation from ward staff increases the family's willingness to consider this option. If the symptom has

become an interlocking part of the pattern that maintains family functioning, why should the family opt for work that threatens to change the whole family pattern, rather than being directed apparently at the symptomatic member only? Berkowitz (1984, p. 229) makes the point that the sensitivity of families with schizophrenic members is such that 'it may take weeks or months to engage a family'. There are two factors related to this question. Firstly, all living systems are required to maintain a balance between morphostasis and morphogenesis in order to survive. It is a truism in the field of psychotherapy that a patient or group of patients will approach a therapy, partly hoping for change and partly hoping for relief from discomfort without being required to change. It is the therapist's task to make an alliance with the change seeking part, so to speak, in order to get a working agreement. We regarded the major tasks of the first session to be engagement and the giving of information, both directly and through indirect means such as setting, style of relating, use of language etc, about what the family could expect from working with us. Secondly, families in this situation often expect to be blamed. This is not surprising because (a) in our culture parents, especially, and other family members tend to blame themselves, and get blamed for the ills that befall those close to them; (b) the term 'family therapy' may implicitly convey the view that the family is ill and requires curing; (c) family members may have been blamed overtly (Terkelsen, 1983). For example, in the first session with a family, the members described their anger at having been told by a professional worker that their symptomatic member would never get better unless they all admitted their own pathology; such a family requires considerable amount of work before they can feel engaged enough to agree to work with a therapist.

We paid considerable attention to all the above issues in order to maximise the possibility of the family's agreement to work with us. The invitation asked family members to come to a meeting to discuss the difficulties they had all been having in relation to their symptomatic member and to explore with us possible solutions. We explained that we found it useful to hear the views of everyone closely involved with the symptomatic member. Some family members responded to this by saying, 'Thank God, I thought no one would ever ask!' We were careful not to call what we did family therapy, to the extent of being involved in a long and farcical dispute with two categories of hospital workers about who was allowed to remove the wooden sign saying 'therapy room' from the door of the room we used. The kinds of questions we asked and language we used were all designed implicitly to convey the view that we did not think blame was a valid concept. If asked our opinion on this outright, we would respond with a direct answer. In addition, the issue of the therapist's personal impact is an unquantifiable but crucial element in determining whether a family with a schizophrenic member, and therefore by definition rigidly organised will feel sufficiently hopeful, respected and connected by the end of the first session to agree to continue work with the therapist. The impact is likely to depend on the therapist's style and personal attributes, as well as experience, and is unlikely to be implemented successfully by novice therapists (Selvini Palazzoli and Prata, 1983).

Working structure

The approach used drew mainly on the work of the Milan team as described in 'Paradox and Counterparadox' and other works (Selvini Palazzoli et al, 1978) and on Jay Haley's approach to work with 'disturbed young people' (Haley, 1980). I will not attempt to recap these two complex approaches here: our implementation of their ideas will be evident in the description of our work which follows. The team met before each session to formulate our working hypothese, either on the basis of the referral information or of the previous session(s). The therapist saw the family while the team observed the session via a one way screen. A consultation between the therapist and team took place towards the end of each session, after which the therapist would return to the family to conclude the session, normally with a formal statement of the team's views and perhaps a task. After the session, the team would again meet briefly to assess the status of our hypotheses and to make some predictions and plans for the next meeting. The techniques of circular questioning and therapist neutrality (Selvini Palazolli et al, 1980b) were employed as standard during all the sessions, with deviations from this due to idiosyncratic therapeutic style and family/therapist intereaction. These will be discussed more fully later. Intervals between sessions varied from one to eight weeks, depending on our assessment of the family situation and the length of time required for our intervention to be processed by the family system (Selvini Palazzoli, 1980); sessions ranged from two to eight, with a formal follow up at six months.

Assumptions

We made the assumption that it was not essential for clinical purposes to discover what had 'caused' the designated patient to behave in ways resulting in a diagnosis of schizophrenia. This view would, where relevant, also be communicated to the families.

We assumed that the symptomatic behaviour of the designated patient was part of the family pattern, and could be seen as maintaining and being maintained by it, though not necessarily unilaterally caused by it.

We assumed that our role as therapists was to disrupt the family pattern in such a way that it would be difficult for all family members, but particularly for the designated patient, to continue to behave as they had previously done. If we succeeded in this, we assumed the family would reorganise themselves in a way coherent with their history, belief systems and relationships, but that this reorganisation, due to our intervention would in future allow for more flexible options and problem solving.

It follows then that we had no fixed assumptions about how the family should function after therapy; we did have opinions about how they should not function. We hoped that our intervention would make it unnecessary in future for 'psychotic' behaviour to appear as a viable option to family members. In the case of particular families, we did of course within the team hold opinions about family relationships: 'the bond between mother and son seems over close', 'the other siblings do not seem independent enough', 'the marital relationship does not seem to function well without a third person as a "distance regulator"', 'he thinks he can be a better husband than his father', etc. We attempted by clear articulation of these value stances in the team to guard against imposing our personal criteria for happy family life on the families with whom we worked.

CASE DISCUSSION

Description of family history and our perception of family patterns (case A).

This family consisted of five members. Mr. Morris, aged forty eight, was the son of very poor immigrants. He had started his own market stall at the age of ten with a loan from an uncle. Since he had already been working in family enterprises before this, he had had very little schooling and described himself as illiterate. He now ran a successful inner city retail business with his wife. This had been the source of considerable stress over some years due to vandalism and decline of the neighbourhood. Mrs. Morris had done very well at junior school and obtained a scholarship for prestigious secondary education which she had to give up to work in the family business because 'learning does not matter for girls'. She had started showing severe agoraphobic symptoms four years previously, coincident with a hysterectomy that did not go well, and which resulted in traumatic bleeding in public after she had visited her sister in hospital. She blamed her childhood jealousy and violence for her sister's physical problems now. David was the oldest child. He was described as being very special to his mother from birth, and still lived at home. He had been asthmatic all through his childhood and missed a considerable amount of schooling, so that up to the age of thirteen he was described as illiterate. At his Bar Mitzvah, he announced to his father, 'I am going to be a somebody', he had then been sent to a 'cram school' and had by the age of nineteen obtained sufficient 'O' and 'A' levels to be admitted to a degree course; he was in the second year of study at the time of his admission to hospital. He was described as having been depressed for two or three years before admission, slept very poorly and experienced extreme anxiety and difficulty in concentration. David and Mrs. Morris alternated their twice weekly visits to the GP where, according to David, 'I would talk to him about her problems and she would talk to him about mine'. Medication over a period of two years had proved ineffective.

Janice, aged eighteen, lived at home and had been working since the age of sixteen. She was regarded by the family as a very quiet girl who was no trouble. She had a regular boyfriend, but not much other social life. Ruth, aged sixteen had just started work in the same firm as her sister and was the more outspoken of the sisters. Neither of the sisters had done particularly well at school, nor had they been expected to.

In the summer before David's admission to hospital, he and his sister Janice had both started discussing with their parents separate plans to move away from home. While on a family holiday during the summer, there had been a sexual incident involving Janice which caused considerable family upset. Mrs. Morris had in particular confided in David her concerns about this, as she said her husband would get too distressed. From this time on, there was a dramatic escalation in David's symptoms, culminating in hallucinations, delusional ideas (he thought his dead grandfather was commanding him to take his mother into the park, where only he would have the power to cure her agoraphobia) pressure of speech, sleeplessness and extreme confusion. The family was particularly alarmed, since an aunt of Mrs. Morris had a history of 'mental illness'. David was admitted to hospital after a domiciliary visit by the consultant psychiatrist with a diagnosis of acute schizophrenia.

In our view, this was a family which placed considerable value on closeness, and in which issues of difference, separation and competition (especially between mother and father) could not easily be acknowledged (cf. the discussion on families in schizophrenic transaction in Selvini Palazzzoli et al, 1978). Mrs. Morris and David, who formed a close knit pair in the family, were the only two who could discuss competitiveness in a dramatic and jocular way, and this only in relation to which of the two was the 'craziest' and who required therapy. David was mother's special favourite from birth and was very jealous of, and rivalrous towards, Janice; as it seemed to us father was of mother, and mother had been of her sister. We hypothesised that in the past, David's asthma had both preserved stability in the family and expressed its conflict. Because he was asthmatic, he could not get on with life like Janice and Ruth, could not threaten father by becoming academically succesful as his mother had wished for him, but could usurp father's place in the marital relationship, therefore probably also helping to maintain a desirable distance between Mr. and Mrs. Morris. Thus, David's symptoms, asthma, a clinging and babyish relationship with his mother, illiteracy until the age of thirteen and psychotic behaviour, dramatised the family taboos around closeness and differentation. The girls in this family also seemed not to feel able to develop autonomously, there were clear injunctions about having academic interests or being in conflict. They worked together and were always under pressure to be each other's best friend. The family assumption was 'Janice and Ruth will stay at home until they marry'.

I am interested in attempting to understand the what and how and why of events, to test the logical coherence of my ideas and professional belief systems, and to participate with others in the field in the continual clarification of our thinking. As a therapist, however, I am faced with the requirement to do something about problems for which neither I nor anyone else (to my satisfaction) can offer a full explanation. I am therefore, often content to act pragmatically, knowing that a particular way of thinking and interacting is likely to alleviate difficulties, while struggling to understand why. I am not certain of the 'truth' of the so called functional explanation of family dysfunction e.g. David prevented himself from succeeding in order that his family balance should not be disrupted, but I find it useful to act as a therapist 'as if' this way of thinking is true. It seems to me more likely to be true that David and his family members had together established a 'fit' over time (Maturana, 1978, 1980) without there necessarily being any intentionality attributable to the particular pattern. However, human beings are in the habit of attributing meaning to behaviour, and the joint construction of new meaning (between team members and between team and family) enables the participants in the therapy to attribute an explanation of the situation which does not necessitate assumptions of incurable illness in one member or blame in another, but enables changes in organisation to be made.

One could say that David was caught in a double bind (Bateson, 1972): on the one hand to grow up, be successful and surpass his father; and on the other hand not to triumph over his father and leave his mother. These demands were covert and until coming into therapy, discussion of them did not seem possible to the family. One could also say that something about David's genetic/neurological make up made him vulnerable and therefore precipitated his breakdown (Bateson, 1972). There seems to me nothing necessarily incompatible about any of these views, each is shaped in part by the vantage point of the person describing the situation and it is the therapist's task to decide which point of view coheres best with their own practice and which leaves most room for manoeuvre.

Aspects of the therapeutic work with the Morris family will be discussed below. Therapist and team met with the family for five sessions over a period of six months. After a follow up meeting six months after termination of family therapy, Mr. and Mrs. Morris were seen a few times to deal with the remnants of her agoraphobic symptoms. It is generally agreed in the literature and from experience with young patients diagnosed as schizophrenic, that the first six weeks to six months after discharge is the period in which a very high rate of relapse and readmission (the 'revolving door') is expected (Goldstein et al., 1978). A few months after the final session we got in touch with the family to request permission to use the family data for teaching and publication. Mrs. Morris wrote to us with permission from all family members and for two years after this wrote approximately once a year to bring us up to date with family events. Thus, although our habit was to do formal follow ups only at six months after discontinuing therapy, in addition to informal monitoring of the professional network over a period of four years to check for readmission or other professional contact in all cases, in this case we have more detailed information. About two and a half years after stopping therapy David started post-graduate studies, having successfully obtained his first degree. He was still living at home, had joined Mensa and was making friends through this. There was much good natured joking about him having inherited his brilliance from his father. Janice was married, Ruth had announced her intention of not marrying for the time being, had spent some time on a kibbutz with her boyfriend (announced by the end of therapy) and was now living away from home and pursuing professional training. Mr. and Mrs. Morris had sold their business immediately after stopping therapy and bought a much smaller one in a quiet neighbourhood, but had decided after a period relatively free from tension that they were bored and had expanded again. Mrs. Morris said that she occasionally still felt anxious in social situations but 'just let it flow over' her and reminded us that her occasionally dependent behaviour in relation to her husband helped to maintain a good balance of competence between them!

COMMON THEMES IN FAMILY WORK WITH SCHIZOPHRENICS

Interviewing skills

a) <u>Circular questioning</u>. I consider, in common with the Milan group (Selvini Palazolli et al, 1980b) that circular questioning is a powerful change agent in its own right. Just as the organisation of the family and the 'pattern that connects' (Bateson, 1979) becomes visible to the therapist team in the process of questioning, so the family, too, have the experience of talking and thinking about their interactions and the interconnectedness of symptoms with the family system. Thus, they too, gain a new perspective, and unspoken 'rules' and assumptions become overt.

b) <u>Dealing with 'bizarre' behaviour</u>. The occasional use in this paper of the word 'bizarre' to describe behaviour reflects two usages. Firstly, it refers to terminology used in hospital casenotes describing behaviour before and during admission. Secondly it represents the therapist's experience of certain interactions. For example, during the first session with the Wright family (outlined below) Teddy suddenly interrupted the discussion by saying to the therapist, 'Ah, now I see what you're doing, you're trying to handle me'. There then followed a copious flow of words to do with whether he could be handled (apparently in reference to manipulative and sexual handling), obscure challenges to the therapist regarding his and her relative competence to handle the door handle, culminating in Teddy kneeling on the floor in front of the therapist with his head bent, pulling his hair in different directions, and demanding that she should handle his head. To this the therapist responded by saying (in what is known to her colleagues as her adolescent-inpatient voice), 'No, I don't want to handle your head now, Teddy, please sit down'. He sat down and the session continued. By and large, our practice was to ignore behaviour of this kind overtly and to continue with the question and answer flow of the session on the assumption that all participants were capable of comprehending and responding to the discussion, while nevertheless taking a very keen interest in the timing and metaphoric significance of such 'crazy' behaviour. Our assumption was that such events are interesting pointers to difficult or taboo family subjects, in the same way that the therapist may be alerted to the fact that family tension has risen by a three year old who suddenly starts screaming or insists on going to the toilet.

Normalisation, reframing and positive connotation

Even though the focus of family meetings is on helping with the difficulties experienced by the designated patient, the decision to invite all family members to attend and the inclusion of family history and behaviour in the questioning has a normalising effect on the way the troubles of the designated patient are viewed.

For example, in the Morris family (case A), we discussed David's dependent and 'over close' relationship with the family and with his mother in particular, but we also talked about Janice and Ruth's closeness to the family, the family rules constraining their independence and permission to differ, Ruth's desire to adventure away from home before settling down to marriage, Mr. Morris' jocular diffidence, etc.

In the Wright family (case B), an older daughter, Margaret had bought her own flat and moved away from home, leaving her young brother, Teddy, living with his unhappily married, severely asthmatic mother and busy father. At a time when Teddy's sporting success was about to take him away from home, threatening the precarious equilibrium of the parents' marriage, Teddy started to behave bizarrly and was admitted to hospital and Margaret sub-let her flat and moved home 'temporarily'. In this case, the team expressed their concern that just as Teddy was not as 'mad' as he seemed, so Margaret might not be as 'well' and independent as she seemed, and they were thus able to describe Teddy's 'sacrifice' as an act serving the apparent welfare of all the family members (cf. case discussion below).

In addition to implicitly drawing comparisons between the behaviour of the designated patient and 'well' siblings, the team also made overt normalising statements. Mr. and Mrs. Morris (case A) asked in session two whether they should continue to be careful not to upset David, and the sisters said they were fed up with the way everyone 'pussyfooted' around him, enabling him to dominate all family interaction. The therapists advised the family from then on to act 'as if he was normal'. The family subsequently confirmed that this statement, together with a phrase from the ward charge nurse describing David's experience as 'this episode', (which for the family meant it was not an illness and would not necessarily be repeated), constituted for them an experience of liberation from fear and uncertainty which enabled them as a family to put their lives together again. Obviously, these normalising statements will not automatically shift a family's beliefs but derive their apparent power from the careful structuring of the context. The idea that the designated patient should be treated as 'normal' contrasts with the approach of Berkowitz (1984), Falloon et al, (1981) and other workers using the concept of expressed emotion.

The decision to stop 'pussyfooting' around the designated patient, which also occurred in other cases, might well on occasion lead to increased family stress in as much as family members' insistence on the designated patient's normal participation in family life might be met with refusal, leading to escalation of argument and high emotion for a period of time. However, it was our experience that such confrontations led (with our help) to resolution and therefore, after a short while, to long term diminution of stress. It was also clear to us that the assumption that the designated patient was ill, and therefore could be held responsible for his/her actions, created over time an atmosphere of intolerable tension, stigmatisation and anxiety in all family members, including the designated patient. The positive connotation (Selvini Palazzoli et al, 1978) of all family behaviour, but particularly that of the designated patient and the reframing of the 'psychosis' enable the family to abandon their lineal (see note 1 at end of paper) punctuation of events, particularly around responsibility 'I am responsible for his mental illness...because I protected him too much...because my aunt is psychotic and thus it runs in the family' etc.. This also serves to challenge family belief systems regarding the possibility of unilateral control of the family's destiny by the patient, by the 'illness' or by the 'guilty' parent.

'Yes-but' reframing seems particularly useful in giving positive recognition to the motivation of actions while discouraging their continuance.

During session two with the Morris family (case A), David repeatedly interjected whenever questioning touched on the parents' relationship, with apparently irrational and 'crazy' statements about his power to cure his mother, his dead grandfather's view about this, etc.. The therapist paid little attention to this during the course of the session, but at the end after the team consultation said that the team took very seriously David's statement about his belief that he could cure his mother. However, we thought he had misunderstood the situation. This was understandable, as he was only a young man and thus not sufficiently experienced to understand the subtleties of adult relationships. From what we had seen of his parents' relationship, we had no doubt that his father was competent in supporting and helping his mother.

Leaving home

The team assumed that in Western culture, there is general agreement that children in their late teens or early twenties should become emotionally, if not physically independent of their families. While it is always important to check this assumption against the culture of particular families, this focus informed much of our work (Haley, 1980).

It was striking how many of the designated patients in the families we saw had experienced events highlighting the demand/opportunity to leave home shortly before the behaviours which precipitated admission to hospital. Mary Johnson (case C) and Teddy Wright (case B) had been offered opportunities to turn their athletic prowess into professional careers by joining national sports teams. Alan Cohen (case D) spent three months on a kibbutz, had his first passionate love affair and proceeded to train as a Hassidic Rabbi. At a time when David Morris (case A) and his sister Janice had both started taking steps towards moving away from home, Janice's distressing sexual misadvanture seemed to both of them proof of the dangers awaiting young people away from their parents' protection. Simultaneously, the families of these young people frequently adhered to a powerful family norm of extreme closeness while, covertly, there were many splits, differences and desires to separate, which were apparently secret but known to all. It was therefore not beyond understanding that the designated patients, in a perhaps heightened and unrealistic sense, concluded that their dramatic 'sacrifice' of themselves as the focus for family concern was all that was keeping their families, and perhaps especially their parents, together.

Prescribing the system

There are two particular consequences of using the range of intervention techniques generally lumped together, often inaccurately, under the term 'paradoxical prescription':

1) The therapist team recognises the constraints of the family system (interactional patterns, history, beliefs, rules, etc.) as experienced by the family members. By describing the team's understanding of these constraints and the apparent inevitability of symptomatic behaviour to the family, the therapists enable the family to obtain, perhaps for the first time, an overview of their situation. This not only makes it hard for family members to continue as before (Selvini Palazzoli et al, 1978) but alters the family's view of events which has been focused on a search for lineal explanations.

2) Having recognised the constraints of the family pattern, it follows logically that the therapist should recognise the importance of continuing as before, until new options can be found. The intensification of the 'sweat box' effect (Hoffman, 1981) thus produced makes it likely that the family will reach into their (unused) repertoire for new solutions.

Teddy Wright (aged twenty two) (case B) demonstrated in the sessions that he had an extremely close, sexualised relationship with his mother, who was severely asthmatic, and whom he assumed would not survive if Mr. Wright left, as he threatened to do once the children were no longer at home. There was also considerable discussion about how close Teddy and his father had been in the past, but how unpleasantly rivalrous their relationship had become since Teddy had become adult, particularly around his very glamorous sporting prowess, which Mr. Wright had originally encouraged. We speculated that Teddy's psychotic behaviour could be seen to perform a number of services for the family; (a) it kept the parents from making a decision about whether or not to end their long drawn out embattled marriage for the time being; (b) it enabled Margaret to return home while still regarded as functioning well by her parents and by returning she could regain the closeness with her father which meant so much to her and which she had 'lost' when she moved into her own flat and her own social life; (c) it removed the competitive element of the father-son relationship to a metaphoric level which could be disregarded as Teddy's 'crazy talk'; (d) it enabled Teddy to leave home (by living in hospital) without leaving home (by still requiring concern and active support from his parents) (Haley, 1980).

The therapist had described the team's view of (a), (b) and (c) above to Mrs. Wright, Margaret and Teddy, and was beginning to discuss (d):

THERAPIST: (after some meanderings about general expectations regarding leaving home and the potentially disastrous consequences, in Teddy's view, if he did). We think you've found a very original solution to this problem. Teddy...

TEDDY: Yes I know. If I'm in hospital I'm kind of away from home and I have some space and there's not so many fights but I'm still sort of home because I still need them both and they have to visit me all the time.

THERAPIST: (rather taken aback but rallying). Yes, that's what I mean...

TEDDY: And I reckon I should do it for another year or maybe five years and then I can still get back to my sport.

THERAPIST: Well, I don't want to depress you because I think you're doing a very impressive job and making a big sacrifice. It may be that you're right and it will take a year or five years, it may even take less - it may take six months or even one month or less - but we see a lot of people with your dilemma and I have to tell you it may take much longer. A sacrifice like this is not a light one and you may have to make up your mind to give your whole life to it...etc.

The response to this was dramatic, Teddy went home for Christmas, having asked his father, with support from the therapist, to make the decision as to whether he should be allowed home, and from there he informed the hospital that he would not return. At follow up he had returned to work and had no recurrence of symptoms.

Tasks

The therapist's choice of questions, comments and tasks in general aimed to realign family relationships in ways that would strengthen the parental/marital dyad, increase differentiation amongst family members, de-triangulate the designated patient, strengthen sibling equality and support, interrupt rigid patterning, rehearse the family for dealing with predicted relapse and diminish the special role of the designated patient in the family. For example, in session two with the Morris family (case A), Janice had said she was fed up with always having to 'put myself and my boyfriend down' because David did not like to have him in the house and produced bizarre tantrum like behaviour whenever her boyfriend visited. The family were instructed to invite Janice's boyfriend to dinner, rehearsed in the ways David might sabotage this arrangement, and a plan of action was drawn up in which father instead of mother would deal with any difficult behaviour from David, leaving mother free to be the hostess.

In the Johnson family (case C), father was given the task of helping his athlete daughter regain her former physical and emotional fitness by taking her jogging in the mornings, while leaving the emotional and cuddling support to his wife, which the team defined as more gender appropriate. This served to loosen the intense and sexually flavoured, though defined as tomboyish, relationship between Mary and her father, while not expecting them to give up all specially close activities, and increasing closeness between mother and Mary, who had become trapped in a habit of apparent aloofness from each other.

Idiosyncracies

I find the families of schizophrenics in general interesting and stimulating to be with, and the generally layered, metaphoric talk and tendency to behave in 'odd' ways provokes in me some of my own 'crazier' aspects (Napier and Whitaker, 1978). Having the security of a team behind the screen who will anchor me to a consensus view of reality and remind me that I'm a therapist, frees me at times with such families to allow my own sillier flights of fancy to emerge. These behaviours on the therapist's part cannot, in my experience, be produced to plan, but when they emerge from a resonance between therapist and family, and reflect something of the therapist's ability to participate in the family style while still flexibly moving between family 'craziness' and team professionalism, they usually prove to make a considerable impact for change (Papp, 1984). Humour can be one manifestation of the transcontextual syndrome (Bateson, 1972) and a powerful agent for change (Cade, 1982).

In the third session with the Morris family (case A) all the family members reported that things were going very well. The therapist had spent some time obtaining detailed descriptions of improved family interactions and had then moved on to questions about what they all felt they had learned and gained from the experience of David's hospitalisation and the events preceding it (this line of questioning was prompted by family statements). All the family members were eloquent about their many gains, but David could only say that he had gained 'not to be mad any more'. The therapist experessed herself very dubious about this, pointed out how much he had gained in terms of power, excitement and being the focus of all attention by 'being mad', and said that in her opinion he seemed to have lost more than he had gained. (The obvious concern for the therapist was that if this accurately reflected David's perception, his 'improvement' was unlikely to last). She then asked the family questions to establish how David had gained family attention, particularly Mrs. Morris' as it transpired, in the past and how he might do so again. This produced a considerable amount of giggling amongst the siblings, with the girls prompting David, 'go on, tell her' and David refusing and asking what the therapist would pay to divulge this important secret. The therapist allowed herself to become infected by the general silliness, refused to pay David the £500 he demanded on the grounds that his deposit account was larger than hers, but offered to bribe him with a five week interval between sessions. David then proceeded to enact, with considerable prompting and stage directing from his sisters, his usual technique for achieving a 'tete a tete' with his mother. He would study at night in the kitchen. After his father had gone to bed, usually quite early, David would call out, 'Mummy - tea' in a babyish voice (this was replicated for the therapist with considerable exaggeration and gales of laughter), and his mother would then come down stairs, make him tea, and the two of them would embark on a discussion of their woes, symptoms and dissatisfactions, until the early hours of the morning.

It seemed most unlikely, after this recounting, that David would ever again be able to embark on this or similar behaviours with his mother or that she would be able to respond, without them and the rest of the family experiencing it as absurd. However, the team also instructed that if David was ever to call for baby-tea again, his mother was to relay the call to his father who would get up and make tea for his studious son.

DISCUSSION

I assume that there is a genetic factor in the aetiology of the syndrome we call schizophrenia. (Bateson, 1972). However, since this also seems to me to be true of most other propensities, capacities and vulnerabilities, this does not seem an adequate reason for failing to work psychotherapeutically with people diagnosed as schizophrenic. Some of the salient contributions in our field derive from the study of schizophrenia (Boszormenyi-Nagy and Framo, 1965; Selvini Palazzoli et al, 1978; Selvini Palazzoli and Prata, 1983; Scheflen, 1981). Traditional thinking in the psychiatric field has assumed a discontinuity between those mental afflictions which are similar to the ones 'we ourselves' suffer (neuroses) and the psychoses which are regarded as being different in kind. Thus, change procedures regarded as useful with one client group will be assumed useless with another. However, many years' experience in psychiatric settings has not convinced me that this view is valid. Rather, it has often seemed to me to paraphrase Hitchock's dictum that 'murder is for people who have scruples about breaking family rules'.

We have found this approach useful with a range of cases (seventy four during the life of the team), including cases where the designated patient is a member of the youngest generation with diagnoses other than schizophrenia (manic depressive psychosis, acute anxiety states, toxic psychoses, depression) and where the designated patient is a member of the parent generation (with a range of psychiatric diagnoses). We have been most successful with relatively acute cases, i.e. where the designated patient has been hospitalised once or twice (or, with increasing confidence among our referrers, never) and where the diagnosed behaviour has been in evidence in acute form, for not longer than about five years. Bearing in mind our rough and ready criteria for success (cf.p.1), about ninety to ninety five percent of these cases were concluded successfully. Although we have had some successes with more 'chronic' cases i.e. where the designated patient has been hospitalised numerous times (ten to thirty times) over a period of many years (up to twenty to thirty years), we have also had a larger number of failures with these cases. About a third of these cases were concluded successfully. Boscolo (in Selvini Palazzoli et al., 1983) makes a thought provoking comment on the relative ineffectiveness of family therapy approaches to the treatment of chronic schizophrenia. Reading the case discussions of Berkkowitz (1984) and Falloon et al (1981), I wonder whether these are perhaps the cases where they have found their method to be particularly applicable. On the other hand, the Milan trained workers in Bologna (Castellucci et al, 1985) are reporting considerable success in working with chronic cases where the designated patient has been hospitalised for twenty years or more. Our subjective impression of the reasons for our failure accord more with the thinking of Castellucci and her colleagues in that our judgement was that we often did not manage to obtain sufficient leverage with the professional system with which the designated patients and their families had become complexly interlocked over many years of treatment and readmission. Our attempts to work with the families only in these cases meant that we were working with too small a part of the significant system, and since we were very much part of the professional system we did not feel able to address it from a meta-perspective. Obviously, this is a speculation based on personal judgement which could well be explored (Dell, 1980). While the term schizophrenia remains a useful descriptive shorthand amongst professionals but is not yet an explanatory term, it is our responsibility as workers to use whatever skills are to hand that can be of use in particular cases. Paying attention to the family organisation, the life events and developmental stresses of the designated patient and family, and mobilising the family and individual resources for change has proved useful. I will continue to believe that I can serve clients better by working with them according to the premise that they may be able to engage fully in life, having gained strength and flexibility from successfully negotiating potentially disastrous experiences. This view, for me, is best summed up by Bateson's words:

> First, that severe pain and maladjustment can be induced by putting a mammal in the wrong regarding its rules for making sense of an important relationship with another mammal, and second, that if this pathology can be warded off or resisted, the total experience may promote creativity.
>
> (Bateson, 1972).

Note 1. Family therapy literature in recent years has incorrectly adapated the use of 'linear' when 'lineal' is meant. 'Linear is a technical term in mathematics describing a relationship between variables such that when they are plotted against each other on orthogonal Cartesian co-ordinates, the result will be a straight line. Lineal describes a relation among a series of causes or arguments such that the sequenece does not come back to the starting point. The opposite of linear is non-linear. The opposite of lineal is recursive' (Bateson, 1979, p.242).

ACKNOWLEDGEMENT

I would like to express my gratitude to my colleagues, Loretta Shoben, Anne Richardson and Liz Bennett.

REFERENCES

Bateson, G., (1972), Steps to an Ecology of Mind, Chandler Publishing Company (reprint in Paladin Books, 1978), Granada Publishing Ltd., London.

Bateson, G., (1979), Mind and Nature: A Necessary Unity Wildwood House, London.

Berkowitz, R., (1984), Therapeutic intervention with schizophrenic patients and their families: A description of a clinical research project. Journal of Family Therapy, 16, 211-233.

Boszormenyi-Nagy, I. and Framo, J.L. (eds.), (1965) Intensive Family Therapy, New York, Harper and Row.

Cade, B.W., (1982), Humour and creativity, Journal of Family Therapy, 4, 35-42.

Catellucci, A., Fruggeri, L. and Marzari, M., (1985), Instability and evolutionary change in a psychiatric community in Campbell, D. and Draper, R. (eds.),

Application of Systematic Family Therapy: The Milan Approach, Grune and Stratton, London.
Dell, P.F., (1980), Researching the family theories of schizophrenia: An exercise in epistemological confusion, Family Process, 19, 321-335.
Falloon, I.R.H., Liberman, R.P., Lillie, F.J. and Vaughn, C. E., (1981), Family therapy of schizophrenics with high rate of relapse, Family Process, 20, 211-221
Goldstein, M.J., Rodnick, E. H., Evans, J.R., May, P.R.A. and Steinberg, M.R., (1978), Drug and family therapy in the aftercare of actue schizophrenics, Archives of General Psychiatry, 35, 1169-1177.
Haley, J., (1980), Leaving Home: The Therapy of Disturbed Young People, McGraw-HIll, New York.
Hoffman, L, (1981), Foundations of Family Therapy: A Conceptual Framework for Systems Change, Basic Books, New York.
Maturana, H.A., (1978), Biology of language: The epistemology of reality in Miller, G.A. and Lenneberg, E. (eds.), Psychology and Biology of Language and Thought. Academic Press, New York.
Maturana, H.R. and Varela, F.J., (eds.) (1980), Autopoiesis and Cognition: The Realistion of the Living, Reidel, Barton Crucible, Harper and Row, New York.
Napier, A.Y. and Whitaker, C.A., (1978),The Family Crucible, Harper and Row, New York.
Nitsberg, L., Patten, J., Spielman, M. and Brown, R., (1985) In-patient hospital systemic consultation: Providing team systemic consultation in in-patient settings where the team is part of the system in Campbell, D. and Draper, R. (eds.) Application of Systemic Family Therapy: The Milan Approach, Grune and Stratton, London.
Papp, P., (1984), The creative leap: The links between clinical and artistic creativity. The Family Therapy Networker, 8, 20-29.
Selvini Palazzoli, M., (1980), Why a long interval between sessions? The therapeutic control of the family therapist supra system in Andolfi, M. and Zwerling, I. (eds.), Dimensions of Family Therapy, Guildford Press, New York.
Selvini Palazzoli, M. and Prata, G., (1983), A new method for therapy and research in the treatment of schizophrenic families in Stierlin, H., Wynne, L.C. and Wirching, M. (eds.), Psychosocial Intervention in Schizophrenia, Springer Verlag, Berlin.
Selvini Palazzoli, M., Boscolo, L., Cecchin, G. and Prata, G. (1978), Paradox and Counterparadox. A New Model in the Therapy of the Family in Schizophrenic Transaction, Jason Aronson, New York.
Selvini Palazzoli, M., Boscolo, L., Cecchin, G. and Prata, G. (1980a), The problem of the referring person, Journal of Marital and Family Therapy, 6, 3-9.
Selvini Palazzoli, M., Boscolo, L., Cecchin, G. and Prata, G. (1980b), Hypothesising-circularity-neutrality-: Three guidelines for the conductor of the session, Family Process, 19, 3-12.
Scheflen, A.E., (1981), Levels of Schizophrenia., Bruner

Mazel, New York.
Terkelsen, K.G., (1983), Schizophrenia and the family. II Adverse effects of family therapy, Family Process, 22, 191-200.

Three approaches to working with families with a schizophrenic member

A. MILLER

INTRODUCTION

As William Macfarlane (1983) points out, family therapy has had relatively little to say about the treatment of schizophrenia, despite the fact that it was observations of 'schizophrenic communications' which made a profound impact on American psychiatry in the 1950's, and were a major impetus to the development of family therapy over the next twenty years, the impact of circular epistemology eventually arrived at by the Palo Alto group of Bateson, Haley Jackson and Weakland (1962) and the wholesale adoption of systems thinking, has, in many instances been limited. Seekers for alternative aetiologies of schizophrenia (e.g. Theodore Lidz, R.D. Laing) missed the point and substituted one linear causal explanation for another. Paul Dell (1980) claims that much of the research on thought disorder and on family communication has also remained within a tradition of Aristotelian (linear) epistemology. The field has been bedevilled by failures to distinguish adequately two domains of enquiry: (i) the question of the aetiology of schizophrenia (linear epistomology) and (ii) the question of the connection between schizophrenic functioning, or behaviour, and systems interaction (circular epistomology). There have also been many practical problems in the family therapy approach to schizophrenia, and they may be summed up in Murray Bowen's rather gloomy remark (quoted in MacFarlane, 1983) that the families in his practice did not seem to be amenable to change, and the patients just went right on having psychotic episodes. The narrow definition of the family as the relevant social system to treat has also had its limitations and the problems inherent in ignoring the larger social context, including the treatment system in the maintenance of schizophrenic patterns, has been accompanied by a subtle accusation and demoralization of the family. One only has to think of the disproportionate number of young black males in psychiatric hospitals at the present time to be shaken out of the complacency of believing that the family system is the only relevant system to consider. From the stand point of ordinary practitioners however, attempts to find good solutions to the problems of working with schizophrenic people and their families continue.

Two very important approaches are presented within this volume: (i) the educational approach related to 'expressed emotion' (EE) which is syntonic with the medical model of schizophrenia defining it as an illness, helping families maximise the functioning of the 'sick' person in their midst, and (ii) work based on the circular epistemology of the Milan approach with its emphasis on 'normalising' the schizophrenic person and creating areas of shared meaning through the use of reframing and prescription of system functioning. The first approach is one which, broadly speaking, represents a point of view which divests the schizophrenic's experience of any other meaning than that of an illness, a kind of 'benign neglect' of the details of schizophrenic functioning. The second approach is an attempt to find connection and invest with meaning the disconnected parts, relating the behaviour of the schizophrenic person in meaningful ways to the behaviour of the rest of the family. I will come back to these points after presenting some ideas of three practitioners, one of them myself, working in a London Clinic. Each approach is experimental, representing work in progress rather than fully worked out models. A central issue for us is how the level of functioning of the schizophrenic person is related to the kind of treatment approach adopted.

First approach

This will be illustrated by a family referred some time ago to me, by a social worker in a large psychiatric hospital. She said the family wanted help in working out some of their problems in being together, specifically tensions between husband and wife exacerbated by the unruly behaviour of two of their three children. The wife, a black woman of thirty five, had received a diagnosis of schizophrenia on her second admission to hospital when she was hearing voices telling her to leave her husband, and when she announced she could heal all sick people through prayer. On meeting them for the first time they were a very attractive family and she a beautiful and well dressed woman. Her manner was, however, extremely remote and she sat withdrawn amid the quite remarkable hurly burly created by her husband (who was white) and the children. Gradually I started to define problems with them (the children were both worried about and disrespectful of the mother, clearly seeing her as the patient) and to make fairly simple moves to restructure the family. To my surprise, expecting rigidities so characteristic of the family with a schizophrenia member, they started to change, mother and father started to exert joint authority in relation to the children, and the children's undisciplined and disruptive behaviour started to subside. I focussed on supporting the woman more or less unconditionally as she was clearly disqualified by the family as a functioning member, and disqualified herself. Outlined below are extracts from a session. Members present were Mr. John and Mrs. Beth Jones, Gerard (twelve), Olivia (nine) and Simon (seven), (the names and some details have been changed for reasons of confidentiality). After initial greetings and general remarks, Mr. Jones opened with the statement that he would like to talk about what happened when his wife's sister was with them for three or four days the previous week.

THERAPIST (to Mrs. Jones): Do <u>you</u> want to talk about it?
MRS. JONES: I don't mind.
OLIVIA: It was five days, no it was three days, no it was four days and a bit.
MR. JONES (immediately to wife): During that time you were out and about, but as soon as she went, you relapsed back to normal.
MRS. JONES (flatly): I can hardly go out on my own to the cinema.
MR. JONES: But you led a sort of active existence, you weren't lethargic all the time.
MRS. JONES: I was tired then.
MR. JONES: But nowhere near as much. After she left, it was almost as if you were drained, well both of us were a bit drained, both of us were very tired, but after that I feel we flopped back whereas you were able to transform yourself whilst she was here and I wondered if there was any way of preserving that...way of being, is that worth talking about?

At the point at which the wife apparently abdicates her interest in the conversation (I don't mind), Olivia reinforces the disqualification of her mother as a participant by declaring her right to redefine father's terms and take over her mother's part in the adult discussion, matching her father in tone and pace.

The therapist's opening remark, acknowledging and confirming the wife, sets the stage for an increasing focus on the disqualification of the wife both by Beth herself and by her family. Note Mr. Jones' elegant disconfirmation 'You relapsed back to normal', and the flurry of confusion with which he counters his wife's substitution of the normal term 'tired' for his more symptom orientated 'lethargic'.

MRS. JONES - looking straight ahead, silent.
MR. JONES: Well?
MRS. JONES: I don't know.
MR. JONES (attempting to engage the therapist in a discussion of his wife's behaviour): When her sister was here, they

went out a lot and had a good time.
THERAPIST (to Mr. Jones): Do you know if Beth wants to talk about this or not?
MR. JONES (shrugging): Well, she said she didn't mind.
THERAPIST: When Beth says she doesn't mind, do you know if she minds or if she doesn't mind?
MR. JONES (bristling slightly): She doesn't mind. If she does mind, she says so (turning to her) Don't you?.
MRS. JONES: Mmm.
THERAPIST: I see. (to wife) So you are straight. You say what you think. If you mind, you tell him.
MRS. JONES: Yes.
THERAPIST (to Mr. Jones) So Beth not minding, does that mean she wants to talk about it, she thinks it's a good idea to talk about it, or she doesn't mind if you talk about it but she would rather be quiet?
OLIVIA (quick as a flash): She doesn't know.
MR. JONES: That's right, she doesn't know.
THERAPIST (to Mrs. Jones): Isn't that interesting. Olivia thinks that she has to talk for you...I wonder where she gets that idea from....that she's got to be your voice.
OLIVIA (overlapping): Cos Daddy said.
MRS. JONES: Daddy said what?
OLIVIA: I said first... and then...Daddy said. (Looking down).
MR. JONES: But Miss Miller asked why you said anything.
OLIVIA: Because I wanted to.
MRS. JONES: Do you think I wanted you to say something?
OLIVIA: I didn't know....because she was asking.
THERAPIST (to Mrs. Jones): She answers for you. I don't know if she does it all the time but just now that's what she did. Do you need her or want her to do that? Or you don't mind.
MRS. JONES: I don't mind.
THERAPIST: O.K. that's fine.

The Therapist does not attempt to challenge the wife, accepting her definition. There was some further discussion about how Olivia speaks for other people in the family.

THERAPIST: I don't know Beth what you take your husband to mean when he says that you were very lively when your sister was here and collapsed when she left. I don't know whether you think he is kind of criticising you for the way you are now, or whether he is praising you for the way you were then, and whether that's something you want to talk about. I don't know still...
MRS. JONES (animated): I was surprised that he brought up the subject...he hadn't discussed this with me before, he hadn't said any of it before and um, I felt he was being a bit unfair to say I had relapsed, because when she was here it was right that I should take her out and I didn't know that he expected me to carry on in the same way once she had gone.

THERAPIST: O.K., you obviously had a number of ideas about

him bringing this up.
MRS. JONES: Mm. (Nodding).
THERAPIST: What would happen if you were to say to him 'I think it's a bit unfair that you brought this up because you hadn't talked to me about this first?' What would he do?
OLIVIA: (attempting to activate father): Ask him.
MRS. JONES (ignoring Olivia while her husband smiled at the child): He would defend himself.
THERAPIST: Mm mm...Because you see it's interesting to me that he brings it up and you say you don't mind.
MRS. JONES: Mm (nodding her head).
THERAPIST: Whereas clearly you do mind. Somehow or other with him you speak with a forked tongue, on the one hand you say you don't mind, on the other hand you kind of secretly mind. Now I don't know what he does that gets you to deal with him in that roundabout fashion. I imagine he does something that gets you to deal with him in that way, do you know what it is? (This comes as a surprising relocation of the problem from one located in Beth to one that suggests the husband requires it. Neither, and both of course are 'true').
MRS. JONES: I know what you mean...well I feel that he is the sane one in the family.
THERAPIST: Oh! I see, he is the sane one...so, by implication... your're what? the crazy one?
MRS. JONES: Yes.
THERAPIST: So if he brings up something...
MRS. JONES (overlapping): If he brings something up it must be worthwhile talking about.
THERAPIST: I see, goodness, what an interesting situation to get into. So if you were to say 'Mm, this is not what I want to talk about', then...you would be in trouble.
MRS. JONES (smiling): Yes.
MR. JONES (moving uncomfortably in his seat and smiling sheepishly).
MRS. JONES: He would say to me in the car on the way home why did you refuse to talk about it, it was very important.
Therapist: It's a tricky issue how you are going to resolve that because otherwise you are going to have to go on through life with these fixed jobs for you (to husband) to be the sane one and you (to wife) to be the crazy one.
MR. JONES: Yes, it's something that goes on a lot. I notice that I say things being rational and fair, but there is a dimension of impatience and intolerance in my voice to her.
Therapist (to wife): Is he any good at being crazy?

Both husband and wife laughed, looked at each other and for the first time in this session Mrs. Jones seemed very natural.

MRS. JONES: When he shouts at the children, I sometimes think he is crazy. You've got to be crazy to shout at them the way he does.

Subsequently Mrs. Jones remained active and assertive for

several weeks and was not withdrawn. She then decided to stop her medication so that she could enjoy a holiday without the uncomfortable side effects. What followed was a psychotic episode and another hospitalisation.

What I had not sufficiently considered was the powerful system with which the family were connected all along, namely, the psychiatric system supporting a medical definition of her state represented by the psychiatrist in the original hospital who saw her regularly to renew her prescription. There could be several explanations of her psychotic episode and the biological one is obvious. Another is that the family responded to family therapy with an apparent move in the mother's position away from patienthood. However, there remained throughout this process another, more powerful system, maintaining the definition of her as a patient. When she decided to take a holiday from being a patient by stopping medication, the balance of the family system was truly threatened, and only restored for all of them when her psychotic episode and subsequent admission firmly reinstated her as a patient. The family at this point dropped out of therapy despite invitations on my part to continue, interestingly enough the given reason was that they felt things had changed quite a lot and the husband in particular was now becoming rather worried about what he perceived as my 'feminist' position. When they re-referred themselves a year later they did so because they were both expressing alarm at the psychiatrist's recent statement to them that the woman would be better to stay on medication indefinitely. This time, a joint interview with the psychiatrist and the family helped to clarify and forge some new possibilities for defining the situation. What subsequently emerged in the work with the family could in many respects be understood in terms of the way in which the definition of self for the woman was constructed between herself, her husband, her children, the extended family, black and white, and the medical world. The connections between her 'mad' state, in which she divested herself of the identity of wife and mother and took on the identity of healer with its relationships to her family of origin was gradually illuminated as the work continued and further psychotic episodes have not occurred.

SECOND APPROACH

Rosine Perelberg's (Anthropologist and Family Therapist, Marlborough Family Service), work with families of schizophrenic people, seems to me to be on a continuum with her approach to other families (as opposed to the disjunction between work with schizophrenic and nonschizophrenic families that characterise Heiner Schuff's work, outlined below).

She starts from the premise that the schizophrenic person has many signifiers which are not connected to signifieds, and that the process of connecting one to the other or of creating symbols, can be achieved through rituals. The background to these ideas is in social anthropology and in particular in the work of Levi Strauss. Her interest is in the extent to which the identified patient and the family share meanings, and her first step as the therapist is to uncover the extent to which this is the case. While noticing en passant the structures currently operating in the family, she does not, like Cloe Madanes (1980) in strategic therapy, focus particularly on hierarchy. The universe of meanings in the family is the centre of operation and her interest in structure is related to how meanings are supported and developed (as opposed to unsupported and diminished) by structure. In the family therapy of a woman who believed herself to be possessed by the devil for example, she first discussed in detail with the family, including the quite young children what their understanding of events had been. She discovered that the family had been highly connected to the local minister who had performed exorcism on the woman. She therefore invited this minister to the family meeting to discuss (respectfully) the nature of his understanding of the woman's belief and the ritual which he had carried out on the basis of their shared meanings. It is notable that the therapist's meanings are quite submerged in this part of the work, except in so far as she exhibits a careful respect for all that is revealed to her. In this sense I think the work is coherent with the Milan Group's notion of neutrality but her method of interviewing is quite different. After an initial stage of exploring meanings, which may last for several sessions, or may be concluded in one, she will offer a meaning to the family (a reframing of the situation) which may be linked to one or more rituals. However, she will only inject a specific framing once the family has already done so. She seeks out the conflict of values which coming to the clinic or hospital represents for the family, exploring those values which they would not otherwise readily have brought to (or thought relevant in) a psychological or medical context. She looks rather for the context which invests the schizophrenic person's symptoms with meanings for the family. What she brings to the work in relation to rituals is the concept that one of the functions of rituals is to create an identity. Another important function is to resolve contradictions. In the case just mentioned she prescribed an elaborate ritual whereby the woman in question would have a context carefully prepared in which she would explain to her mother and father as much of her psychotic experience as she was able to do. She would do this in the presence of her husband and children, who would act as witnesses to this and the husband would have an additional role as helper. All of this was within an original framework of the woman having lost her voice.

In another example (Perelberg, unpublished) the schizophrenic person in question was a young man from a family of nine children of African Asian Hindus. The parents had not spoken to each other in this family for some twelve years before they came to the session and the behaviour which worried his family was that the young man had become silent and rarely got out of bed. Two years previously he had become involved with a Muslim guru who had converted him to Islam.

During the first session two versions of his problem were put forward. The father, who had more or less lost his position in the family since their emigration to this country, thought that his son had become 'kinky like' after his contact with the guru. Although the therapist worked with many layers of the way in which this family operated around these symptoms and the parents' silence, I will focus on one. The therapist eventually labelled the young man's silence as an expression of the fact that he did not know who he was. She then enquired as to whether anyone in the family would know of a ceremony that might be the correct one, if the young man chose it, to allow a reinstatement of the Hindu religion. The father turned out to be the only person in the family who was knowledgeable in this matter and during the following sessions, the young man and the father discussed his possible reconversion to Hinduism. The father eventually organised such a ceremony and the young man underwent it a few months later. Throughout the process the therapist never requested the parents to talk to each other directly. It is interesting to speculate on the connection between these events and the birth of the child as a fruit that Gisela Pankow (below) talks about. However, in Rosine Perelberg's terms it is the connections between structures in the family which support certain meanings that are the focus of her work.

THIRD APPROACH

Heiner Schuff (Consultant Psychotherapist at St Albans Hospital, Locum Psychiatrist, Marlborough Family Service), is experimenting with the ideas of a German analyst, Gisela Pankow. Her ideas include the following notions: the fragmentation of the schizophrenic is profound and can be understood in terms of body experiences or body image; the schizophrenic does not have an experience of a body as a container with an external outline; the other feature of body image, the internal content of the body, is also missing so that they do not have any experience of containing parts. There is no difference between inside and outside as there is no form. Consequently there is no structure of self as a person with symbolising functions in relationships.

In order to help the schizophrenic construct a form or a body that has organic unity, she uses concrete forms of communication including clay modelling and painting:

> How does one enter the world of the schizophrenic, this world where there is only himself and nobody else? Even if the schizophrenic speaks about other persons and we think that they could be important figures in his life history, we discover sooner or later that what he, for instance, calls 'father' is only a part of himself. Therefore, it is useless to elaborate association concerning his life history because in this way the psychotic material increases, and there is no longer any basis on which to work. In psychosis we need another kind of technique. I ask

> the patient to take modelling clay and to model something for me. This clay work is a message revealing the manner in which a patient, in relation to his analyst, lives in his body. Therefore, the clay model is equivalent to the body image and implies the two fundamental functions that I have described elsewhere. First, the body image reveals the manner in which the patient lives, that is, experiences the reciprocal relation between the part and the whole in a spatial figure and espcially in his own body. This attempt at the spatial structure of the body image is elaborated by means of the external outline in the sense of a container. The other function of the body image concerns the internal content as the thing signified by a container and leading to historical structures...The recognition of the internal content leads the patient to understand that a container has a content. If this container is, for example the patient's body he has to recognise that the inside of his body is differentiated, as well as other parts of his body, and belongs to him as a person. Thus, the reciprocal relation between to be and to have introduces the one who has and the one who does not have. Thus the other person can appear, and interpersonal relationships are possible.
>
> Pankow, 1976

Her view of the relationship between the schizophrenic and their family is one which fits well with the concept of enmeshment (very familiar to family therapists). Her metaphor is a vivid one:

> When they (the parents) are able to renounce their infantile relationship with their own parents, they can become parents themselves. At this moment they can recognise their child as the 'fruit' that means something that is different from themselves. In this way the schizophrenic child can get permission to exist.
>
> Pankow, 1976

Although she comes perilously close to the notion of the schizophrenogenic mother and also, I think, adopts a linear cause and effect model in relation to aetiology (although she does make disclaimers from time to time about aetiological explanations), her phenomenological descriptions are compelling. Heiner Schuff has adopted her ideas in two contexts. One is in individual work with schizophrenics either on his own or in joint work developed with Kathy Killick, an Art Therapist at Hill End Hospital, St. Albans (Kathy Killick has also developed an original approach to art therapy with schizophrenics (1987). The other is in his work with the families of schizophrenics. It is the latter on which I would now like to comment.

His view is that the truly fragmented, schizophrenic human

being (he uses this term deliberately to distinguish 'personhood' as a separate phenomenon) does not share with the rest of the family or with the therapist, personhood. If we think of the disconfirmation of communication as described by the communication theorists, the transactional messages are of the nature 'You are not here' (I am not here)'. A more accurate statement of the position is seen by Heiner Schuff as 'Not here, not there' - or no - where. In other words there is no I and no You. The interpersonal consensually validated basis on which we stand is blown by the schizophrenic experience. The problem in therapy is that the therapist shares the communication system of the non-psychotic members and is nobody or anybody for the schizophrenic. One of the most powerful processes maintaining and intensifying the fragmented 'no-where, no-body, anybody' experience of the schizophrenic, and thereby its 'crazy', defensive organisations are the constant, so-called positive attempts by the environment to induce, retrieve and demand personhood where there is 'nobody', which often turns into the so-called negative version 'the person we knew, who makes him/herself (as a person) unavailable to us, turns against us'. In both cases the fragmented human being is forced to be a person which she/he cannot be, and sometimes, in momentory, rudimentay states of personal self organisation, the schizophrenic will comment on his/her environment as being crazy or driving him/her crazy. He would see that many of the family therapy models imply that there is just interpersonal behaviour and personhood is taken for granted. If one takes these ideas to their logical conclusion, as I think he does, the work with the families is quite unusual. Unlike the work I presented of my own where, following the example of Minuchin, the therapist adopts the strategy of supporting the schizophrenic person more or less unconditionally, Heiner Schuff would relatively speaking ignore the schizophrenic human being in the presence of their family and talk only to the family. What can be seen as 'ignoring' is a concrete acknowledgement of the current reality of the schizophrenic being, an avoidance of the demand to be a person and behave interpersonally and a concrete message to the family which is quite consciously adopted by the therapist. It is not to say that the therapist does not look at the schizophrenic person or make and allow body contact with them but he in no way attempts to engage them in conversation and exchanges of meaning. If the schizophrenic human being joins in, the therapist will acknowledge this movement but will not focus on it. Instead he talks to the family. The focus of this talk is on examining with the family their difficulties in dealing with the now so different human being who used to be a person among persons, the results of their attempts to make him/her a person and their experience of not succeeding. Inevitably, using various forms of interviewing, framing and reframing, a point is reached where neither casual explanations, nor interpersonal meaning in terms of knowledge and, importantly, no claim of either family and therapist can be upheld which perpetuates the (crazy) idea that 'anybody can change a nobody'. The usually achieved aim is that the family acknowledges 'differentness', maintains contact to the schizophrenic being without 'forced normalisation' or 'forced pathologizing' and allows the schizophrenic independence with the choice to remain fragmented or to engage in specialised, individual psychotherapy in a setting and with methods which attempt to meet the schizophrenic at the structural and functional level of fragmentation. It is clear that Heiner Schuff believes in the necessity of both working with the family and offering an individual, potential space for therapy to the schizophrenic at the same time.

The work with the schizophrenic human being in constructing a self will take place at the moment outside the family therapy session. Schizophrenia in this model is seen as an existential condition in which illness is irrelevant. Family therapy is focussed on helping the family acknowledge profound 'differentness' by ceasing attempts to change it. One might argue that although this approach comes from a completely different theoretical and ideological background, the effect of this kind of intervention on the family in fact has some parallels with the interventions based on the notions to do with EE. A characterisation of the schizophrenic human being as ill and the methods used to decrease EE in the family could be seen as disconnecting the family's attempts to create meanings with the schizophrenic which are irrelevant and create intolerable tensions. The difference is that it also inscribes a rigid, extrapersonal illness framework which imprisons both the family's true acknowledgement of human 'differentness' and the schizophrenic's organismic and structure determined choice and ability to make a self.

CONCLUSION

In presenting these three approaches, a fundamental question is raised: are we talking about the same schizophrenia? We think not, despite the fact that all the cases mentioned had received a diagnosis of schizophrenia. It is clearly not a unitary concept. The woman possessed by the devil, and the woman with the 'sane' husband established a level of functioning socialised enough to allow them to marry and raise children. They were clearly not experiencing the same kind of fragmentation as the 'human beings' with whom Heiner Schuff is working. It may well be argued, as Schuff does, that in those cases, a family therapy aimed at making connections is likely to be either irrelevant or worse, a part of the process maintaining the schizophrenic in their profound disconnection. At higher levels of personal organisation, work aimed at 'interfering' in family patterns which threaten to disrupt more established, though precarious personal functioning, can afford to encourage positive moves away from the disqualification of self engaged in by the schizophrenic person and by those in their context. Further enquiry is called for.

ACKNOWLEDGEMENT

I would like to extend my sincere thanks to my colleagues, Heiner Schuff and Rosine Perelberg for their stimulating ideas and for their generous permission to describe them in this paper.

REFERENCES

Bateson, G., Haley, J., Jackson, D. and Weakland, J., (1962), A note on the double bind, Family Process, Volume 2, No. 1, pp. 154-161.

Dell, P., (1980), Researching the family theories of schizophrenia: An exercise in epistomological confusion, Family Process, Vol. 19, No. 4. pp.321-335.

Killick, K., (1987), M.A. thesis, available from College of Art and Design, St. Albans, Herts.

MacFarlane, W.R., (ed.) (1983), Family Therapy in Schizophrenia, Guildford Press.

Madanes, C., (1980), Prevention of rehospitalisation of adolescents and young adults, Family Process.

Pankow, G., (1976), Dynamic structurisation in schizophrenia in Burton, A. (ed.) Psychotherapy and the Psychoses, Krieger, New York.

Perelberg, R. Familiar and Unfamiliar types of Family Structure: Towards a conceptual framework (to be published).

Family work and the schizophrenic parent

J. WEBSTER

INTRODUCTION

Family oriented treatments are traditionally the province of agencies where the referred 'patient' is a child while adult settings have limited their focus to the referred adult. In the adult psychiatric setting, the usual context in which schizophrenia is treated, the broad purpose of the work might be rehabilitation after a period of hospitalisation. This natural focus on the identified adult patient seldom includes a consideration of the adult patient as parent, although there have been encouraging signs of this in recent years. (Anderson et al, 1986).

This paper will look at the implications of working with a schizophrenic parent, with particular reference to schizophrenic mothers. It may be that the therapists who consider the parenting functioning will be working in different contexts, in agencies that are concerned with children. It is unfortunate that there are few resources which consider both child and adult as referred patients, since such an establishment would be able to consider the sometimes very different needs of parents and children (Cooklin et al, 1983).

FAMILY WORK AND SCHIZOPHRENIA

The emphasis on family work with schizophrenic members, has been with the young unattached adult living with parents

(Leff and Vaughn, 1985; Berkowitz, 1984; Falloon et al, 1984). The task of separating from the family of origin occurs in the first stage of the family life cycle, and is the stage most commonly associated with the onset of schizophrenia. There is now substantial information about family interactions and schizophrenia (Brown, 1962; Vaughn and Leff, 1976; Leff and Vaughn, 1985), which have influenced the form of therapy offered to families with a schizophrenic member. Interventions arising from this research offer information about schizophrenia to families, often as part of the engagement process, in addition to a variety of therapeutic interventions with the family or in groups (Berkowitz, 1984; Falloon, et al, 1984; Leff and Vaughn, 1985).

There is less evidence of work at other stages of the life cycle, although recent attention has been paid to the marital relationship (Anderson et al, 1986). This may be attributed to a lower rate of marriage among schizophrenics (Stevens, 1969), although it may be that the marital relationship is particularly difficult to address with the spouse of a schizophrenic. Dupont et al, 1971 has described the way in which some spouses wish to disassociate themselves from the disturbances of the psychotic episode, when there was a high risk for divorce. By contrast, a few couples have reported improvements in their marital relationship after a psychotic episode! Others have emphasised the need to support the spouse, and to work with both spouse and the schizophrenic patient through different phases of adjustment. After lowering expectations during acute episodes, new adjustments to the 'deficit' role need to be made. Only at a later stage can marital functioning be addressed (Anderson et al, 1986).

At different points in time, attention has been drawn to the plight of the children of the mentally ill. Authors have noted the need to consider the children in their care (e.g. Rutter, 1966). But the care of the sick parent is by professionals with very different orientation from those who may be involved with the care of the children. References in the literature about the need to concentrate on the families of the mentally ill have had little impact despite being available for twenty years (Irvine, 1961; Rice et al, 1971). Research designed to identify the needs of the children has found it necessary to seek out families, since they do not readily ask for help (Rice et al, 1971).

Families of schizophrenics are difficult to engage in treatment interventions (Berkowitz, 1984; Rice et al, 1971) and frequently anticipate blame from professionals (Terkelson, 1983; Jones, 1987). When young adults are still living in their parents' home, the invitation to join in a therapeutic programme may be directed to the parents, who retain some executive responsibility for an adult child in their home. The situation with a schizophrenic parent is different, and the problems may be exacerbated by anxieties about children being removed as the result of poor functioning. Therapeutic approaches that promote heirarchical functioning, i.e. parents caring for and controlling their children, may have limitations at times when it may be more appropriate that another adult takes over the care of the children. Supporting the resumption of responsibility may be best done in closely supervised settings (Cooklin et al, 1983), although in practice, many parents will be expected to resume full care of their children in their own homes from the time of their discharge from hospital.

Why consider children?

Since the peak age of onset of schizophrenia in women is between the ages of twenty four and twenty nine years, (some five years later than the onset of schizophrenia in men, Loranger, 1984), women may well have their first episode of schizophrenia after they have married and had their first child. In fact seventy per cent of women with schizophrenia have been married (Gibbons et al, 1984). This has implications for family work with schizophrenic women, who present at different stages of the family life cycle than that most frequently described (Leff and Vaughn, 1985; Berkowitz, 1984; Falloon et al, 1984; Jones, 1987).

Hafner (1986) emphasises the stresses on a couple in the initial years of marriage, with implications for the onset of schizophrenia. Interventions for the next stages of the family life cycle, which include parenting roles are addressed in this paper.

In a survey of schizophrenics attending one District General Hospital, Gibbons et al (1984) found that in a quarter of the households with a schizophrenic member, there were children under sixteen years, and eight per cent contained children under five years. Little is known about the interactions between a schizophrenic parent and his/her young children in relation to the factors that affect the prognosis of schizophrenia. On the other hand, feelings of incompetence about parenting may contribute to difficulties during a psychotic episode, and may delay recovery. Although some schizophrenic parents will not continue to care for their children, and will be found 'unfit' under the Child Care Act, 1980, these details are poorly recorded and the numbers of such children are not known. Family interventions at this stage of the life cycle may arise from concern about poor parental functioning rather than to influence the course of an episode.

The need to consider the children in the home of a schizophrenic parent may arise from very different positions:
1) The children are potentially at some risk for injury or neglect.
2) The psychological vulnerability of the children arising from difficulty in understanding the changes in their parent.
3) Children may take care of themselves, albeit prematurely, which may have implications for the role of the parent.

Anxieties about the inheritance of schizophrenia, based on misinformation or 'family lore', may colour the way in which a family seeks help for children, or the way in which vulnerable children are perceived within the family. Children identified as being 'difficult' are at risk for emotional problems (Rutter, 1984), but help may not be sought for them because of the denial of anxieties about schizophrenia being 'passed on'.

1) The risk to the children Children of actively psychotic parents may be at considerable risk of injury or neglect. Greger and Hoffmeyer (1969) examined the motives of three women who killed their infants during a psychotic episode. In these cases the killing was associated with the idea of 'the child with them' in a suicide. Winnicott (1961) has argued that there are emotional effects for the child living with a psychotic parent. He distinguishes four categories involving a relationship between developmental stages and parental psychosis: a) Very ill parents, in which case others take over the care of the children and infants; b) Less ill parents, where there are periods during which others take over; c) Those who have sufficient health to protect their children from their illness and ask for help; and d) Those parents who include the child in their illness, so that nothing can be done for the child without violating the rights a parent has over his or her child.

The role of the other parent is crucial in protecting a child at risk, but there is little evidence of the inclusion of husbands/fathers in treatments in adult settings to assess risk. Winnicott's views, though dated, reflect commonly held views of the exclusive relationship between the mother and the child and the lack of consideration for the father. It would be important to know the extent to which he is able to take on the parenting role, and the support he offers his partner.

2) The experience of the child. Anthony (1973) describes two separate kinds of emotional reactions in the children of psychotic parents: a) a sense of alienation, as if of a stranger, with avoidance behaviour, as the parent becomes a different person with bizarre qualities; and b) a sense of abandonment associated with separation anxiety, the child approaches the withdrawn parent without getting responses. He views the child's attempts to be reunited with the well parent as a mourning process, the problem being that the mourning is incomplete, since the parent may be present and there may be a promise of recovery.

The way in which a child or the family will cope depend on many factors, and there is a risk of the whole family withdrawing from social contact (Anthony, 1970). The children are vulnerable, but they may develop survival strategies. The children may 'turn off' the parent and begin to 'mother' themselves. Based on these observations, he moves on to describe a model for intervention aimed at helping the child to have a sense of differentiation of the self (Anthony, 1974).

The vulnerability of the child, as portrayed by Winnicott and Anthony, arises from the child's dependence on the adults. In some ways they share the experience of children of divorcing parents, whose emotional needs are neglected at the height of family disruption, and who receive little explanation for the absence of the divorcing parent

(Mitchell, 1985). The disturbances in parental functioning will affect the child's experience of being cared for. The availability of other family members during periods of crisis offers protection from physical injury or harm but the lack of information imparted to families about schizophrenia is likely to result in even more ignorance in children (Leff and Vaughn, 1986).

3) The role within the family. The spontaneous legitimizing of schizophrenia in some families may allow for lowered expectations. The psychoeducational approaches (Anderson et al, 1986) focus on adjusting to a deficit role during acute episodes, and to lowered levels of functioning subsequently, while maintaining an appropriate role within the family.

CONSIDERATIONS FOR TREATMENT

1) The risk to the children

When children of schizophrenic women are under five years of age, there are real concerns about the care of the children. A few women may have had joint admissions to a Mother and Baby unit (although these tend to be women with chronic schizophrenia who will have their babies cared for by the Local Authority on discharge, Margison, 1982). but this resource is not available for even only slightly older children. Cooklin et al (1983) describes a Family Day Unit which addressed the parenting problems of psychotic parents, together with their children. With this group of families joint care is desirable for different reasons. The care of the children needs to be monitored; and women may well require support and help during this stage of recovery when their capacity to attend to the emotional needs of young children may be erratic, or dulled. Whilst the very young infants may be most vulnerable because of their dependence on adults for all their needs to be met, children of any age may be at risk of injury during psychotic episodes.

Case illustration: A single woman with a three year old child was referred for family assessment, after she had physically abused the child while her social worker was on holiday. The child was removed to a foster family. During the assessment it was observed that the child had been in a nursery from the mother's first hospital admission when he was a few months old. Although the mother, who was still in her teens, appeared to be very well supported by the extended family (whom she visited several times a week) and the social worker (who visited weekly), none of these people saw her with her child. Her poor functioning in the maternal role and her difficulties in setting limits for the child were seldom observed.

The extended family was involved in the treatment, when three major issues were addressed: a) Some information was provided about the diagnosis, which reduced some of the criticisms immediately. This allowed an important shift to take place by the father who had previously been very critical of his daughter for allowing the child to go into care. The criteria for the Place of Safety Order were clarified, b) The family was encouraged to continue their support and c) Open communication began to take place, very tentatively at first. Specific requests were now made so that the family support was provided at times when most difficulties in child management were experienced. The family were able to describe, in retrospect, their longstanding anxieties about the child's safety.

In work with abused children there is a need to have access to facilities which enable mother and child to be together, so that the interactions may be observed and the parent may practice new ways of responding to the child.

2) The experience of the child

With school aged children, different issues arise, which relate in part to the level of functioning of the mother, and in part to the impact on the rest of the family. The access to the husband and the children may depend very heavily on the mother's ability/willingness to allow this to take place.

Case illustration: A man was admitted to hospital following very disturbed, violent behaviour within the family. During his admission to hospital, he returned home, still very disturbed, while the mother was out. The children aged seven and eleven were very frightened by this incident. Their mother was quite preoccupied at the time of the admission, with managing the family with the after effects of the psychotic episode, previously having relied on her husband. The family was isolated for various reasons, partly the result of having moved to England recently, in search of a better life. Their extended family was therefore unable to support them.

The younger child was frightened by ideas about the power of his father. The children were seen together by the therapist, to gain their understanding of the psychotic episode, and for them to express their fears. Through the use of genograms ('playing family trees') the children were able to talk about the family they had left behind, and how they would have been supported by them had they been geographically closer. This work helped the children to keep alive the memory of their family, from whom they had begun to feel estranged. In due course their mother became more accessible to them, as she began to deal with the family's future plans, including her divorce from their father.

3) The role within the family

When the schizophrenic parent is perceived by the family to be 'ill', a view that could be supported by frequent admissions to hospital, there are likely to be serious erosions on the parental role. Such families will attempt to preserve such order as is possible, and in doing so, perpetuate the need to do so. The spouse may assume responsibility for running the home, and the children share the tasks usually performed by the psychotic parent. In one parent families the children may find themselves assuming responsibility for obtaining treatment for the psychotic parent, in addition to assuming other roles within the home.

Case illustration: A mother of two young teenage girls, had multiple admissions to hospital. Her constant poor functioning led to the family assuming roles that she had previously performed. In an interview arranged as part of a survey of such families, each of the family members in turn expressed a wish for the mother to be out of the house, with varying levels of intensity. However, they all felt trapped, and would visit her in hospital daily during her lengthy hospital admissions. Divorce had been discussed by the father with the children, who felt guilty about their wish to be rid of their mother, so the family was unable to explore alternatives.

The domestic arrangements were organised around the mother's absence, so that the children were paid their pocket money for the cooking and cleaning. Modern equipment was bought for the convenience of the family, which the mother could not use or found difficult to master. The youngest child understood that her mother would like to resume her role in the family, but did not feel she could give up any of the tasks assigned to her without getting into trouble from her father.

This family declined the offer of help, and change is likely to be precipitated by the next stage in the family cycle: when the children plan to leave home, or when their (premature) independence allows their father to consider his own future without his wife.

CONCLUSION: CONSIDERING THE FAMILY

With the developments in family focussed work in schizophrenia, and the growth of community based centres, there is a need to develop therapeutic interventions for the families with children. The goals of treatment may be either to do with the course of the parent's episode, or because of real concern for the safety of the children. It may well be that the children play an important protective role with schizophrenic mothers, in a similar manner to the way in which marriage is a protective factor.

Children's vulnerability during a parent's schizophrenic episode results from the chaos and disturbance of the family at the time and from their lack of understanding of the psychotic process, particularly when they are very young and dependent on their mothers. The availability of a father/husband reduces some of the disruption for children, but a father may find it difficult to deal with his own reactions to the psychotic episode as well as attend to the needs of the children. Family interventions with schizophrenic parents need to include the children if the full extent of the problems are to be recognised, and for mothers to receive appropriate support when they most need it.

REFERENCES

Anderson, C.M., Reiss, D.J. and Cahalane, J.F., (1986), Marital therapy with schizophrenic patients in Jacobson, N.J. and Gurman, A.S. (eds.) Clinical Handbook of Marital Therapy, Guildford Press, New York.

Anthony, E.J., (1970), The impact of mental and physical illness on the fmaily life, American Journal of Psychiatry, 138-146.

Anthony, E.J., (1973), Mourning and psychic loss of the parent in Anthony, E.J., Koupernick, C. (eds.) The Child and His Family: Children at Psychiatric Risk, Vol. 3, John Wiley and Sons, New York.

Anthony, E.J., (1974), The syndrome of the psychologically vulnerable child in Anthony, A.J. and Koupernick, C., The Child and his Family: Children at Psychiatric Risk Vol. 3, J. Witney & Sons, New York.

Berkowitz, R., (1984), Therapeutic intervention with schizophrenic patients and their families: A decription of clinical research project, Journal of Family Therapy, 6, 211-234.

Brown, G.W., Monck, E.M., Carstairs, G.M. and Wing, J.K., (1962), Influence of family life on the course of schizophrenic illness, British Journal of Preventive and Social Medicine, 16, 55-68/

Cooklin, A., Miller, A.C. and McHugh, B., (1983), An institution for change: Developing a family day unit, Family Process, 22, 453-468.

Dupont, R.L., Ryder, R.G. and Grunebaum, H.L., (1971), An unexpected result of psychosis in marriage, American Journal of Psychiatry, 128(6), 91-95.

Falloon, I.R.H., Boyd, J.L. and McGill, C.W., (1984), Family Care of Schizophrenia, Guildford Press, New York.

Gibbons, J.S., Horn, S.H., Powell, J.M. and Gibbons, J.L., (1984), Schizophrenic patients and their families: A survey in a psychiatric service based on a D.G.H. Unit, British Journal of Psychiatry, 144, 70-77.

Greger, J. and Hoffmeyer, O., (1969), Murder of several children by schizophrenic mothers, Psychiatrica Clinica 2, 14-24.

Hafner, J., (1986), Marriage and Mental Illness, Guildford Press, New York.

Irvine, E.E., (1961), Psychosis in parents: Mental illness as a problem for the family, British Journal of Social Work, VI, 21-26.

Jones, E., (1987), Brief systemic work in psychiatric settings where a family member has been diagnosed as schizophrenic, Journal of Family Therapy, 9, 3-26.

Loranger, A.W., (1984), Sex differences at age of onset of schizophrenia, Archives of General Psychiatry, 41, 157-161.

Leff, J. and Vaughn, C., (1985), Expressed Emotion In

Families, Guildford Press, New York.
Margison, F. and Brockington, I., (1982), Psychiatric mother and baby units in, Brockington, I. and Kumar, R. (eds.) Motherhood and Mental Illness, Academic Press, London.
Mitchell, A., (1985), Children In The Middle: Living Through Divorce, Social Science Publications, London.
Rice, E.P., Ekdahl, M.C. and Miller, M., (1971), Children of the Mentally Ill: Problems in child care, Behavioural Publications, New York.
Rutter, M., (1966), Children of Sick Parents, Oxford University Press, London.
Rutter, M. and Quinton, D., (1984), Parental psychiatric disorder: Effects on children, Psychological Medicine 14, 853-880.
Stevens, B., (1969), Marrige and Fertility of Women Suffering From Schizophrenia and Affective Disorders Oxford University Press, London.
Terkelson, K. G., (1983), Schizophrenia and the family: II Adverse effects of family therapy, Family Process, 22, 191-200.
Vaughn, C and Leff, J, (1976), The influence of family and social factors on the course of psychiatric illness, British Journal of Psychiatry, 129, 125-237.
Winnicott, D.W., (1961), The effect of psychotic parents on the emotional development of the child, British Journal of Psychiatric Social Work, VI, 13-20.

PART V
EMPOWERING THE CLIENT

Editor's note

For several reasons the following chapter proved to be exceptionally difficult to edit. Over the past few years the topics on which papers are invited have invariably been both clearly defined and circumscribed. Even if not necessarily tangible, the subjects described in the chapter titles focus on an aspect of clinical psychology of some familiarity and the papers within a chapter display quite strong and apparent connections.

The Albert Chambwe Memorial Symposium did not respect this tradition. The editors were faced with papers of enormous variation of subject matter, style and length and it was sometimes difficult to distinguish the eulogic from the actual subject of the paper. This may sound like an excuse for a job poorly done, although it should only be regarded in part as such. In fact it was through editorial doubt and difficulty that the editors came to feel in a position to write a short introduction to this chapter.

What became apparent was that at least part of the difficulty was a result of the fact that the real subject of the chapter is the man Albert Chambwe. He was not a famous psychologist in this country (although of considerable renown in Zimbabwe) and neither of the editors knew him. He trained in clinical psychology at Liverpool University and then returned to Zimbabwe taking with him and using the skills he had acquired. He died after a hemi hepatectomy in May 1985 having been appointed Dean of Students at the University of

Zimbabwe only the previous year.

How can Albert Chambwe be regarded in Britain as anything more than a transient figure with commitments to a distant country and career, certainly with no time to contribute to 'British clinical psychology'? Perhaps to answer this question one would have to have known the man himself, but without knowing him, simply by reading the following chapter, one can see that his contribution to psychology in this country was both very real (although certainly not traditional) and has continued beyond his death.

The existance and contents of this memorial chapter prove that although not a famous man, he was enormously influential. Anyone can 'believe' in empowering clients, yet Albert apparently did so in such a way that his energy and commitment to this belief powerfully influenced others. Years after their quite short contact with him, his peers still share a perspective on their remarkably diverse fields which they all attribute to Albert Chambwe. What more appropriate memorial could there be?

David Glasgow
Nadine Eisenberg

Empowering the client? In 1987?

R. WARBURG

INTRODUCTION

I want to start with a bit of recent history. Since the meeting that five of us had earlier this year where we planned this symposium, I have been thinking off and on, latterly more on than off, about what I was going to say today. It seemed to be coming together reasonably well in my mind, so last week I faced the task of writing it down. I had two train journeys that week, so there was the time to do it. It was a lot more difficult than I expected, but as the London train pulled into Piccadilly station, I finished it. The next day I got it out and re-read it. It was awful. Worthy, pompous, and utterly unconvincing. Panic. The only thing to do was to re-write it completely on my research day this week when I again had uninterrupted time. I wrote diligently all day with short breaks for other business and coffee. The result was not quite so bad, but what trouble I had with the conclusions. What moral, what inspiration for the future was I going to draw from the great man's life? Cycling back from the University, struggling with this question, I suddenly had an image of Albert. I choose the word 'image' deliberately, I do not believe in the afterlife or the supernatural. 'Richard', he said. 'Hey, man, you're taking this too seriously'. He was right.

Thinking about it later, I realised that what I had done was very much in the form of a Psychological Report. All I needed was Albert's WAIS scores and it could take its place with the others in my filing cabinet. It is galling, but salutory to realise that the only literary form you are capable of is the psychological report or journal article. There are serious dangers in mistaking for reality the ways we describe, classify and measure human existence.

So I am determined to try to break out of this way of thinking, at least a bit. How successful I will be is for you to judge. But this paper will have no conclusions, observations will be unashamedly personal and selective, and I can promise you there will be at least a moderate degree of bias.

So now to Albert. I have many fragmentary memories of him: his voice, his smile, his mock humility at times 'Please, please...' or 'But, but ...' he would say, lifting a finger like a timid schoolboy, when he really disagreed with something and wanted to smash it. His way of bullshitting out of trouble, slightly evasive answers to questions, and if that didn't work, to sit there mute with a seraphic smile and shakes of the head. His ability to communicate. I found teaching medical students an uphill struggle and a chore. We parted at the end of the statutory hour with mutual relief. Often when I went to find Albert afterwards, his lot of students would still be there, asking questions, unwilling to leave.

So there are a great many things that we could remember Albert for, and I hope we will today in our various ways. I want to draw out one part of my memories, which will require a bit of further explanation.

One of the earliest memories I have of him is a conversation shortly after we began our course in 1979. I had followed the General Election of that year and its aftermath quite closely, and prided myself on my understanding of the issues at that time. The night before this conversation I had been watching speeches on TV from the TUC Annual Conference. Something one of the union leaders had said (I forget which) seemed to herald a serious selling out of a large section of that union's membership. I said as much to Albert, not really expecting he'd be particularly interested, given that he was both a psychologist and from overseas, both of which would make me expect a disinterest in internal trade union politics. But he had seen the speech, was interested, and had in fact thought about the whole thing a lot more deeply than I had. This was the first of many occasions where I was to realise his knowledge and understanding of politics and power relationships, and his ability to relate and integrate very disparate sources of information in his understanding of the world.

Switch now to my last memories of him. He made two brief stopovers here on his way back from international conferences. The first time I met him he was still working for the Ministry of Health. Not tucked away in the basement somewhere, either. Meetings with ministers, travelling to health centres around the country, developing national curricula for psychology and nursing, and I forget what else besides. And this at a time when I (and I suspect some others of our year) was afraid to say 'Boo' too loudly to a consultant for fear of prematurely aborting the career I had struggled so hard to attain.

A letter arrives. He has moved to the University of Harare, student counselling service. Typical Albert, he doesn't say why. Still, I think, 'That's cut you down to size a bit, my friend. You can be a proper psychologist like the rest of us for a while'.

A few months later, Albert is over again. We meet. 'Student counselling service alright for you?' I ask. It turns out he's been promoted. He's Dean of Students, with responsibility for the overall welfare of the whole student body, directly answerable to the Vice-Chancellor. I can now say 'Boo' to a Consultant and feel that life will carry on afterwards, but I think I'm doing well to organise a study day for local psychologists. He has organised a series of televised debates between government ministers and students at the University. Quite an amazing man.

How did he do this? I don't really know, and the two 'psychological reports' I have written don't really help me. (Do they ever?) I can only try to grope with a very limited understanding and for the rest to acknowledge that there was a lot about Albert that we never really knew.

Albert had to struggle for his education in a way that certainly I, and I suspect most of us here, never had to. The eulogy delivered by the Vice-Chancellor of the University of Harare after his death in May 1985 records how (aged seventeen) he was forced to withdraw, along with all the other African students from Bulawayo Technical College 'on some technicality which was typical of those oppressive times'. He came to this country in 1970, and obtained the SRN certificate in 1974, and in 1976 got the certificate in Psychiatric Nursing, 'A' Levels, and completed the Open University foundation course, from whence he went to Sussex University.

Throughout this time, he was also involved in the Zimbabwean liberation struggle. I don't know a lot about the nature of his involvement, for Albert never said a great deal about it. I presumed for reasons of security, and I didn't want to press him.

So I imagine that from these joint struggles, both for his own personal development and his country's liberation, (I am sure he did not see them as separate, but as two aspects of the same thing), Albert had to draw upon, and develop, resources, skills, and a level of political understanding that most of us do not achieve. His career when he returned home was in this sense a natural extension of his career here. It is tragic that it was ended so prematurely.

When we met to plan this symposium, there seemed to be a general agreement almost as soon as it was suggested that 'empowering the client' would be an appropriate title and theme. The dictionary that Albert left behind, with me, because it was too heavy for the plane, defines 'empower' as 'To give power to' or 'To give a person capacity, enable, to perform some physical or mental activity'. In a psychological context, the mental activity in question is, I think, to make choices or decisions. Defining 'the client' is potentially more problematic: who is the client? The individual referred to us for treatment? His or her family? Or increasingly these days, the overall system by which services are provided to particular client groups? Or the potential client, the one who needs and could benefit from services we provide, but does not get past the gatekeeper to the services. Or who perhaps does not even know the gate exists? So 'empowering the client' could mean a wide range of things depending on the definition of clients. It could mean individual work of a particular type, with clients, family or group work; working to change the system; health promotion; or public education. Indeed, all these aspects of work seem to be represented in this symposium today. Looked at this way, almost any activity that clinical psychologists undertake could arguable be seen as 'empowering the client'. If this is so, then what is all the fuss about? The title of this symposium could equally be 'Clinical Psychology in the late Eighties' or 'What wonderful things psychologists do'.

So what is special about the notion of 'empowering the client'? For me, as I think it would have been for Albert, it is because it has a political dimension to it. This is not to say there is not a professional, psychological aspect to it as well, clearly there is a need to try to develop in 'the client' certain skills of decision making, information gathering and so on so that they may develop and exercise an ability to choose among different possibilities and to generate options for their life where previously none existed. This presupposes that real, positive choices do exist, or can be brought into existence, and the difficulty that faces us in 1987 is that, despite the Government's rhetoric about freedom and choice, positive options (in the sense of choices that are in some way better than their current situation) are diminishing, rather than increasing for a large proportion of our clients.

The health district in which I work, for example, faces a cut in revenue in cash terms over the next few years. Manchester City Council has been ratecapped, and faces a shortfall in revenue of about 100 million in this financial year. Inevitably, there will be severe cuts in health and social services, housing, and leisure and occupational facilities.

To concentrate on the technical or psychological aspects of empowering the client in these circumstances could, I think, be a betrayal of their real interests. It hardly makes sense to talk of 'empowering the client' or 'enabling them to make choices' if the ultimate choice is between the Salvation Army Hostel and a grubby private boarding house, or between hanging about the railway station all day or looking at the shops in the Arndale Centre.

In addition to the psychological techniques and the existence of positive choices, there are other necessary conditions if we are to truly empower the client. One of these is that our primary identification should be with the client, not with a bureaucracy, management structure, or professional associaton. To a degree, I think clinical psychologists have a reasonable record here. Many of us were influenced by ideas in the more optimistic times of the late sixties and early seventies, the anti-psychiatry movement, the women's movement, liberation struggles in various countries, anti-war and anti-nuclear organisations, and so on.

In general, psychologists have taken a leading role in a critique of the medical model with its tendencies to label and stereotype people, to reify and decontextualise behaviour, and its use as a means of social control. Now the worst excesses of behaviourism have been overcome, psychologists generally tend to view a person as a whole, and to see behaviour in relation to the social context in which it occurs. So in terms of experience, attitudes and training, there is the basis of a positive identification with 'the client'. However, this is not the whole story. As Clinical Psychology as a profession develops from its traditional role of assessment and treatment of individual clients to a greater involvement with service development, psychology's agenda for change becomes intermixed and entangled with the government's agenda for change. The former is based at least in part on the idea of increased self-determination and independence for the client, the latter motivated to a very significant degree by intentions of cost cutting and privatisation. It is hard to disagree with the desirability of more effective and efficient use of resources, improved planning and monitoring of services, greater accountability (which are the sweeteners on the government's introduction of general management), and clinical budgetting, Korner information, performance review and the rest of the recent barrage of changes in the health service. However, it is clear that what the professions mean by, say, effectiveness is very different from what the government means. Is an effective service one in which bed occupancy is high and turnover fast, or one in which the patient is satisfactorily rehabilitated?

The danger of course is that by attempting to embrace some parts of the package, for example, evaluation of treatment outcomes, psychologists have traditionally and rightly been concerned that they will become lumbered with the less acceptable parts. This includes the introduction of competition and competitive tendering for services, or clinical budgetting in all its inglory, where service users (i.e. doctors) 'purchase' (and inevitably determine) services from other professional groups. The notion of competition to provide services between groups where inter-professional rivalry is already excessive raises horrendous visions of corruption and patronage, and a struggle to 'sell' professional services at the expense of rival professionals. In these circumstances, multi-disciplinary teamwork and the vision of the client as a whole person must inevitably disappear, and the services provided become those which can be 'accurately' weighed, measured and determined services which in general are 'given or done to' a client, quite the opposite of a joint exercise in decision-making.

A further condition for successful empowerment work is that the climate in which the work is done should be right. Not that one can expect unconditional positive regard from everyone with whom the client comes into contact, far from it, but there should be some reason to believe that the climate of opinion is turning, or can be made to turn, the client's way. Otherwise, one may run the danger of using one's clients simply as cannon fodder for pre-formed ideas of the way things should be.

What is the situation in 1987? It is undeniable that 'community care' in a very general sense is fashionable. My instincts usually tell me that whatever the government (of whatever political persuasion) is in favour of should be regarded with the greatest suspicion. My feeling is that 'community care' in its present under-resourced, over-hasty and ill-planned form will fail, and will inevitably have the effect of filling prisons, hostels, private boarding houses and flop houses with the deprived, the depressed and the demented. In the present climate of reaction and intolerance of deviance, this will lead to further demands for containment and repression of these 'social misfits'. Psychologists, along with other professionals, will be called upon to supply their expertise as agents of social control in privatised institutions of correction and containment.

This may be (I hope it is) an overly pessimistic view, but the Marxist dictum 'History tends to repeat itself: the first time as tragedy, the second time as farce', is probably as applicable here as elsewhere, and the way out of the circle is certainly not clear to me at present. But if we are to break out, we will need people with the breadth of vision and the commitment of Albert Chambwe. If his death seems a great loss to us, how much greater a loss must it be to his own family and country.

But despite my sadness at the realisation that I will never see him again, I am so very glad to have known Albert, for the time that I did. To me, he was someone who instinctively and unswervingly bore in mind the interests of 'the client', in its broadest sense of people who are oppressed, disadvantaged, or handicapped by oppressive social structures, and who dedicated his life to opposition to such structures by every means at his disposal. Although he is tragically no longer with us in person, he will not be forgotten.

Teaching mentally handicapped people to make a choice

K. NG AND F. KENNEDY

INTRODUCTION

It is difficult to imagine what life would be like if one was entirely unable to make choices. By 'making choices' we are referring to a complex activity which seems to be an essential part of acquiring and maintaining some degree of control over one's environment, of interacting with the world rather than reacting to it. A person without such control would be unable, cognitively, to progress past the sensorimotor period (Hogg and Sebba, 1986). In terms of development of a self, that unique 'I' which is considered by many to be the essence of being human would surely never emerge. Competence, 'knowing how' rather than 'knowing that' (Connolly and Bruner, 1974) would not be acquired. 'Incompetent' would be an accurate, if pejorative, description of such a person.

A first search for component skills which are necessary for the successful making of a choice yields the following:

a) A certain amount of previous experience and knowledge

b) Perception (anticipation) of a range of possible responses to a given situation.

c) Anticipation of the consequences of making each response, involving the activation of existing knowledge.

d) A system of values.

e) Ability to compare alternative responses in view of anticipated consequences and their 'goodness' or 'badness' as valued by the individual.

f) The ability to act on the decision reached.

Most non-handicapped individuals, according to Slovic (1972) and Hogarth (1975) make suboptimal decisions due to limited memory, attention and reasoning capacities. For the individual with a mental handicap, these limitations also apply, along with a host of others. Significant amongst these are lack of opportunity to make choices, lack of motivation and punishing consequences as a result of making choices.

The following account divides factors affecting choice making by a person with a mental handicap into three categories: 'primary disenabling' factors; 'secondary disenabling' factors; probable consequences of choice making behaviour.

'Primary disenabling' factors

Intellectual disability, the condition which, we presume, has earned the individual that dreadful title 'mentally handicapped' comes in so many varieties it is impossible to generalise about its effects. In and of itself it usually means experiences of failure for the person affected. Additional handicaps or sensory impairments such as visual or auditory deficits, physical or motor disabilities such as cerebral palsy or epilepsy increase the problem enormously. These 'primary disabilities' very often result in communication problems, a much greater than average failure to achieve desired aims and can lead the individual to experience the world as essentially uncontrollable (Brinkler and Lewis, 1982). Experience of lack of control leads to a declining motivation to try to exercise control or express choices. This learned helplessness along with the original disability means that the number of opportunities to express choice is greatly reduced. As a result, choice making skills are not learnt. Without such skills, as discussed in the introduction, development in all areas of competence is severely impeded, thus exacerbating the initial, 'primary disabilities'.

'Secondary disenabling' factors

Turning to the social and emotional experiences of people with a mental handicap we find the situation worsens. The label of mental handicap is itself a certificate of incompetence. It is difficult to imagine how one might accept such a label and simultaneously retain one's self esteem (Edgerton, 1967). In reality, one's competence is generally underestimated by others and by oneself. Experiences of failure as mentioned above, contribute to this negative self perception and also to a fear of the consequences of failure.

Social deprivation can exist in the institution or in the home. Experiences of being 'done for' and 'seen to' rather than acting for oneself are commonplace. Growing up in such an environment leads an individual to assume that this is the way of the world and that there are always others who will take the decisions. We see people with a mental handicap often engaged in an active search for other people to make decisions and choices for them (although it should be noted that this behaviour is by no means confined to this group!). Learning to look for other people to do it for you is one way of escaping from or avoiding choice making situations. Fear of failure is another factor contributing to escape/avoidance behaviour, and takes a multitude of forms. Choices may be made abruptly, with apparently no attention to the options presented; at random or governed by simple rules, such as 'always choose the first or last option'; straghtforward refusal to choose or, the person may structure life in such a rigid way that options almost never arise. Escape/avoidance behaviour means, of course, that opportunities to choose are reduced greatly and that choice making skills are not learned. This increases the effects of social deprivation and confirms the individual and society at large, in the opinion that the label 'incompetent' is indeed accurate.

Probable consequences of choice making behaviour

The essence of choice making is that it is an expression of self, an exercise of will. Simple acts like choosing one's own breakfast cereal can throw an institutional regime into chaos. For example, the cook may be adamant that no resident be allowed in the kitchen; the domestic staff see cereal spilled and trampled on the floor; the manager is worred that it contravenes Health and Safety regulations and creates a 'precedent'. More vital choices, like choosing a sexual partner or learning to drive a car, can have devastating effects on parents, professional carers and society at large. The drive for normalization is directed towards changing these very phenomena and holds firm to the belief that attitude changes will follow. For the present, however, punishing consequences as a result of parental, professional or societal attitude can be severe, with the consequences that a decrease in choice making behaviour occurs and is maintained while the punishment contingencies are perceived to remain. This process is likely to handicap the individual further and have secondary consequences all of which are detrimental to the person. Extreme expressions of such consequences include the phenomena labelled as behaviour disorders including challenging behaviour, self injurious behaviour, bizarre behaviour or psychotic episodes, the re-establishment of escape/avoidance behaviour or a withdrawal into learned helplessness and depression. Surprisingly often, however, the positively reinforcing consequences outweigh the effects of punishment. In addition to the reinforcement intrinsic to the chosen course of action, social reinforcement occurs originating from peers, care staff or parents and siblings. This is obviously very important and empowering, for in the face of all the handicapping factors and aversive consequences discussed above, people with a mental handicap are increasingly making their own decisions and developing their 'selves' with a determination we can only envy.

IMPLICATIONS FOR INTERVENTIONS

These analyses suggest a broad range of possible interventions which could contribute towards enabling people with a mental handicap to exercise choice including: the amelioration of primary disenabling conditions; deinstitutionalization; consciousness raising for all members of society (including people with a mental handicap) as to the nature handicap, the problems it presents and the strengths possessed by those affected; provision of opportunity to make choices and helping people to acquire all the necessary skills.

Whilst acknowledging that all of these are vital, it is intended to focus on the last mentioned intervention. The reason for this is that although progress in other areas is apparent, a systematic method for teaching choice making skills has not developed. In the following section the beginning of such a teaching method is presented.

Decision analysis - the state of the art

The method of intervention to be presented is called Decision Analysis. It is a practical approach based on the normative models of behavioural decision theory. It is already widely used in business and management (e.g. Metheson, 1970), in industry (Pessemier, 1966), in military settings (see Brown et al, 1974) and more recently in the clinical setting (e.g. Emerson et al, 1974).

In decision analysis, the decision maker is assumed to have a number of choice alternatives or options, from which an optimal choice can be made. What the decision maker has to do is to evaluate systematically the consequences associated with the perceived choice alternatives. The basis for deciding an optimal choice is determined by the axiomatic principles of Subjective Expected Utility Theory. The axioms of the theory are relatively straightforward and uncontroversial. For example, one axiom, called 'transitivity' states that if you prefer outcome A to B and also prefer outcome B to C, then you should prefer outcome A to C. (For a more detailed review of the axiom system underlying Subjected Expected Utility, see Edwards, Lindamn and Phillips, 1966).

The procedure of the decision analytic technique usually involves a number of logical steps, which can be describes as follows:

a) <u>Drawing</u> <u>a</u> <u>decison</u> <u>tree</u>. The first step is to reduce the complexity of the decision problem into a number of manageable components. This involves drawing a decison tree in which the perceived choice alternatives and their consequences are represented. The essence of this procedure is to 'force' the decision maker to define the problem clearly, by specifying all the feasible choice alternatives and consequences.

b) Evaluating risks and payoffs. The next task a decision maker has to do is to evaluate the relative risks and payoffs of the consequences associated with each perceived choice. The payoffs (or risks) are often expressed in terms of subjective utility values, although in some instances, (e.g. in business) they can be represented in concrete monetary terms.

c) Assessing uncertainty. At this stage, the decision maker has to evaluate his/her degree of belief that the outcome events will occur. In decision analysis, it is assumed that uncertainty can be quantified in measurable probabilistic terms, either in terms of objective frequency or in subjective probability.

d) Determining the optimal choice. Having quantified his/her opinion regarding the risks and uncertainties, the decision maker is required to calculate the expected utility value of each choice alternative by combining (multiplying) the estimated probability and payoff of each outcome event. By trading off the relative expected utility value of each perceived choice, all the alternatives will be eventually eliminated except the alternative with the maximum expected utility value.

An example of a real life decision problem

The application of decision analysis to a real life decision problem can be illustrated by the following situation. Imagine one Saturday morning an individual has to decide whether to spend the day going picnicing or staying at home to do the housework. The weather, however, looks uncertain even though the sun is out at present. If the weather is sunny, the individual would rather go picnicking with a friend but if it rains, staying at home would be the preferred choice.

Figure 1 is a decision analytic representation of the decision problem. The decision tree shows that there are two possible courses of action: go picnicing or stay at home. For each course of action there are three possible outcomes: the weather may stay sunny, or it may rain, or it may be overcast but not rain.

The first task the individual has to do is to estimate the probabilities of these outcomes (P1, P2, P3 for sunny, overcast and rainy respectively). Given the probability estimates, the individual is required to assign appropriate subjective payoffs in numerical terms for each outcome (A1 to 6). With the probability estimates and the individual's

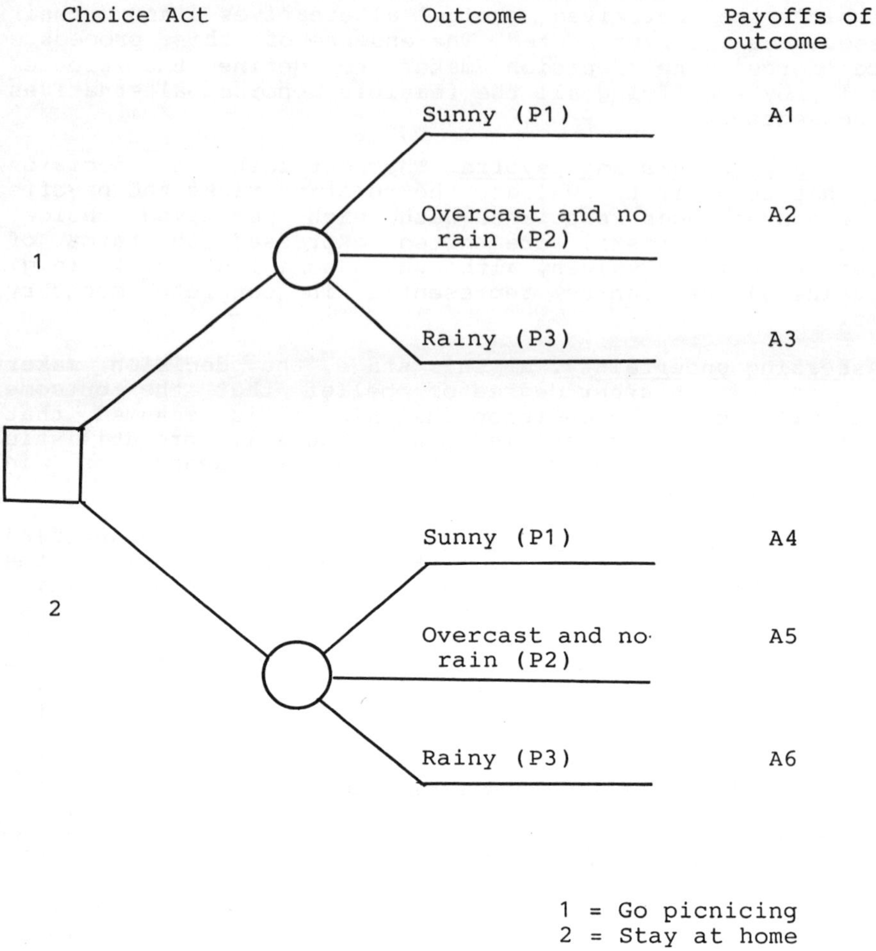

If expected utility of going picnicing > Staying at home, then choose picnicing

If expected utility of staying at home > Going picnicing, then stay at home

Figure 1. A decision analytic representation of a real life problem subjective payoffs, it is possible to caluclate the expected utility value for each course of action. The course with the highest expected utility should therefore be the logical choice for the individual.

TOWARDS DEVELOPING A BEHAVIOURAL PROCEDURE FOR PEOPLE WITH A MENTAL HANDICAP

Clearly, decision analysis is potentially a useful tool for teaching people with mental handicap how to make choices rationally. However, in its present form, the procedure can be rather complicated even for the 'sophisticated' decision maker (Phillips, 1983). Yet, so far, there is frustratingly little information in decision research on how the technology can be translated to aid 'unsophisticated' and 'untrained' people (Beach et al, 1976). In terms of work with people with a mental handicap, we have yet to discover any research in this area.

The task is, therefore, to develop a behavioural decision procedure that would be appropriate for work with people with a mental handicap. Bearing in mind the primary and secondary disenabling factors as discussed above, there are several major considerations in the design of our procedure:

a) It would have to capture the essence of the decision analytic approach, i.e. structuring the decision problem into separable components of perceived options and consequences (the wisdom of which is clear from literature Winkler and Murphy, 1973).

b) It would have to be flexible enough to accommodate varying degrees of abilities and disabilities. Visual or pictorial cues may have to be used to increase the saliency of the decision tree.

c) It would have to be relevant to the individual's knowledge and values.

d) It would have to be non-threatening and enjoyable, if possible, in order to reduce escape or avoidance behaviour.

e) Complicated procedures, such as quantifying uncertainty and risk, would have to be simplified where possible.

The problem of expressing risk and uncertainty.

One major problem in the development of a procedure has been how risk or uncertainty should be communicated. In formal decision analysis they are required to be quantified in measurable probabilistic terms, which are regarded as a prime input for optimal choice making (Raiffa, 1968). The ability to elicit and assess correct probability estimates is therefore a crucial process. However, most subjective opinions on risk and uncertainty are often not measurable

(Knight, 1921). Moreover, it is commonly acknowledged that people in general do not think or communicate in numerical probabilistic terms. Thus, despite the availability of many elegant methods for quantifying uncertainties, many people still prefer to express themselves verbally and non-numerically (Budescu and Wallesten, 1987). It has also been suggested that numerical probability estimates are not always superior to non-numerical expressions. In fact, recent research has shown that probability assessments are prone to heuristic biases (Tversky and Kahneman, 1974), cultural and subcultural effects (Wright and Phillips, 1979; Wright et al, 1978), and unstable ephemeral influences (Howell and Burnett, 1978). These would often result in inaccuracies (Lichtenstein et al, 1977, 1982) inconsistencies (Winkler, 1967), and unreliability (Wallesten, 1983); the more vague and uncertain the information, the poorer the probability assessment (Einhorn and Hogarth, 1985).

To quote from a committee of the US National Research Council:

> (there is an) important responsibility not to use numbers, which convey the impression of precision, when the understanding of relationships is indeed less secure. Thus, while quantitative risk assessment facilitates comparison, such comparison may be illusory or misleading if the use of precise numbers is unjustified:
>
> National Research Council, 1981, p 15

With these views in mind, it is our contention that probabilistic information can be processed optimally using non-numerical means. For simple day to day decision problems, most people would understand and respond better if information is presented in verbal rather than numerical form. Indeed, as Zimmer (1983) has pointed out,

> it was not until the 17th century that probability concepts were formally developed yet expressions for different degrees of uncertainty existed long before then...
>
> cf Budescu and Wallesten, 1987.

In view of the intellectual and cognitive difficulties that may be experienced by people with a mental handicap, we feel it would be better to have a simplified procedure using non-numerical means to both assess and express probability and risk.

A FEASIBILITY STUDY

In order to evaluate the feasibility of our method, the evolved procedure will be described and illustrated with a case study. The subject of our case study, M. was a twenty seven year old man with an estimated I.Q. of sixty. He could not read or write except to recognise a few simple words. However, in spite of a speech difficulty, he could count reasonably well but was unable to handle simple additions and subtractions. Likewise, he was unable to handle simple financial transactions although he could discriminate the value of money of different denominations.

The decision problem M faced was whether or not he should regulate his spending and save money as he tended to spend more than he received from his weekly supplementary benefits. Most of his money was spent on C B radio components, stereo equipment and records. His mother understandably felt that he had been squandering his money and this had been a source of conflict between M and his family particularly when his demand for more money was not being met.

Method of intervention

Step 1 Eliciting knowledge: our first task was to elicit information from M and his family in respect of his choice problem: whether or not to control his spending. This was done during two separate interview sessions. The information obtained from the interview was transcribed onto index cards; each card represented a statement of an event relating to his choice problem. Two decks of cards were constructed: the first deck contained possible choice alternatives; the second were outcome events associated with the choice alternatives. As M was unable to read, visual and pictorial cues were used to assist him in understanding the meaning of each card e.g. a picture of Tower Bridge represented the statement of going to London.

Step 2 Clarifying choice alternatives: M was presented with the first deck of cards (option cards), which consisted of a number of possible courses of action in relation to controlling his spending. He was asked to study the cards closely and any card (i.e. option statement) deemed inappropriate or unclear was discussed, modified or eliminated if necessary. When this was completed a final deck of 'option' cards evolved. He was asked to study them again and to familiarize himself with all the available options.

Step 3 Card sorting, matching outcomes to options: At this stage, M was presented with the second deck of cards, the 'outcome' deck. Each card contained a brief description of a consequence. Once again, pictorial cues were used to facilitate M's understanding of the statements on each card. The cards were presented to M one at a time and after he had studied each card, he was required to match the 'outcome' card to one of the 'option' cards. The result of this procedure was a hierarchy of choice alternatives and outcomes. This hierarchy served the same function as a decision tree representing available options and the individual's perception of the likelihood of respective outcomes. Table 1 gives the hierarchy which evolved from our work with M.

Step 4 Evaluating payoffs: A simple procedure was devised in which M indicated his subjective payoff value for each card with 'ticks' or 'crosses'. (Red tick to indicate positive value, red being his favourite colour; and a black cross to denote negative value with black being his least preferred colour). The relative strength of the payoff value was represented by the number of 'ticks' or 'crosses' assigned with three red ticks indicating maximum positive value and three black crosses to indicate maximum negative value.

Step 5 Determining the optiminal choice: This was done by calculating the total expected utility associated with each choice alternative. The complicated multiplication procedure used in decision analysis was replaced with a simple additive rule. What M had to do was simply count the total number of 'ticks' and 'crosses' for each choice alternative. The preferred choice was then determined by the choice with the most number of 'ticks' and the 'least' number of 'crosses'.

The result of our case study was encouraging, with M showing little difficulty in using our 'simplified' procedure. Further details of the result are presented on table 1.

CONCLUSION

The present paper argues that even in its simplified form, the decision analytic approach can provide a coherent and didactic framework for aiding people with a mental handicap to make choices rationally. The significance of the approach is that it imposes a logical structure upon the individual's choice behaviour. Through its step by step approach, it 'forces' the individual to consider the pros and cons of all the available options. Furthermore, by bringing the important issues of the choice problem into focus, it makes explicit the usually implicit process of choice making, thereby enabling the individual to 'see' the logical implications of the chosen behaviour.

Finally, a note of caution: the structure of a decision problem, if inappropriately presented or 'framed', can strongly influence or bias the judgement of the individual (Tversky and Kahneman, 1981). To this end, more investigation and refinement of our procedure is required before a satisfactory format is established. The present paper, we hope, will provide the first step towards enabling people with a mental handicap to take control of their own lives through the making of rational choices.

Table 1

M 's Decision hierarchy of options and outcomes

Decision Problem — To save or not to save

Options	1. Mother to control spending	2. Save £5 weekly in building society	3. Save nothing
Outcomes	Being controlled by Mum XX	A chance to visit London ///	have more CB radio and stereo equipment //
	More arguments with Mum XXX	A chance to visit Llandudno ///	More rows with Mum XXX
	May upset elder Brother XX	Little chance of extra CB radio and stereo XX	May upset elder brother XX
	Good chance to visit London ///	Fewer rows with Mum //	No London trip XXX
	Good chance to visit Llandudno ///	Unlikely to upset brother /	No Llandudno trip XX
	Money saved in Mum's account X	Money saved in own account /	No saving X

Total Expected Utility of Option 1
(Mother to control spending) = 6 ticks (/) and 8 crosses

Total Expected Utility of Option 2
(Save £5 weekly) = 10 ticks and 2 crosses

Total Expected Utility of Option 3
(Save nothing) = 2 ticks and 11 crosses

The 'Preferred' Option
i.e. Choice with Maximum Expected Utility = Option 2

REFERENCES

Beach, L.R., Townes, B.D., Campbell, F.L. and Keating, G.W., (1976), Developing and testing a decision and for birth planning decision, Organisation Behaviour and Human Performance, 15, 99-116.

Brinker, R.P. and Lewis, M., (1982). Making the world work with micro computers: A learning prosthesis for handicapped infants, Exceptional Children, 49. 163-70,

Brown, R.V., Kahr, A.S. and Peterson, C., (1974), Decision Analysis-An overview, Holt, Rinehart and Winston,

Budescu, D.V. and Wallsten (1987), Subjective estimation of precise and vague uncertainties, in Wright, G. and Ayton P. (eds.), Judgemental Forecasting.

Connolly, K. and Bruner, J., (1974), Competence, its nature and nurture in Wright, G. and Ayton, P. (eds.), The Growth of Competence, Connolly, K. & Bruner, J. (Eds.), Academic Press, London.

Edwards, W., Lindman, H., and Phillips, L.D., (1966), Emerging technologies for making decisions in Newcombe, T.M. (ed.) New Direction in Psychology 11, Holt, Rinehart and Winston, New York.

Emerson, P.A., Teather, D., and Handley, A.J., (1974) The application of decision theory to prevention of deep vein thrombosis following myocardial infarction, Quart, J. Med., New Series, XLIII, 171-389.

Edgerton, R.B., (1967). The Cloak of Competence: Stigma in The Lives of The Mentally Retarded, University of California Press, Berkeley and Los Angeles.

Hogarth, R.M., (1975), Cognitive processes and the assessment of subjective probability distribution, J. Amer. Stat. Assoc., 70-721

Hogg, J., and Sebba, J., (1986) Profound retardation and multiple impairment, Vol. 2, Education and Therapy, Groom Helm, Kent.

Howell, W.C. and Burnett, S.A., (1978), Uncertainty measurement: A cognitive taxonomy, Organis. Behav. Human Perform 22, 45-68.

Kaufman, G.M. and Thomas, H. (1977), Modern Decision Analysis, Penguin.

Jungerman, H., and Thurning, M., (1987). The use of mental models for generating scenarios, in Wright, G. and Ayton, P. (eds.) Judgemental Forecasting,

Knight, F.H., (1921), Risks, Uncertainty and Profit, (reprint 1971), Chicago, University of Chicago Press.

Lichenstein, S., Fischhoff, B., and Phillips, L.D., (1977), Calibration of probabilities: The state of the art in Hungerman, H. and De Zeeuw, G. (eds.), Decision Making and Change in Human Affairs, D. Reidel, Amsterdam.

Metheson, J.E., (1970), Decision analysis practice: Examples and insights, in Kaufman, G. and Thomas, H., (1975), Modern Decision Analysis, Penguin.

National Research Council, (1981), Governing Board Committee on the Assessment of Risk, U.S. in Wright, G. and Ayllon, P. (eds.), Judgemental Forecasting, 1987.

Pessemier, E.A., (1966), New Product Analysis - An

Analytical Approach, New York, McGrew-Hill.
Phillips, L.D., (1973), A theoretical perspective on heuristic biases in probalistic thinking, in Humphreys, P., Svenson, O. and Vari, A. (eds.), Analysis of Aiding Decision Processes, New York, North Holland.
Raiffa, H., (1968), Decision analysis, Introductory lecture on Choice Under Uncertainty, Reading - Mass., Addison-Wesley.
Slovic, P.C., (1972), From Shakespeare to Simon: Speculation and some evidence about man's ability to process information, Oregan Research Institute, Res. Bull, 12.
Tversky, A., and Kahneman, (1974). Judgement Under Uncertainty: Heuristic and Biases, Science 185, 1124-31.
Tversky, A., and Kahneman, (1981), The framing of decision and the psychology of choice, Science, 211, 433-458.
Winkler, R.L., (1967), The assessment of prior distribution in bayesian analysis, J.Amer. Stat. Assoc., 66,776-800.
Winkler, R.L. and Murphy, A.H., (1973), Experiments in the the laboratory and the real world, Organ. Behav. Human Perform., 10, 252-270.
Wright, G.N., Phillips, L.D., Whalley, P.G., Choo, G., Ng. K. O., Tan., I. and Wisundha, A., (1978), Cultural differences in probabilistic thinking, J. of Cross Cultural Psychology, 9, 285-99.
Wright, G.N. and Phillips, L.D., (1979), Personality and probabilistic thinking, An exploratory study, B.J. Psychology, 70, 295-303.
Wright, G.N. and Ng. K.O., (1981), Three methods for improving clinical decision making in Main, C., (ed.), Clinical Psychology and Medicine - A Behavioural Perspective , Press, New York and London.
Wright, G.N., (1984), Behavioural Decision Theory, Sage Publication, Beverley Hill.
Wright, G.N. and Ayllon, P., (eds.), (1987), Judgemental Forecasting.
Zimmer, A.C., (1983), Verbal vs. numerical processing of subjective probabilities, in Scholz, T.W. (ed.), Decision Making Under Uncertainty, Amsterdam, North Holland.

Combatting powerlessness in the face of AIDS

J. WILKS

Toward the end of 1981, occasional reports began to appear in the press of a strange new disease occurring among gay men in the USA. Since then, the Acquired Immune Deficiency Syndrome has claimed thousands of lives and has come to be perceived as public enemy number one. It appears in the mass media almost daily and has spawned a range of social and political responses which are often characterised by such panic and hyperbole that it is sometimes difficult to remember that seven years ago nobody knew AIDS existed. In the light of this, one might think that to talk about AIDS in the context of a symposium on 'empowering the client' is a contradiction in terms. I will attempt to argue that, on the contrary, issues of personal power and control can be seen as the bottom line to many of the problems that the syndrome presents.

The devastating and life-threatening nature of the physical consequences of AIDS is certainly one reason why people feel so fearful and powerless about it. Recent advances in medical technology have lulled people into the expectation that ultimately medicine will cure all ills. This encourages much abnegation of responsibility for one's own health and susceptibility to disease, and has made it difficult for people to accept that there is no simple cure or vaccine for AIDS. Furthermore, death has become increasingly more hidden from most people than in the past, and this tends to increase fear and denial of one's own mortality. However, there are other life threatening illnesses, and it is not simply the relative youth of most people with AIDS which exacerbates our difficulties in dealing with it. More important in this is that AIDS is unique in the number of psychosocial issues and problems it highlights, which greatly compound the difficulty, for both individuals and societies, in dealing rationally with the problems it presents. A major reason for this is rooted not in the virus's method of attack, but in its means of transmission. It is a sexually transmitted and blood-borne virus, and for this reason it has become particularly endemic in certain groups of the population, some of which were already heavily stigmatised and marginalised. It is obvious, but nevertheless important to stress, that this is not because HIV has some salacious interest in homosexuality or intravenous drug abuse, but simply because any virus which is transmitted in this way (e.g. hepatitis B) will leave these groups particularly vulnerable to infection.

PSYCHOSOCIAL EFFECTS OF AIDS

The particular demographic spread of AIDS has had several effects, each of which to some extent adds to the general air of powerlessness. These include:-

a) Labelling of people with AIDS as 'innocent' or 'guilty'.
b) Increase in anti-gay prejudice.
c) Delay in recognising the risk of heterosexual transmission.
d) Confusion of morality with public health.

a) Discussion about AIDS, particularly in the press, has frequently involved a division of people with AIDS into 'innocent' victims (e.g. recipients of blood products) who merit some sympathy (although they still suffer the same discrimination in employment, housing etc.) and those whose AIDS is seen as retribution for socially deviant and/or sinful behaviour. This distinction can sometimes be internalised by people with AIDS/HIV themselves, which increases their own difficulties in regaining some sense of self-efficacy and power in the face of their illness. Research in San Fransisco found that gay men who blamed themselves for having AIDS, and those who had not 'come out' as gay to families and workmates (who were therefore less likely to discuss their health problems with others) had particular difficulty in coming to terms with their diagnosis (Mandel 1986). As the gay community gradually comes to terms with AIDS, self-blame may be becoming less likely in those diagnosed. However, as more heterosexuals contract the disease, high levels of anger and self-blame are likely in this group. For example if they have ignored the publicity campaigns around AIDS they may feel that they deserve to have become infected and will need support and understanding in reaching an acceptable explanation for this. Also, therapists have a difficult task in acknowledging people's anger and facilitating its expression without reinforcing notions of blame of particular groups.

b) Related to the above, AIDS has led to a backlash against gay rights (which was probably already brewing in the social climate of the early '80's, a period of economic recession and increased intolerance of liberal ideas) and has eroded many of the limited gains made by the gay community during the decade following the 1967 Sexual Offences Act (which provided for an albeit limited decriminalisation of male homosexual behaviour). The most extreme examples of this include pronouncements from religious fundamentalists that AIDS represents the wrath of God against homosexuals; there have also been reports of an increase in violent attacks against gay men, and in many countries AIDS has been invoked as a reason for legal sanctions against homosexuality. The State of Georgia recently defended its antisodomy law on the grounds that it served public health by combatting the spread of AIDS, despite the fact that the law was enacted in 1816! The fact that such responses are a result of already existing homophobia and not in any way a logical response to AIDS is demonstrated (if such proof were needed) in the increase in prejudicial reactions to lesbians as well, despite their being the group currently at lowest risk of infection. Perhaps even more serious is the fact that using AIDS as an excuse for further repression of homosexuality is not only offensive to civil liberties but is a highly dangerous move from the perspective of public health. Any move which makes it more difficult for gay men to openly discuss their sexual behaviour and gain accurate information about risk reduction or come forward for treatment will put them even more at risk and increase the spread of AIDS. A major reason that gay men as a group have been more successful than heterosexuals in reducing their risk-behaviour is that many of them are part of a social network of others in the same position (including many with AIDS/HIV, thus making the threat indisputable to them) and so have had mutual support to talk over what they need to do and how to do so. At greater risk are those who are still 'in the closet' and have less access both to the necessary information and to the social supports that help in working through what it means in their lives. It is also worth noting that much of what is now understood about AIDS/HIV has been learned because people with AIDS and gay men have cooperated willingly with researchers; gay men have also been at the forefront of developing support services for people with AIDS/HIV. Repressive measures against them would obviously greatly impede both these areas. Indeed, AIDS is yet another reason to expand full civil rights to the gay population; but the opposite view is more usually expressed. Taking power over AIDS therefore demands that people confront their own fears and prejudices about homosexuality to an extent that relatively few heterosexuals seem ready to do.

c) The initial view of AIDS as a gay problem led to a false sense of security among heterosexuals, so that if they felt powerless about the illness, neither did they feel threatened by it. In fact evidence that AIDS was transmissable heterosexually appeared in medical journals fairly early on in the epidemic (e.g. Harris et al, 1983) but it was not until the 'gay plague' angle ceased to be newsworthy and the tabloids announced that AIDS had 'gone straight' that the majority of heterosexuals took notice of this. This led to a new set of reactions which again militated against people developing any sense of power over the issue. These have been characterised by much resentment and blame toward the high risk groups, who are now seen as the 'cause' of everyone else being at risk as well. Particular targets for attack have been people in the 'bridging groups' (those from whom the virus is considered most likely to move from the risk groups to infiltrate the rest of the population) i.e. bisexual men, users of injectable drugs, and prostitutes (particularly those who are also drug users, many of whom finance their drug 'habit' by this means). It is still relatively early days in this shift of emphasis, but epidemiological research suggests that the rate of new seroconversion is now much higher among injecting drug users than among gay men (who have as a group greatly modified their sexual behaviour to reduce risk) and that drug users will form the next major wave of the epidemic (Moss, 1987). If, as is likely, this coincides with a heightened awareness of the risks of heterosexual transmission, drug users may come in for blame and punitive attitudes of a ferocity that might even surpass the anti-gay reactions which have already occurred. People working in the drugs field have for many years experienced the dilemma of being expected to offer both treatment for drug users and social control of the drug problem; this (conflict) is likely to be sharply heightened by AIDS which may lead to untenable external demands on their work practices and policies. Gay men, particularly in places like San Francisco with a large organised gay movement, have to some extent been able to create their own treatment constituency with regard to AIDS, including lobbying for resources, exploring alternative and holistic treatment approaches and demanding accountability from health service providers. This is much more difficult for users of illegal drugs, and drug workers are faced with the task of being both advocates for their clients and dealing with the demands of governments' and authorities' policies for dealing with the problem. The emphasis of drug treatment policy has changed in recent years, toward time-limited withdrawal and more focus on abstinence. AIDS necessitates harm-reduction measures which are often inconsistent with what has been considered good practice in drug treatment in the 1980's. This has tended to delay the implementation of appropriate policies and facilities (e.g. outlets for free needles and syringes) and there is still much debate within drug treatment services about what changes are required in the light of AIDS.

d) The pattern of AIDS/HIV infection has provided many people with ostensible validation for their prior moral views. The use of AIDS as an excuse to moralise in the guise of public health has already been noted above in the context of homosexuality; it is also an aspect of reactions to the perception of AIDS as a heterosexual threat. AIDS has been invoked by right-wing and religious groups to condemn heterosexual permissiveness as well as homosexuality and to promote their views on chastity and the sanctity of marriage. Although the government has kept a discreet distance from this and presented information in strictly factual, non-moralistic terms, the focus of public education has been monogamy and reduction of partners, with 'safer sex' (usually presented as simply the use of condoms) being presented as a poor second-best for those who do not stick to celibacy or an exclusive relationship. This has led to a very negative slant on safe sex (which is virtually always in terms of what people should not do rather than the wide range of activity they can engage in completely safely) and has also meant that the relative safety of different activities has been very unclear to most people. Since for many people monogamy is neither a realistic nor preferred option, this can lead to much anxiety engendered by lack of knowledge about the degree of risk they may be taking. This also fosters a sense of powerlessness and may even encourage more risky behaviour, since if condoms are seen as an inadequate substitute for monogamy they may be dispensed with altogether, in ignorance of the prevailing evidence that if used carefully they can be highly effective in blocking transmission of HIV (Wellings, 1986).

As with attitudes toward homosexuality, it seems that AIDS is being used to bolster a morally reactionary viewpoint which was already gaining support before the AIDS epidemic, in particular the stress on marriage and the family (which has always been a central point of Conservative Party policy, for reasons which have much more to do with economics and ideology than disease). This has social implications which may not become clear for many years but there is a risk of many people forming and remaining in unsatisfactory relationships because of their fear of AIDS, with consequent negative effects on the emotional health of themselves and their children. The whole issue of safer sex is of course even more problematic when dealing with young people. Most of the AIDS information available is based on the assumption that the recipients have some sexual experience. For young adolescents the issues are more complex; sexual initiation has always been fraught with emotional and interpersonal difficulties. For those who are grappling with this at the same time as society struggles to comes to terms with AIDS, a great deal of support is needed, both to help them consider ways in which safe sex might be possible and enjoyable, and allow them to express their anger at feeling they are being denied the freedoms of the previous generation.

ALTERNATIVE RESPONSES TO AIDS

In the light of all the above, it is not surprising that current responses to AIDS involve a degree of fear and confusion which is out of proportion in relation to the known facts about HIV. The important aspect of AIDS to stress in this context is that although it was only recognised as recently as 1981, medical research has already developed a considerable body of knowledge about the nature of HIV and the means by which it is transmitted. This should in theory permit anyone who is not yet HIV-positive to make a considered decision about how the existence of AIDS affects them, and what modifications may be indicated for their lifestyle in order to avoid infection or at least reduce their risk to a minimum. Despite the expenditure on mass media campaigns it is doubtful whether this basic message has got across to very many people.

What may be needed is a quite different slant on publicity and education around AIDS, which while not denying that AIDS is an unmitigated tragedy, recognises that it can be viewed as a challenge to which positive responses are possible, rather than solely as a menacing threat. The dramatic effects of television adverts with sombre voiceovers and falling tombstones is hardly conducive to encouraging such a perspective. As anti-smoking research has found (Leventhal and Cleary, 1980) repeated exposure to highly fear-laden messages can lead to denial and desensitisation against the fearfulness of the message. The publicity campaign has also underemphasised the many ways in which the virus is <u>not</u> transmitted, and did not make any attempt to encourage people to respond supportively and sympathetically to people with AIDS. However, there is a dearth of knowledge about what does constitute effective public health education, and hence an important task for psychological researchers is to clarify which components lead to attitude and behaviour change. Friedman et al (1986) point out that AIDS education should consist not merely in delivering a single set of information, but should be thought of in terms of maintaining behaviour change over an indefinite time period. This may be better facilitated by strategies used in commercial advertising, of repetition through as many sources as possible of varying messages with a consistent theme.

The first important point that must be understood in beginning to develop a position of power with regard to AIDS, is that HIV is fundamentally a difficult virus to catch. It is very fragile, does not survive well outside the body and is destroyed by bleach and detergent. Although most people are probably now aware that expert opinion is unequivocal on the fact that HIV cannot be transmitted by casual social contact, many people's behaviour (e.g. the donning of 'spacesuits' by Prison Officers escorting HIV-positive prisoners) suggests that they have not really taken this knowledge in at an emotional level. Even among health care workers who have to be in close contact with infectious body fluids, there have been only a handful of cases of seroconversion as a result of work with HIV-positive people and these have almost always involved serious needlestick injuries (i.e. direct inoculation with infected blood) rather than mere proximity (Geddes, 1986). Yet the reactions to people with AIDS/HIV even by health care workers (outside specialist AIDS services) have often included degrees of panic and misinformed reactions which suggest that people's response is not based on their logical appraisal of the actual risk, but on other aspects of AIDS, (e.g. the perception of it as invariably fatal, or prior views about certain high-risk behaviours) which can overcome people's better judgment. Searle (1987) found that health care staff were generally in favour of serotesting prior to hospital admission even though this is usually neither in the best interests of the patient nor necessary to prevent virus transmission in hospitals.

Once people have come to the basic realisation that they are only at risk from HIV if they behave in a number of specific ways, the major area in which changes will be needed is the sexual arena. Certainly this was bound to be fraught with difficulties. Even in the so-called permissive era few people are confident about discussing sex in a frank and unembarrassed way, even with (perhaps especially with) their partners. Safe sex demands changes in sexual behaviour that challenge many aspects of prevailing mythologies about sex: e.g. that it should be totally spontaneous and unplanned, that people should know instinctively what pleases their partner, and that 'real sex' equals penetration. However, the fact that such changes can be made is indicated by the experience of many gay men. The impressive aspect of much of the gay literature on safer sex has been the attempt to frame it in a reasonably positive and erotic light, with a strong emphasis on the large number of sexual activities permissible within a safer sex framework, rather than just a set of proscriptions of what is high-risk. That this is a better strategy than focussing on what is prohibited is supported by tangible evidence that, as a group, gay men have considerably changed their behaviour in ways to reduce risk, i.e. the reduction in other STD's among gay men (Gellan and Ison, 1986)and more recently the levelling off in the rate of new seroconversion to HIV in this group (Moss, 1987).

Serious consideration of sexual possibilities in the age of AIDS must include much more discussion about mutual pleasure, less focus on conquest and seduction, and a validation of non-penetrative sex as not merely foreplay but a legitimate form of sexual expression. This could lead to a greater equality in sexual relationships and help protect women in particular from risks they have always had to face, such as cervical cancer and unwanted pregnancy (Richardson, 1987). If AIDS forces us to question many of our assumptions about sex this may not necessarily be restrictive, despite the difficulties involved. The need to communicate more with partners about sex and be more imaginative about alternative forms of sexual expression can lead to enrichment rather than impoverishment of sexual relationships.

THE ROLE OF CLINICAL PSYCHOLOGY

There is clearly a great need for everyone to be sufficiently informed and aware of issues and facts about AIDS in order to make the decisions needed to take control over the problem, both to avoid the spread of infection and to prevent the development of repressive social policies around AIDS (which, although they are bound to be counterproductive, are more likely to be considered by authorities if there is evidence that people are not changing their behaviour). It is therefore particularly important for clinical psychologists to make a rational response to AIDS and to take responsibility for confronting their own fear, prejudice and lack of knowledge, because they have some influence over social institutions (particularly the NHS) and because they will find AIDS occurring more and more frequently in their clinical work. In each of these areas we need to develop a perspective which is empowering to both our individual clients and the society in which they live.

a) Social and institutional responses to AIDS

In the early years of the AIDS epidemic people generally underestimated the extent to which the disease would become an issue of widespread concern and would impinge on nearly every social institution and agency. It was generally left to those who had developed some expertise in the field (due to working in specialities and geographical areas where they came into contact with Britain's first large numbers of people with AIDS/HIV) to advise government departments and other agencies on appropriate policy. These professionals (mostly in London) had already, relatively early on, worked with enough clients with AIDS-related illnesses and HIV-infection to have come across many of the worst types of social and interpersonal responses to AIDS. They had seen many of their clients lose their jobs and homes, be rejected by family and friends, have trouble finding general medical and dental care, and be hounded by the press. They had therefore developed an acute awareness of the fact that however ravaging and painful the medical consequences of AIDS, the social consequences can be equally devastating.

Current official policy (DHSS, 1986) is that HIV-infection should be dealt with under the terms of the Venereal Diseases regulations; this means that unless the patient has given their consent, information on their HIV-status must not be disclosed to anyone for any purpose other than the health care of the person, except where such disclosure is necessary to avoid the spread of infection. Although this is somewhat ambiguous and open to interpretation, in practice it means that the medical records of Genito-urinary clinics are kept separate from other medical records and even the person's G.P. will not be told their results without the person's permission. As testing should not take place without pre-counselling and informed consent, if someone declines to be tested the advice to surgeons and dentists is to use appropriate clinical procedures to avoid transmission of HIV, as if the result were known to be positive. This is in fact safer than relying on the test due to the time-lag between infection and seroconversion; a negative result does not mean that standards of clinical hygiene can be lowered with impunity.

If AIDS did not invoke such a legion of negative emotional

and social reactions, these precautions might not be necessary; but until society has reached the point where people can tell friends and professionals that they have HIV infection and be reasonably confident that the other person will respond on the basis of accurate knowledge and lack of irrational fear, they will require the protection of such rules, which also ensure the safety of others. These principles of confidentiality and informed consent enable people to have some control over who has access to information on their HIV-status and in what circumstances it is disclosed. This greatly increases their chances of seeking necessary medical help and of feeling that they still have some power over their situation, even in the face of a virus which erodes so much control over their lives and health.

In the last couple of years AIDS has moved further and further from being the province only of a small number of experienced workers and their clients, and with some rapidity has become part of the public domain and as such a legitimate topic for public debate. This shift was absolutely necessary to encourage the changes needed to reduce the spread of infection, and indeed it only occurred because of the vocal concern of those specialising in the field who had for a long time been issuing warnings to the effect that everyone had to consider the issue. However, it appears to have contributed to some negative shifts in the balance of professional opinion, in the direction of more repressive responses. This is most clearly demonstrated by the decision at the BMA meeting in July, 1987 (later overturned) that doctors should have the right to test patients' blood for antibodies without their consent or knowledge, despite the fact that this is completely contrary to DHSS guidelines, would discourage people from seeking medical help, and may even be illegal.

One aspect of the argument in favour of testing is based on improving health care, insofar as if someone is known to be positive they can be given advice on maintaining their health, and infections may be picked up and treated earlier. However, this is not inconsistent with allowing the individual to make the decision about being tested, particularly given the possible social and emotional implications of a positive result, the fact that any health care advice offered is based more on sound common sense than documented evidence, and there is nothing that can be done to guarantee future health. The more sinister side of enforced testing is whether a positive result will exclude people from basic medical and dental care. Searle (1987) found that a considerable percentage of physicians erroneously believed that they could refuse hospital admission to patients from high-risk groups. In the argument about testing the issues of what is best for the patient and what is for the apparent reassurance of doctors are frequently confused. These issues can be effectively separated by offering anonymous testing sites for those who want the test but are concerned about confidentiality. Anonymous testing is available in some areas of the USA but is very rare in the UK.

Some aspects of this debate reinforce the view that even

professionals in health care are not immune to the prejudices and fears that inform (or misinform) many lay people's reaction to AIDS, and that these can cloud their judgments of appropriate medical and ethical reactions. There is a real danger that the official response to AIDS may change dramatically in ways that will ignore the experience of the last few years and may drive people with AIDS and those at risk away from sources of information and help; thus fuelling not only increased panic but also increased spread of infection. Psychologists in the NHS need to consider this area and ensure that they take a well-informed stance when they are in a position to influence local or national policy.

Controlling infection also, of course, requires continued education and support to HIV-negative people to help them to modify their behaviour to minimise their risk of infection. This must be everyone's responsibility, not just that of those infected. Miller et al (1986) point out that the sexual spread of infection requires a tacit compliance between two people, one infected and one not, and that behavioural change in both is the most effective way to avoid infection. Repressive measures around AIDS reflect a response that has occurred in earlier epidemics of disease, where society has sought to protect itself by isolating the victims (Kirby, 1986). Quite apart from the ethical problems it is totally impractical to effectively isolate HIV-positive people; and they will find it more difficult to avoid high-risk behaviour if others in the community are not equally aware and informed about how to avoid infection.

b) Clinical responses to AIDS

It is not the intention of this section to attempt a synopsis of how to work with clients (which requires much more in-depth reading and experiential training) but to focus on those aspects of clinical work which are particularly useful because their emphasis is on the empowerment of the client. Clinicians offering a service around AIDS need to be: (i) fully aware of up to date knowledge of medical and psychological aspects of AIDS and HIV, (ii) in possession of therapeutic skills which can enable clients to cope with the emotional and interpersonal effects of AIDS and (iii) aware of the wider social and political issues raised by AIDS (iv) able to confront their own negative attitudes toward the risk-behaviours, and also consider the implications of AIDS for their own lifestyle. It is easier to appreciate the difficulties which clients face, in altering their behaviour to reduce risk and in dealing with their fears about AIDS/HIV, if we have made some consideration of these issues for ourselves.

For non-specialist psychological therapists, particularly outside areas where there is a high concentration of infection, the first type of AIDS-related referrals they are likely to have encountered are the 'worried well' i.e. people who have no real reason to think that they have AIDS but who have severe anxiety about it, perhaps engendered by exposure to inaccurate and sensationalist medical coverage.

Clarification of what they think may have put them at risk may indicate that their chances of having been infected are minimal or nil, and explaining to them why this is so may be sufficient to allay their anxiety. Where there are some grounds for their fear, or where it is part of a more long-standing hyponchondriasis, more detailed counselling will be necessary. Equally importantly, their presence in therapy provides an opportunity to correct misinformation and to help them come to a better understanding of why AIDS tends to provoke such strong fear. If this enables them to take control over their own likelihood of future infection it is clearly an important piece of preventive health care.

Clients who are at higher risk of infection (because they have engaged in high-risk behaviour) present more complex problems. Their chances of having already contracted HIV are higher and they may need to consider the pros and cons of being tested. The ability to make an informed decision about this depends on them being fully aware of what the test does and does not mean; the implications of a positive result and whether they anticipate being able to handle this; and whether they need to know where they stand in order to reduce their risk-behaviour even though any modifications needed in their behaviour will be the same whether the result is positive or negative. With some people, knowledge of the result will facilitate appropriate decisions about how to behave in ways that minimise the risk of contracting/ transmitting HIV. Others will be able to change their behaviour without knowing their HIV-status and may feel that the emotional and social consequences of a positive result are more than they could deal with and might even hinder their ability to take control of their risk behaviour.

Effective behaviour change requires that people really believe that they can take a position of power over their own risk of infection. This will often require much more than the provision of information alone, and it is important to explore any difficulties that the client may have in putting it into practice and help them to work on these. Morin et al (1984) describe support groups for gay men which included practice of sexual social skills and assertiveness, including how to negotiate a 'safer sex agreement' with prospective partners.

Even in communities where awareness of AIDS is very high (e.g. among gay men in San Francisco), a minority continue to engage in high risk practices, supporting the view that knowledge alone may be insufficient to lead to behaviour change. There is a need to identify what psychological processes are operating that allow people to maintain this without unbearable cognitive dissonance. Psychologists possess skills in assessing factors which maintain maladaptive behaviour and those which facilitate behaviour change; they therefore have a crucial role to play in clarifying influences which impede risk-reduction and developing ways of tackling these. People may be less likely to change if they disbelieve the facts, do not see the issue as applying to them, or if they do not believe that they have the necessary social skills or self-efficacy to change.

Rejection of the facts may in some cases represent the person's way of rationalising their perceived inability to change. It is also important to assess the person's level of anxiety about AIDS. If this is very high, it will inhibit their ability to take in the necessary information and/or lead to denial and hence interfere with behaviour change; but too little anxiety may also increase risk if it leads to information being ignored (Friedman et al, 1986).

All these areas should be open to psychological intervention, aimed both at helping the person to clarify the issues and their feelings by supportive counselling, and using specific techniques such as stress management, problem solving and assertion training to help them develop a sense of mastery over the situation. This requires clinicians to develop a more active, educational role than they may be used to.

The issue of power is particularly acute in dealing with drug-takers since they are already, almost by definition, an isolated and powerless group, existing outside many of society's conventions and institutions, especially the law. Also, at a more individual level, people who have experienced dependency on drugs are likely to have a particularly low sense of self-efficacy with regard to all areas of their lives, and hence may be less likely to perceive themselves as able to control their risk-behaviour, particularly since they have two areas of risk, sex and drug use, to tackle. In this context it is important to note that the spread of HIV among drug users is caused not by drug abuse per se, but by a particular mode of use, i.e. injecting (specifically, sharing needles and syringes). It is therefore logically possible to reduce the spread of HIV in this group without necessarily reducing the level of actual drug-taking. Both drug users and those working with them need to be aware of this distinction and not confuse treatment of problem drug use with attempts to reduce AIDS. However, this raises the question of whether drug-users can do anything to change their drug-using behaviour other than stopping using, which has rarely been addressed in the drugs field. (Because of the illegality of drugs such as heroin, the issue of controlled use versus abstinence which has caused so much controversy in the alcohol field has hardly been open to debate in the drugs field). Attempts to educate drugtakers about the risks of HIV infection, and practical support for this by increasing the availability of sterile injecting equipment, is based on the assumption that drugtakers can control some aspects of their drug using behaviour even if they are unable or unwilling to stop using drugs. Initial evidence suggests that indeed they can. Friedman et al (1986) found that fifty nine percent of drug-users interviewed in New York had made some behavioural changes to avoid AIDS (e.g. reducing needle sharing or cleaning their injecting equipment). It is possible that this experience of partial control may have a positive spin off for some drug users, in that if it increases their self efficacy they may develop greater confidence in their ability to increase their control over other aspects of their drug-using lifestyles.

Tragically, for an increasing number of people, empowerment with regard to risk-reduction will come too late. Clinicians are likely to get an increasing number of referrals of people who already have AIDS/HIV-infection and will be required to offer a therapeutic response to help these individuals come to terms with this and work on how they can adapt to life in as fulfilling a way as possible within the constraints placed on them by the virus.

Although there has as yet been little research into the efficacy of psychological therapy with people with AIDS and HIV-infection, the kinds of approach that are recommended by experienced clinicians in the field are characterised by a strong element of empowering clients by enabling them to structure the various areas in which AIDS affects their lives and work on how they can increase their control of each of these. For example Acevedo (1986), discussing how people can work on the problem of whether to tell others that they are HIV-positive, suggests that the object is to empower the client; the decision about disclosure is therefore framed in terms of whether it will help them feel more in control. Green and Miller (1985) suggest that the reinstatement of a feeling of control is the key factor in overcoming depression among people with AIDS.

This poses a considerable challenge to both clinician and client since there are so many aspects of AIDS which undermine one's sense of control, particularly the frequent recurrence of episodes of illness and new infections, as well as some of the reactions of other people. In many ways people with AIDS/HIV may feel that the virus is in charge of their lives and severely limits what they can do and what they can expect from a curtailed future, and this real uncertainty is not something that will be affected by psychological therapy. Therapeutic support can however help the person to feel that they still do and can have considerable control both over their physical health, e.g. by improving their diet, reducing stress and avoiding drug-use and other infections since these can all affect immune response; and over their psychological health, e.g. by exploring what changes may be needed in their goals, activities and priorities. People who make considerable changes in their lifestyles in an active attempt to cope with their illness have been found to be less distressed and more hopeful than those who make few changes (Mandel, 1986). The basic task of the therapist is to help the client to structure the issues they have to face so that they can make a relevant and effective response to each (Miller, 1986), so that they do not feel so overwhelmed as to be powerless to do so. This will include working on practical and emotional issues around dying; however the major goal is to increase the quality of life. Namir (1986) cautions against concentrating too much on issues of death and dying and forgetting about life and living.

Underlying many of the emotional difficulties caused by AIDS is a strong sense of uncertainty, regarding the course of the illness and its treatment, or in the case of asymptomatic seropositive people, whether they will go on to develop AIDS-related illness. To a large extent this uncertainty reflects the current state of medical knowledge and is also perhaps inherent in a syndrome with such a wide range of manifestations. However, it is vital that clinicians should be honest with the patient about their diagnosis and what is known about it. Evading giving people bad news may feel more comfortable for staff, but generally makes adjustment more difficult (Miller, 1986). In order to regain any sense of control in their lives, people need to know where they stand, and what they can do to try to protect their future health. This is another area where more research is needed to identify co-factors which increase the likelihood of disease or influence its course, as well as psychological factors which contribute to health-promoting or damaging behaviour (Coates et al, 1984). Even when we can be reaonably sure of what the person should avoid (e.g. stress, other infections, drugs) the same issue arises as with risk-reduction i.e. the provision of information alone may be insufficient. If the person feels that their life is out of their control and is predicated on the virus, this may lead to them feeling helpless to make necessary changes and they will need support and help to tackle this. It is important to note that being honest with clients should not preclude maintaining hope.

Working with people whose lives are affected by AIDS/HIV is highly stressful and brings up many personal issues for staff. There is obviously a risk of their own feelings of helplessness and despair obstructing their ability to be supportive of clients. Empowering the client therefore also necessitates adequate support systems for staff of all disciplines. Psychologists can have an important role in facilitating this, both for other staff groups and for ourselves; but this means that people in the 'helping professions' (who often seem much better able to deal with other people's problems than their own) need to discard the fallacy that admitting to any symptoms of stress or burnout is a sign of inadequacy or incompetence.

GENERAL ISSUES RAISED BY AIDS

In conclusion, I would like to stress three issues which are crucial to combatting powerlessness in the face of AIDS. The first is the need to distinguish between public health (risk reduction) and morality (personal views of right and wrong). The search for value-free psychological therapy may be an unattainable goal, but in the area of AIDS it is particularly crucial that we separate a rational appraisal of the known facts from our personal tendencies for moral posturing, whatever our particular moral stance. It may be easier for liberally minded psychologists to be aware of gay issues and to be highly critical of those whose heterosexism has infiltrated their clinical practice; but will we be so sympathetic to, for example, the male client who is at risk because he goes to prostitutes, and is equally in need of unbiased advice to protect himself and his sexual partners?

AIDS has thrown up a rather uneasy alliance between civil

and gay rights activists on the one hand and the 'moral majority' on the other (rather like the one between the latter and feminists with regard to pornography). In both cases, the important point to stress is that any superficial resemblance between the messages being conveyed is merely coincidental. This point is often insufficiently recognised, even by radical commentators; e.g. Tatchell (1986) who considers that there is no alternative to the restrictiveness of safe sex having unfortunate echoes with the puritanism of the new right. As argued above, safe sex could be achieved by revolutionising sexual relationships in ways that bear no resemblance to right wing moralism.

Many people have capitalised on AIDS as an excuse to expound their preferred set of moral prescription and proscriptions. Medical and health education workers need to beware of being inadvertently used to push a particular morality in the guise of public health, and to ensure that what is necessary for risk reduction is kept separate from value judgments. The confusion of risk-reduction with morality is dangerous. People will reject the health message if they feel preached at. For both HIV-positive and negative people, it is difficult to accept restrictions on sexual behaviour (which for seropositive people is life-long), therefore guidelines on safer sex need to be given in a well thought out and sensitive way, not as rigid do's and don't's that may be interpreted as prescriptive moralising (Miller et al, 1986). Also, as argued above, repression could drive AIDS underground and further out of control. Neil Blewitt, Australia's Health Minister, (quoted by Hancock and Carim 1986) has pointed out that the over riding criterion in judging any legislative action in relation to AIDS is

> not whether it will or will not calm the hysterical; not whether it will or will not infringe civil liberties; not whether it will or will not make the government popular; (but) whether it will or will not impede the spread of the disease.

Secondly, there is a great need to keep AIDS in perspective. Comparisons with the medieval Black Death, and extrapolations from current figures in ways which imply that whole generations or nations will be wiped out, go far beyond current knowledge, fuel panic and repressive measures, and deflect attention from a host of equally pressing social and public health problems.

It is, however, very difficult to know where to draw the line about AIDS. In trying to reduce the moral panic caused by AIDS by appealing to a rational appraisal of the facts, there is a risk of returning to complacency. Any discussion of how serious the AIDS threat is and how we should respond is complicated by the fact that it is very much a 'moving target', with new epidemiological and medical findings changing the picture almost daily. The important point to stress is that whether AIDS ever does come to justify the label of 'the worst public health disaster ever' is largely up to us: whether we change our behaviour to limit its spread, and whether we put enough resources into the search for a vaccine and cure.

Finally, I would like to reiterate and discuss the view that AIDS, in highlighting so many of societies' most problematic issues, presents us with a set of challenges to which positive outcomes are at least possible. At an interpersonal level, among the many negative responses to AIDS based on fear, prejudice and misinformation, it has also evoked compassion and increased understanding among many health care workers, many of whom have successfully confronted their own heterosexism and developed a much greater understanding of gay lifestyles and problems, and are beginning to do so with drug users. It has inspired thousands of committed and dedicated volunteers who provide emotional and practical support to people with AIDS, and who have often been a catalyst to state-funded responses, and in many cases families and friends have discarded lifelong prejudices to help loved ones cope with dying (U.S. Institute of Medicine, 1986).

At a medical level, research prompted by AIDS has already led to considerable advances in immunology and virology, and the search to find a vaccine and effective treatments will undoubtedly have positive spin-offs for many other areas of medicine. AIDS has also given a boost to the emerging study of psychoneuroimmunology (Mandel, 1986) which will increase our knowledge of psychological aspects of many other illnesses.

At the wider social level, it may be harder to see any cause for hope, but although AIDS currently seems to be helping to swing back the pendulum to social and sexual repression, in the long run it may not be as devastating, even for gay rights, as it may seem. Hancock and Carim (1986) quote an American gay rights activist as pointing out that 'AIDS is the one thing that demonstrably seeps under the closet door'. If the invisibility of the gay community has contributed to discrimination in the past, this is clearly eroded by AIDS statistics which, while they represent thousands of individual human tragedies, also force people to face the fact that gay people are everywhere and make up a far larger minority than many people imagined. This may force people to confront the irrationality of their prejudice.

There is obviously a danger in looking for 'silver linings' to the grim reality of AIDS, in that it can sound as if one is welcoming one of the most unpleasant illnesses around. Certainly many people with AIDS and HIV-infection themselves have responded by making positive changes that they feel have enriched their lives, but although this may be the most effective way to cope with and attach some meaning to a traumatic situation, it does not mean that they would not gladly roll back the years and not have contracted the virus. Spence (1986) quotes one person as saying:

> I realise that this diagnosis of AIDS presents me with a choice...either to be a hopeless victim and die of AIDS, or to make my life right now what it

always ought to have been.

Much as that is a moving and courageous response to AIDS, it is a dreadful indictment of the society we live in (particularly the quality of life of some of its minority groups) that it is often only in the face of illness and death that people fully appreciate and make the best of their lives.

The attempt to throw a positive slant on AIDS can be particularly offensive when it comes from people who do not have the virus, and may represent their own psychological denial of the reality of the threat. Altman (1986) quotes one commentator who suggests that gay men with AIDS may be 'luckier than those whose lives are frittered away hanging out in gay bars, tricking with new bodies every night'. Quite apart from the fact that this does not represent the lifestyle of most gay men, Altman points out that the insistence on extracting good from a horrible event is ultimately insulting. Those who 'hang out in bars', or abuse drugs, may at <u>some</u> point choose to do otherwise; whereas those who have AIDS have no choice about their illness.

Nevertheless, to rise to the challenge of AIDS and make a positive response is not to deny the tragedy and loss that is being suffered. Like nothing else in our time, AIDS has pushed us, personally, medically and socially, to our limits; so far it has found our ability to respond sadly lacking. There may be few grounds for optimism; indeed, things will probably get worse before they get better. However, it is just possible that we could respond to the AIDS crisis by really examining the attitudes and values of our society, and replacing them with a tolerant, compassionate and non-oppressive understanding of different lifestyles, human relationships and sexualities. Only then would the thousands of deaths not have been entirely in vain. AIDS will undoubtedly bring about huge changes in medicine, society and interpersonal relationships; time will tell whether we allow this to empower us or to further limit our horizons.

REFERENCES

Acevedo, J. (1986), Impact of risk reduction on mental health in McKusick, L. (ed.)<u>What to do About AIDS: Physicians and Mental Health Professionals Discuss the Issues</u>, University of California Press, Berkeley.

Altman, D., (1986), <u>AIDS and the New Puritanism</u>, Pluto Press, London.

Coates, T.J., Temoshok, L. and Mandel, J., (1984), Psychosocial research is essential to understanding and treating AIDS, <u>American Psychologist</u>, 39(11), 1309-1314.

DHSS, (1986), AIDS Booklet 3: Guidance for surgeons, anaesthetists, dentists and their teams in dealing with patients infected with HTLV-III, DHSS, London.

Friedman, S.R., DesJarlais, D.C. and Sotheran, J.L., (1986), AIDS health education for intravenous drug users, <u>Health Education Quarterly</u>, 13(4), 383-393.

Geddes, A.M., (1986), Risk of AIDS to health care workers, British Medical Journal, 292, 711-712.

Gellan, M.C.A. and Ison, C.A., (1986), Declining incidence of gonorrhoea in London: A response to fear of AIDS?, Lancet, October 18.

Green, J. and Miller, D. (1985), Psychology and AIDS in Britain, American Psychologist, 40(11), 1273-1275.

Hancock, G. and Carim, E., (1986), AIDS: The Deadly Epidemic, Gollancz, London.

Harris, C., Small., C.B. and Klein, R.S., (1983), Immunodeficiency in female sexual partners of men with the Acquired Immunodeficiency Syndrome, New England Journal of Medicine, 308, 1181-1184.

Kirby, M.D., (1986), AIDS, legislation - turning up the heat?, Journal of Medical Ethics, 12, 187-194.

Leventhal, H. and Cleary, P.A., (1980), The smoking problem: A review of the research and theory in behavioural risk modification, Psychological Bulletin, 91, 370-405.

Mandel, J., (1986), Psychosocial challenges of AIDS and ARC in McKusick, L., (ed) op cit.

Miller, D., (1986), Psychology, AIDS, ARC and PGL in Miller, D., Weber, J. and Green, J. (eds.), The Management of AIDS Patients, MacMillan, London.

Miller, D., Jeffries, D.J., Green, J., Harris, J.R.W. and Pinching, A., (1986), HTLV-III: Should testing ever be routine?, British Medical Journal, 292, 941-943.

Morin, S.F., Charles, K.A. and Malyon, A.K., (1984), The psychological impact of AIDS on gay men, American Psychologist, 39(11), 1288-1293.

Moss, A., (1987), AIDS and drug use. Paper presented to conference on Drug Misuse, May 15, University College Hospital School of Medicine, London.

Namir, S., (1986), Treatment issues concerning people with AIDS in McKusick, L. (ed.) op cit.

Richardson, D., (1987), Women and the AIDS Crisis, Pandora Press, London.

Searle, E.S., (1987), Knowledge, attitudes and behaviour of health professionals in relation to AIDS, Lancet, January 3, 26-28.

Spence, C., (1986), AIDS: Time to Reclaim Our Power, Lifestory, London.

Tatchell, P., (1986), AIDS: A Guide to Survival, G.M.P./ Heretic, London.

U.S. Institute of Medicine, (1986), Mobilising Against AIDS, The Unfinished Story of a Virus, Harvard University Press, Boston.

U.S. National Institute of Mental Health, (1986), Coping With AIDS: Psychological and Social Consideration in helping People With HTLV-III Infection, Department of Health and Human Services, Washington D.C.

Wellings, K., (1986), AIDS and the condom, British Medical Journal, 293, 1259-1260.

Wells, N., (1986), The AIDS Virus: Forecasting its Impact, Office of Health Economics, London.

Brief interactional therapy in community settings

J. LETHEM

DEDICATION

Of Albert Chambwe's many remarkable qualities, I would like to pay tribute to just one which I particularly valued: his ability to ask challenging questions in such a way as to change the attitudes and behaviour of his listeners. During discussions with the other trainees on the Clinical Psychology course at Liverpool 1979-81, he would often adopt the client's viewpoint, drawing attention to unjust practices within the NHS in relation to race and class, questioning the ethics of the approaches about which we were learning, and challenging us to set ourselves higher standards as clinicians. It is unusual for a working day to pass without one of Albert's questions coming into my mind, an enduring influence upon my work, by which to remember him, with admiration and affection.

I spent November, 1986 as a resident at the Mental Research Institute, Palo Alto, California. My aim was to study Brief Interactional Therapy (BIT), with a view to returning with ideas to share with colleagues and to refreshing my style of working with families. My main concern at that time was the possible need to adapt the approach for British clients and colleagues. Since I returned I have been trying to put BIT and especially my own application of it to the test of the kind of challenges Al used to make of therapies and of therapists, questions of ethics and personal politics. I believe he would have wanted to know whether BIT can empower clients as its practitioners claim.

DEVELOPMENT OF BRIEF INTERACTIONAL THERAPY

BIT which is essentially a problem solving approach (Watzlawick, Weakland and Fisch, 1974; Fisch, Weakland and Segal 1985) represents the refinement and application of ideas first explored in Palo Alto by Gregory Bateson in the 1950's (Bodin, 1980). Bateson and his research colleagues were carrying out studies of communication of various kinds. Their interest in the unusual communication of patients at the local Veteran's Administration hospital who had been diagnosed schizophrenic brought the group into contact with Don D. Jackson, a psychiatrist who believed in 'family homeostasis'. He sometimes saw patients with their families, an unusual practice at that time, and became a consultant to the research project. The 'double-bind' theory of schizophrenia developed out of this collaboration. Although details of this theory have been reexamined critically since its first publication (Bateson, Jackson, Haley and Weakland, 1956) it still represents an important step toward the recognition of the influence of an individual's context on her/his behaviour, and a move away from attributing the development and maintenance of behavioural problems solely to the individual manifesting them. The Mental Research Institute was set up to study schizophrenia and the family, broadening its research and clinical projects in the 1960's as other researchers and therapists joined. The Brief Therapy Centre was founded at the Institute in 1967 to evaluate therapy for specific problems, carried out over a limited number of sessions, utilizing an understanding of the client's social context.

THEORETICAL BASIS

Cybernetic model

The group borrowed concepts from engineering to describe the influence of family members upon one another, likening families to cybernetic systems and their patterns of communication to feedback loops. In BIT, an individual's problems relating to thoughts, feelings or actions are assessed in the context of other people in the individual's system i.e. an interdependent group of people such as a family, a class of children or a professional team. The problem can be viewed as an outcome of patterns of interaction between members of the system, making an interactional description of the problem more appropriate than an individual centred one e.g.' parent and child have difficulty separating so that the child can attend school' would be preferred to the more limited alternative individual descriptions 'clingy child' or 'over protective' parent. Interactional descriptions serve as a reminder that any change will affect both parent and child.

When the attempted solution becomes part of the problem

John Weakland has said that when life seems like 'one damn thing after another' that does not indicate problems just the rigours of everyday life. However, when life seems like 'the same damn thing' over and over again, then there is a problem. He and his colleagues in the Brief Therapy Centre suggest that problems are often maintained by vicious cycles of repeated inappropriate attempts to solve them on the part of the members of the system and that the therapist's main task is to alter this pattern i.e. to interrupt the failed attempted solution. The sleep disturbance problems of small children are often vivid illustrations of this concept as a child's waking at night may be unintentionally rewarded by his/her parents' escalating attempts at settling with drinks, food, cuddles, toys, music etc. night after night.

In some cases professionals may have joined in a 'more of the same' pattern with a succession of individuals (health visitor, G.P., therapist) repeating the same advice to a family about management of a problem. However sensible the advice seems, if the family has gone on rejecting it and keeping the problem, then advice giving may have become part of the viscious cycle and another approach might be more productive. Those who have devised and developed Brief Interactional Therapy believe that strategies aimed at altering attempted solutions can effect improvement rapidly and their research in which a maximum of ten sessions per client is offered supports this claim.

PRACTICAL APPROACH

Defining the complainant, the problem and the aims of therapy

The therapist's first tasks are to identify the individual in the system who most desires change and the nature of the problem. Where a referral has been made on the basis of the referring agent's view that there is a problem the family members, (or other system members) do not acknowledge, then a flexible approach to problem definition may include the referrer as part of the problem for example, 'I have a problem with my G.P. (referrer) and my spouse nagging me to stop smoking' contrasts with the referrer's perspective 'this patient has a smoking problem'. It is possible to conduct BIT with only the complainant present with the therapist. The therapist elicits a clear description of the problem (and the interactional context) for which the client wants help, using questions like 'in what ways is that a problem to you and your family?', 'could you give me an example of the last time this occurred?'. Details of the interactional patterns within the family (or other system) are also obtained. Next he/she is asked what they are hoping therapy can achieve, 'how much improvement?', 'what will be the first sign of recovery?'. Similarly detailed descriptions of attempted solutions are also elicited. The therapist tries to encourage clients to give this information in concrete terms so that both the problem and the goal of treatment can be monitored. When vague or abstract concepts are used then further questioning attempts clarification e.g. 'if a Martian with no notion of abstract ideas was watching what could they observe about you that is different with the problem/without the problem?'

Learning the client's values and culture

Throughout assessment, the therapist attempts to gain information about the client's value system, figures of speech and understanding of the problem. They may be asked directly 'what's the reason you are stuck with this problem at present?' The therapist may make use of a 'one-down' stance, minimizing her/his status as an expert to encourage the client(s) to give their own views. This one-down position can also be useful at the later stages of intervention. Clients are asked to imagine what the disadvantages to them or their families would be of losing their problem. Their answers provide further information about their view of the problem and may also reveal genuine disadvantages in families where a problem has been serving a function of some kind.

Intervention

The aim of this approach is to devise an intervention, using language and ideas that are congruent with those of the client, which is designed to alter the pattern of failed attempted solutions which has been defined during the assessment. Thus interventions are individually tailored to the system's problem and style of communication. However, strategies may be grouped under a number of headings:-

a) Reframing: Some clients are able to make use of the therapist's direct advice to change behaviour surrounding the problem and thus move from a repeated pattern of unsuccessful attempts to solve the problem to a more effective strategy. However, many may find it difficult to follow advice unless it is couched in terms which correspond to their own values. For example, parents who have been attempting to solve the problem of their child's substance abuse by reasoning and pleading with the child in an escalating cycle of more abuse and more entreaties may find it difficult to break this pattern if they view reasoning and pleading as their duty as caring parents.

Reframing involves redefining a problem and unsuccessful attempts to solve it, using language and concepts that are meaningful to the client(s), to enable a change in problem solving strategy that does not threaten their belief system e.g. the parents in the example above might be told that in the therapist's opinion their child appears to have developed an attention problem along with the substance abuse habit. They have been so caring and reliable in their gentle challenges of the behaviour that the child has difficulty attending to what they say. Until they do something surprising and unpredictable the child will not learn the wisdom of the parents' words. The therapist might then suggest a task which would break the usual cycle in some surprising way, and initiate a more effective approach to stopping the child's substance abue.

b) <u>Taking a one-down position</u>: Arguments rarely solve problems and may become an example of a failed solution that maintains a problem i.e. the more arguments offered, the greater the resistance of the opposition in response. Similarly in therapy, arguing with a client or repeating unwelcome advice is likely to be met with an unwillingness to accept new ideas or to change behaviour in any beneficial way. If the therapist takes a one-down position i.e. playing down the 'expert' role; deferring to the client when possible and being open about the therapist's own limitations, then such resistance can be avoided. This approach also conveys to the client that he/she is viewed as a resourceful person who can take an active part in the therapy process. It usually improves trust between client and therapist and may provide a model to the client, of a way to be persuasive while avoiding arguments, which may be a useful problem solving strategy in the client's everyday life.

c) <u>Counter-intuitive strategies</u>: Clients with problems that fall into John Weakland's category of 'the same damn thing' repeated have often been making very strenuous attempts to conquer a problem only to find that the harder they try, the less they achieve. This is particularly true of attempts to bring about spontaneous actions by effort. A number of strategies facilitate change by relieving this sense of effort by giving the client(s) advice which appears a counter-intuitive or paradoxical approach to problem solving. For example, (i) the instruction to the client to go slow, to aim for smaller goals, to try to reduce the pace of change; (ii) communication of pessimism by the therapist 'I think you may be overestimating how much I can help you'; (iii) suggestions that the client should focus on the disadvantages, even hazards of changes as well as the advantages, so that hasty change and disruption is avoided; (iv) the prescription of a symptom or suggestion that the client should try to intensify a symptom for a period of time, perhaps in order to understand it better.

Each of these approaches conveys an implicit message that the problem can come under the client's control i.e. if the client can choose to 'go slow' or to intensify a symptom that implies a degree of control which could be turned in a more desirable direction. By communicating this implicit information and by taking the pressure off the client these counter-intuitive strategies frequently facilitate rapid improvement in the problem.

INFLUENCES

The Mental Research Institute (MRI) has drawn its therapists and researchers from a variety of backgrounds, including engineering and anthropology as well as social work, psychiatry and psychology. This may partly explain its tradition of innovative work, although the ideas of two figures not part of the MRI have also made a contribution.

a) Milton H. Erickson

A psychiatrist practising in Phoenix, he developed a highly individual strategic approach to psychotherapy described by Jay Haley in the aptly named book, 'Uncommon Therapy' (1973). His style of communicating with patients resembled hypnosis e.g. careful choice of words and of timing verbal and non-verbal communication to the client; paying close attention to client's responses during the session; using indirect forms of communication such as stories or metaphors; embedding one brief clear instruction in a long confusing statement. His strategies were often directed at enabling clients to make use of skills or characteristics of which they were scarcely aware to produce a very small alteration in behaviour which would be likely to preceed a more extensive improvement in a problem area.

Some of his techniques are useful in avoiding 'resistance' on the part of clients e.g. the technique of pacing and leading. This approach involves the therapist matching the client's mood or behaviour in some way and then gradually changing in such a way that the client shifts to keep pace with the therapist. For example, matching the quietness and minimal eye contact of a shy or withdrawn child until the child is ready to accept the therapist's lead into gradually more active communication.

Therapists using BIT have borrowed strategies from Erickson for motivating clients and for devising problem solving interventions.

b) Heinz von Foerster

A physicist, he describes perception as a construction of reality and suggests that each individual constructs his/her version of reality in a unique way. He has drawn on research by Humberto Maturana on the visual system of the frog to demonstrate that seeing is an active process, not a passive taking in of stimuli as in a camera (Segal, 1986). If this is so then it is necessary for therapist and client to agree on a common construction of reality when they meet if misunderstandings and poor progress in therapy are to be avoided. Therapists and clients often begin a session with very different views of reality, of the purpose of the session and the meaning of objects in the room. For example, a child brought to see a psychologist for the first time in a room in a hospital may expect a similar procedure to the more familiar encounter with a doctor; waiting for the psychologist to do a physical examination; expecting that the case on the desk will contain instruments (rather than bricks, puzzles etc.). Similarly a speech therapist's view of a play session with a child may be that it is therapeutic and directed at improving the child's grasp of symbols and enjoyment of communication games, while the accompanying parent may wonder when the play will stop and the 'real therapy' begin.

In such cases there is much scope for misunderstanding unless the participants discuss their mutual expectations and adjust them accordingly. Understanding the client's construction of reality has become central to the practice of BIT.

THE CONTEXT OF THERAPY

At the Mental Research Institute (USA) Therapists work together as a team for clinical research. One therapist interviews the client(s) while the other members of the team provide live supervision from behind a one way screen. Sessions are usually recorded either on video or audio tape. The team can communicate with the therapist who is with the family, by telephone, during the session, to direct questioning or to suggest interventions. The therapist usually leaves the room to consult with the observers before the end of the session, returning to convey any messages from the unseen team. Occasionally members of the team interrupt the session to speak to the client(s) directly, usually for strategic purposes. The Institute is a well known 'centre of excellence' and clients pay for therapy at the end of each session.

The Mental Research Institute provides training for many local therapists who work in a variety of settings. Lynn Jordan, a social worker trained at MRI, works in the community as part of Child Protective Services in San Mateo County, California, and also does some work with families in which there is a mentally handicapped child. She has been collaborating with John Weakland to study BIT with reluctant clients, families referred to her following abuse or threatened abuse of a child. Such families do not usually welcome professional involvement and she impressed me with descriptions of her use of B.I.T. techniques to overcome reluctance e.g. she used reframing and a one-down stance to convince a family of her honesty; liking for their child and recognition of their point of view, an approach which enabled the family to accept a therapy contract with her. She has also found the techniques helpful in gaining the trust of children usually suspicious of professionals. Her interventions often have to take into account the deprived living conditions of some of her clients. For example, she suggested to one couple that they should in future conduct any rows in the laundry room of the apartment building in which they had a one room flat, instead of in their very small cramped flat where disputes put their children at risk. She also said that for particularly noisy rows they might like to put a nickel in the tumble drier, to conceal the noise from their neighbours, a humourous element to the intervention that served to prevent a number of potential disputes, one of the parents saying 'O.K. who's got a nickel?' early in a disagreement and interrupting the usual escalating pattern of rows.

DISCUSSION

BIT seems to be a sufficiently flexible approach to allow its use in a variety of settings, on both sides of the Atlantic. In its brevity and emphasis on problem solving it fits readily into the repertory of therapies offered by a psychological service in the NHS. Many of its elements make sense to those trained in behavioural or systemic approaches while contrasting more in both theory and practice with psychodynamic approaches. I am still in the process of discovering how much of a place BIT can or should have in my own work. However, practical experience and the reactions of clients and colleagues have highlighted for me some of BIT's unique aspects e.g. the emphasis on the therapist working for the complainant; the one-down stance of the therapist and the focus upon changing attempted solutions.

The ethics of strategic approaches, including BIT have been questioned recently, especially by Andy Treacher (1986; 1987). It is beyond the scope of this paper to discuss each of his criticisms. However, some are relevant to the issue of power and potential abuse of power by the therapist.

The claim has been made for BIT that it can empower clients, through defining their own problems and criteria of improvement. However, strategic therapies including BIT have been criticised as potentially disabling or even abusive (Treacher 1984, 1986) because the approaches are open to the possibility of deceit by the therapist and of covert manipulation of the client. Treacher has suggested that the emphasis on pragmatism has been associated with a neglect of ethical issues, for example the use of interventions for which the client cannot give informed consent. The use of terms like 'strategic' and 'tactical' make explicit the view of some Brief Interactional Therapists that therapy can be a combative process, in which the therapist relies on a supportive, conspiratorial relationship with colleagues while doing battle with clients.

These reservations and criticisms seem more appropriately directed at therapists than at the approach itself which is open to flexible interpretation. While at the Mental Research Institute I had the opportunity to observe different therapists, to discuss their work with them and to attend workshops they gave. I was exposed to some approaches that shocked me, such as giving contradictory information to members of a family each seen separately; lying to clients; use of the 'devil's pact' in which a client is required to agree to follow a therapist's instruction in advance of hearing what the instruction is. I also met and observed therapists who were models of sensitivity toward, and respect for their clients, espcially Lynn Jordan who makes use of positive connotation in a sincere way to help to engage reluctant parents in therapy to help reduce the risk of further abusing their children. While it is clear that BIT, in common with most forms of therapy, is open to abusive practices, there are many choices to be made by the therapist in interpreting the guidelines for conducting BIT. The therapist must take responsibility for the choices made. Listed below are some contrasting interpretations, offered as examples of the therapist's wide range of options at each stage in therapy:

1. Taking a one-down position

At one extreme this position can be attained by the therapist making false statements about him/herself in a spirit of humouring the client while at the other extreme the therapist may make explicit real differences in status between therapist and client which limit the therapist's ability to empathise with the client e.g. 'because I don't live on the same kind of estate as you I may not be able to see the world from your point of view as clearly as you would like me to'.

2. Learning the client's values and culture

The therapist may choose to listen to the client and pretend to accept values she/he does not really hold in a quite cynical way, or on the other hand choose to listen to and acknowledge those values and then reach an arrangement with the client to agree to differ.

3. Counter intuitive approaches

These approaches appear particularly likely to tempt the therapist into an abuse of the power that superior knowledge can offer however, some therapists will ask a client early in therapy 'are you the kind of person who wants to understand exactly how they got a problem and how improvement comes about, or would it be O.K. with you if your problem improved without you understanding how or why?'

I am reminded of the 'therapist variables' shown to be important in facilitating improvement in clients receiving individual therapy of various forms. Similar studies of interactional therapists have yet to be carried out. Ideally such a study should take account of the experience of the clients in therapy as well as outcome. It seems possible that BIT carried out in a flamboyant, calculating, insincere way may be effective in the pragmatic sense. However, the approach offers the possibility of the therapist being genuine as well as effective, an option desirable on ethical grounds.

SUMMARY

BIT is based on a systemic view of problem maintenance. It is an action orientated problem solving approach which makes use of interventions which have been called 'strategic'. The overlapping stages of therapy include: identifying the complainant in the system; learning the client's values and culture; adopting a congruent style of communcation;

obtaining a clear description of the problem and the client's criterion of improvement; interventions which may involve counter-intuitive instructions to the client. Throughout therapy the therapist maintains a 'one down' stance and avoids arguing to minimise resistance on the part of the client. While some BI therapists emphasize the approach's ability to empower the client, BIT and other strategic therapies have been criticised on ethical grounds. It is suggested that the approach is a flexible one, making the therapist responsible for interpreting the approach, in a way which can either abuse therapeutic power or which can empower the client.

ACKNOWLEDGEMENT

I am grateful to the Special Trustees, West London and Charing Cross Hospitals, for their generous support of my residency at the Mental Research Institute, Palo Alto, California, in the form of a Blake Fellowship.

REFERENCES

Bateson, G. Jackson, D.D., Haley, J. and Weakland, J., (1956), Toward a theory of schizophrenia, Behavioural Science, 1, 251-264.

Bodin, A.M., (1980), The interactional view: Family therapy approaches of the Mental Research Institute in Gurnan, A. S. and Kiskern, D.P. (eds.) The Handbook of Family Therapy, Bruner/Mazel, New York.

Fisch, R, Weakland, J.H. and Segal, L., (1982), The Tactics of Change; Doing Therapy Briefly, Jossey-Bass, San Fransisco.

Haley, J. (1973), Uncommon Therapy: The Psychiatric Techniques of Milton H. Erickson M.D., W.W. Norton and Co., New York.

Segal, L. (1986), The Dream of Reality: Heinz von Foerster's Constructivism, W.W. Norton and Co., New York.

Treacher, A. (1986), Invisible patients, invisable families - a critical exploration of some technocratic trends in family therapy, Journal of Family Therapy, 8, 267-306.

Treacher, A. (1987), Family therapists are potentially damaging to families and their wider networks. Discuss in Walrond Skinner, S. and Watson, D., (eds.) Ethical Issues in Family Therapy, Routledge and Kegan Paul, London.

Watzlawick, P. Weakland, J. and Fisch, R. (1974), Change: Principles of Problem Formation and Problem Resolution, W.W. Norton and Co., New York.

Weakland, J.H. and Jordan, L. (1986), Child Protective Services: 'When you have to work briefly with reluctant clients'.

Empower yourself!

J. YOUNG

INSPIRATION

I am very happy that Al Chambwe has inspired us to come together in this symposium and to consider the issue of empowering the client. Al and I had many conversations around the issue of power in therapy and one thing we agreed on was the need for therapists to be prepared to look at themselves, and constantly be open to learning and developing themselves, in order to maximise their potential for working together with and 'empowering' clients.

Having completed my clinical psychology training I still had many unanswered questions and this led me, in 1981 to go to the Far East where I became immersed in the study and practice of oriental medicine and healing. In these disciplines I found a rich source of knowledge and techniques that seemed to me to complement Western Psychology and to have tremendous relevance to understanding everyday life and experience.

What began as a three week holiday became almost five years of study with various health practitioners in Japan, China, Korea, Hong Kong, Thailand and India. Since returning to Britain I have been busy trying to integrate what I have learned for the benefit of clients. This paper describes an integrated model of therapy which my colleagues and I have developed and are now using in London which we believe actually empowers our clients.

THE WHOLE WOMAN CLINIC: INTEGRATED HEALTH FOR WOMEN

Although the clinic was developed as a specialist clinic for women, it could just as well be used for men and children. It is called the 'Whole Woman Clinic' because the idea is not just 'well' as in symptom free (which is the basis of many of the 'Well Women' Clinics), but 'whole' as in a healthy integration of the physical, mental, emotional and spiritual aspects of our lives.

Rather than simply providing the facility of several therapies under one roof, as do many so called 'Holistic Health Centres', we aim to actually integrate the therapies, the therapists and the client so that the client is herself actively involved in all aspects of her health process.

The team

We work as a team of three people. We all originally studied psychology and then diversified, so we have psychology as a common root. One practitioner is a skilled osteopath who also uses cranial work (fine tuning of the body's energies especially in relation to movement of the cranial bones and the sacrum) and has a special interest in the link between disease and emotional problems. The other is a counsellor/stress management specialist who has years of experience of psychiatric group work with the Richmond Fellowship, training in Transactional Analysis, Shiatsu (Japanese massage), co-counselling, an MBA and considerable experience in the business world. I complete the team and am officially the oriental medicine specialist which covers acupuncture, acupressure, herbal medicine and guidance on nutrition and therapeutic exercises, though I also utilise aspects of clinical psychology.

Introductory consultation

When a client comes to us we first of all introduce ourselves, explain briefly our way of working and the format of our first session together and then ask her to tell us why she has come. We first of all encourage her to talk freely about the strengths and weaknesses in her physical and emotional life.

Our osteopath then gives her an osteopathic diagnosis checking the movement and balance of her musculoskeletal system as well as her cranial rhythms. I then give her an oriental diagnosis checking her tongue, pulses, hands, feet and meridian lines (lines of energy of the body) all of which provide information of the functioning and relative balance of the internal organs and the relationship with specific disease patterns and emotional states (more of this later). Finally our psychologist/counsellor asks a number of questions about the woman's support systems, relationships, goals and general life satisfaction.

We then take a short break which enables our client to reevaluate what she has said and to think whether there is anything she would like to add or change. In an interview situation it can be difficult to collect your thoughts and it is a common experience to remember things afterwards that you wished you had said. We have found that our clients value this opportunity for reflection and clarification.

During the break the practitioners talk together and pool diagnoses. We have found that the sum of our integrated team is even greater than the parts for we have found unique blends of diagnostic interpretation that enhance our work and our client's understanding of herself and her current situation.

Treatment plan

Following the break we have a feedback session in which we tell our client the results of our consultation and present her with a sheet with a list of recommendations to improve her current situation. These may include treatments by us, or by other medical or complementary medical practitioners where necessary. They also include self help techniques, nutritional counselling, exercise advice, contact addresses of relevant organisations and relevant publications.

We also attempt to list options for both the present and for the future for we see one of our roles as helping our clients to reach their present desired level of health and well being and then to enable them to redefine it as and when they are ready in order to go on to achieve new levels.

The client chooses from the list of options and together we formulate the Treatment Plan and regularly reevaluate and update it. In this way the client is constantly involved and determines her own treatment. We serve her rather than hold power over her and she gradually learns the skills to help herself and subsequently others.

Case history

One woman came to us with severe angina. She had been hospitalised as an emergency four times in the preceeding six weeks with severe pains in the chest and down the left arm. She had all the standard medical checks on the cardiovasculatory system but no irregularities could be found. She was nevertheless given medication which did not improve her symptoms and from which she suffered side effects including nausea and lethargy.

Our psychologist/counsellor discovered that this woman had had a series of difficult bereavements one of which occurred directly before all the heart trouble started and for which she had received no support or counselling.

In oriental medicine such grieving affects the <u>energetic flow</u>, rather than the physical functioning, relating to the heart and lungs. This explained why her heart tests revealed no physical abnormalities and why she also had a variety of apparently unrelated respiratory and skin problems which in oriental medicine connect with imbalance of energetic function of the lungs.

In addition, our osteopath found severe restriction in the movement of certain ribs at both the front and the back of the chest which corresponded exactly to the acupuncture points relating to the heart. Such restriction appears to often be linked with heart problems. On questioning she discovered that the woman had had a fall in the shower shortly before her friend's death, and had injured that specific area of her back.

None of the above information had been elicited during her extensive medical examination yet they played an important part in our diagnosis and in helping this woman to understand her condition.

In terms of our combined diagnosis it appeared that this area of the woman's body had been weakened due to depression and emotional disturbance following her first bereavement and was then further injured during the fall. As a result of the fall, movement of the ribs and corresponding energetic flow was severely restricted, and as it was untreated, this lead to a more severe reaction in the body after the second bereavement. The whole situation was further exacerbated by inadequate nutrition because of poor diet due to her depression.

This woman's treatment plan therefore included: (a) counselling for her bereavement, help in making contact with outside support organisations such as CRUSE, assistance in building up her personal life and making new social contacts; (b) osteopathy, to free the affected ribs; (c) nutritional counselling and help in building up her diet; and (d) acupuncture/acupressure to balance the energetic flow relating to the heart and lungs, in order to remove her uncomfortable physical symptoms, and to build up her energy generally thereby enhancing her confidence and ability to partake in the other activities.

We believe that this kind of combined physical/ psychological help which recognises the link between physical and mental/emotional systems provides the client with the maximum opportunity for relief as well as growth and development.

ORIENTAL MEDICINE

Oriental medicine provides a unique link in this form of integrated treatment as its system combines both emotional and physical health.

Energy lines

The basis underlying oriental medicine is that humans are energetic beings. Sources of energy are supplied by, for example, the air we breathe and the food we eat, and are regulated in the body by means of our physical exercise and movement and also our mental and emotional states, our thoughts and feelings.

The body is coursed by lines of energy known as 'meridians' the nature of which have been investigated by experimental and clinical methods (Motoyama 1975, 1978, 1980, 1984). They have been located in the connective tissue of the skin, where they interlink with but are independent of, the nerve and blood vessel systems, and carry a form of bioelectrical energy that can be measured. The meridians have external pathways, along the surface of the body, and also internal pathways where they link up with each of the internal organs. Along each meridian there are certain points, known as acupoints, which have been found to have specific effects on both the flow of energy within the meridian itself and the functioning of the internal organ to which the meridian corresponds (Manaka et al, 1983; Mann, 1962).

In Oriental medicine a healthy, well person is someone who has a free flowing balance of energy within each of the meridians and the body as a whole. When imbalance occurs, as a result of say poor nutrition, bad posture, inadequate or faulty exercise, or emotional trauma, disturbance first occurs in the meridians and subsequently in the functioning of the internal organs themselves. Acupuncture and acupressure use fine needles or fingertip pressure respectively to regulate and balance the energy within the meridians. Oriental exercise techniques, herbs and nutrition may also be used for the same purpose.

Irregularities in the meridians and certain and signs, symptoms and patterns of disorders, all appear <u>before</u> actual physical malfunction. Thus oriental medicine may be used not only to alleviate present and chronic conditions, but also to prevent disease in the future.

Diagnosis of fingers and toes

In oriental medicine each individual body part is thought to reflect the body as a whole, and changes in their appearance are used for oriental diagnosis (Kushi, 1976). One form of oriental diagnosis is based on analysis of the fingers and toes. This is because the majority of the meridians start or terminate in the fingers and toes and many important acupoints are located in these areas. The fingers and toes may therefore be used to determine the level of functioning of individual meridians as well as for accurate diagnosis of past, present and possible future health disturbances. Figure 1 shows the relationship between individual fingers/toes and the corresponding meridians and internal organs.

Some of the diagnostic signs to look for are as follows:

a) Shape of fingers/toes and nails. If any individual digit is unusual in length, deviated in shape, weak in movement, or has an abnormal nail of any kind this usually signifies an imbalance in the corresponding meridian.

b) Colour and Temperature: If any digit is unusually pale in colour or cold, this generally signifies a deficiency in energy in the corresponding meridian, while a dark or red colour and heat signify an excess.

c) Spots, marks and signs: There are many signs with individual significance. Amongst the more common are: dark

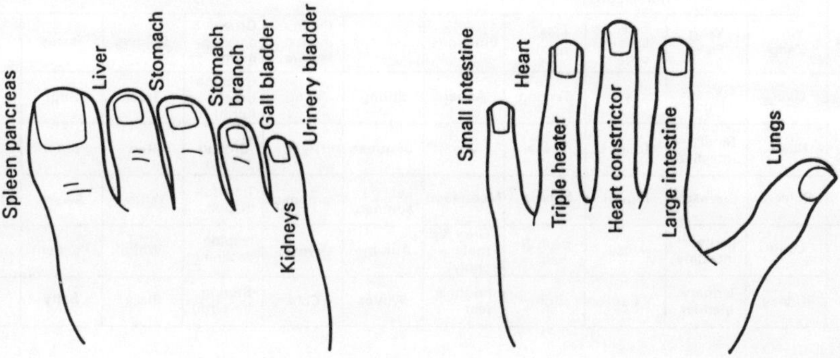

Figure 1. Diagnostic acupoints of the fingers and toes

brown spots (indicating stagnation of energy); white spots and hairs (indicating deficiency); and red spots (indicating inflammation, pain and acute conditions). Scars or cuts can also lead to problems in energy flow.

This kind of diagnostic interpretation is an intricate skill which cannot be learned overnight but most people are able to determine basic indicators for themselves. It is then possible to see the link between these indicators and one's health balance as a whole by using the following table of correspondence (table 1)..
In this table each of the meridians/internal organs is linked with specific elements of nature, seasons, tastes, and colours as well as emotions, and other physical systems namely the tissues and sense organs. The table is based on the theories of Yin and Yang and the Five Elements. These are the systems of classification according to the nature and qualities of living things based on observation and deduction, which form an integral part of Oriental Medicine (Kaptchuk, 1983)..

By combining the diagnostic information yielded by the fingers, toes with the information in table 1. general patterns of health can be determined. For example, someone who has abnormalities of the thumb with a small ridged nail, small hairs growing on the joint and/or the presence of white or brown spots on the skin may be puzzled to see that this links to the lungs. They may have no apparent lung problems,

Table 1
The five elements and their correspondences

Five elements	Human body					Nature					
	Yin Zang	Yang Fu	Five sense organs	Five tissues	Emotions	Seasons	Environ-mental factors	Growth & develop-ment	Colours	Tastes	Orien-tations
Wood	Liver	Gall bladder	Eye	Tendon	Anger	Spring	Wind	Germina-tion (birth)	Green	Sour	East
Fire	Heart	Small intestine	Tongue	Vessel	Joy	Summer	Heat	Growth	Red	Bitter	South
Earth	Spleen	Stomach	Mouth	Muscle	Meditation	Late summer	Dampness	Transfor-mation	Yellow	Sweet	Middle
Metal	Lung	Large intestine	Nose	Skin & hair	Grief & melan-choly	Autumn	Dryness	Reaping (declining)	White	Pungent	West
Water	Kidney	Urinary bladder	Ear	Bone	Fright & fear	Winter	Cold	Storing (re-birth)	Black	Salty	North

however, they may suffer from constipation, hay fever annually in the autumn, thin, lustreless hair, eczema and a tendency to depression. None of these may be significant enough for the person to go to a doctor or complementary medical practitioner, but all prevent full functioning and optimum health and the person may always feels a bit below par.

From table 1, it can be seen that these health problems are interlinked and all result from an energetic imbalance relating to the lung. The second and third columns of the table show that the meridian which is paired with the lung is the large intestine (all the meridians are grouped in specific Yin/Yang pairs) and if there is an imbalance in the lung meridian the large intestine is also affected and generally constipation, piles or diarrhoea results. In addition the lungs link with the sense organ the nose and the season autumn, so it would be expected that in the dryness of autumn the person's nasal function would be affected and in this person it manifests as hay fever.

The tissues connected with the lungs are the skin and hair. Imbalance would result in skin problems, such as eczema, rashes or dryness; and hair that is unhealthy in appearance and possibly receding or breaks easily. Finally, the emotion relating to energetic function of the lungs is melancholy so the person would have a tendency towards depression and brooding.

Thus it can be seen that rather than having many minor health worries, the person has a simple pattern of health imbalance and rather than taking a regime of laxatives, inhalants, skin creams, hair tonics and/or antidepressants, the person's whole health could be improved by working directly on the lungs' energetic functioning by means of oriental medicine, acupuncture, acupressure, herbal medicine or breathing exercises according to individual needs.

Interpretation

There are many more complex ways of applying and interpreting this table which require skill and training but many people are amazed to find the link between their apparently diverse physical and emotional problems. By helping people to see these links and to realise that they have perhaps one, rather than many, problems to tackle and that their problem is not just 'all in the mind' or 'all in the body', they already gain a valuable insight into their situation and positive direction towards resolving it.

Oriental medicine therefore provides a valuable interface between psychological and physical problems and between therapies such as counselling and osteopathy, as in the case described above. The system also enables the client and therapist to know themselves better and to understand the links between say, nutrition, exercise, posture, breathing and certain disease states so that positive choices for change may be made together.

REFERENCES

Kaptchuk, T., (1983), The Web That Has No Weaver: Understanding Chinese Medicine, Congdon and Weed, New York.

Kushi, M., (1976), An Introduction to Oriental Diagnosis, Red Moon Press.

Manaka, Y. and Urqhart, I., (1983), The Layman's Guide to Acupuncture, Weatherhill, New York.

Mann, F., (1962), Acupuncture: The Ancient Art of Chinese Healing and How it Works Scientifically, Vintage Books.

Motoyama, H., (1975), How to Measure and Diagnose the Functions of Meridians and Corresponding Organs, I.R.P. Press, Tokyo.

Motoyama, H., (1978), An electrophysiological study of prana (Ki), Research for Religion and Parapsychology, Vol. 4, No. 1, Japan.

Motoyama, H., (1980), Electrophysiological and preliminary biochemical studies of skin properties in relation to the acupuncture meridians,Research for Religion and Parapsychology, Vol. 4, No. 1, Japan.

Motoyama, H. and Smith, W., (1984), Pre-polarization resistance of the skin as determined by the single square voltage pulse method, Psychophysiology, Vol. 2, No. 5.